THE WORLD
OF THE
OLD TESTAMENT

THE WORLD
OF THE
OLD TESTAMENT

Edited by

JAMES I. PACKER, A.M., D.PHIL.
Regent College

MERRILL C. TENNEY, A.M., Ph.D.
Wheaton Graduate School

WILLIAM WHITE, JR., Th.M., Ph.D.

THOMAS NELSON PUBLISHERS
Nashville • Camden • New York

Third printing

Copyright © 1980, 1982 by Thomas Nelson Inc. Publishers

Published in Nashville, Tennessee, by Thomas Nelson, Inc., Publishers and distributed in Canada by Lawson Falle, Ltd., Cambridge, Ontario.

Printed in the United States of America.

Library of Congress Cataloging in Publication Data
Main entry under title:

The World of the Old Testament.

  Includes index.
  1. Bible. O.T.—History of Biblical events.
2. Bible. O.T.—History of contemporary events.
I. Packer, J. I. (James Innell) II. Tenney,
Merrill Chapin, 1904-   III. White, William,
1934-
BS635.2.W67 1982   221.9′5   82-12563
ISBN 0-8407-5820-0

TABLE OF CONTENTS

Introduction vii
1. The Ancient World 1
2. Old Testament History 15
3. Old Testament Chronology 33
4. Archaeology 67
5. Pagan Religions and Cultures 103
6. The Egyptians 123
7. The Babylonians and Assyrians 143
8. Ugarit and the Canaanites 161
9. The Persians 181
   Footnotes 204
   Acknowledgements 206
   Index 207

INTRODUCTION

The World of the Old Testament is an introduction to the peoples who affected Israel's history during the Old Testament period. It also provides the student of the Bible with the events of Israel's history and the meaning of those events in light of God's complete revelation of Himself in the Bible.

The Old Testament describes a world that is both like and unlike our own. We certainly hold the basic elements of life—birth, growth, death, the family, the nation, the farmer, soldier, magistrate, teacher, physician—in common with that world. But the lack of any of the mechanical and electrical devices with which we have become accustomed places the Old Testament world at a great distance from our own.

As we study the people and events of the Old Testament we are better equipped to judge our own lives and societies by the standards of God's law. Our study can also help us to see the clear evidence of God's mighty work in history, for each of the people that touched Israel's life was an actor on the great stage of civilization. In viewing their drama we can see the unending conflicts of blood feuds among small polygamous clans, observe the collapse of societies that were dedicated to unbridled hedonism, and rejoice with the eternal triumph of those who were faithful to God when the vast majority of mankind was not.

Beyond all the values and lessons which may come from knowing this history lies the fact that the people and events of the Old Testament pointed to the coming of the Messiah, Jesus Christ, and to the fulfillment of history in Him. The underlying theme of the Old Testament—as well as the New Testament—is Creation-Full-Redemption-Restoration. It is in the lives of the people and nations that fill its pages that we see this drama moving toward its fulfillment.

In *The World of the Old Testament*, the student of the Bible will see that these people actually lived through the experiences recorded in the Old Testament; they were not the literary creations of some imaginative writer. The more we come to know of the Old Testment world the better we will understand its events. Hopefully, also, our imaginations will be fired and our appetites will be whetted to study God's Word and allow it to illuminate our hearts.

1
THE ANCIENT WORLD

The Bible gives us reliable information about people, places, and events that other ancient books do not mention. It even tells about kingdoms that have disappeared from the face of the earth. In fact, it reaches into a time that many scholars call "pre-history." A simple illustration will suggest the great length of time that the Bible covers.

Let us say that one day represents a generation (about 25 years). On that basis, World War II ended only last night. The Civil War was fought only four days ago, and the thirteen American colonies declared their independence only last week! On the same basis, Jesus was born in Bethlehem about three months ago, and Moses led the Israelites out of Egypt only two months before that. The oldest books of the Near East were written about seven months ago.

On this imaginary calendar, human history would have begun rather more than ten months ago. And the Bible covers it all! The Bible begins with God's creation of the world; it leads us through many centuries of ancient and classical history; and it points us toward the end of time.

This game of imagination makes us realize that we tend to be overly concerned with current events. Modern technology has blinded us to the depths of the past. But ancient cultures had a highly developed sense of the past; they respected the many generations behind them. The Sumerians, Egyptians, and Babylonians often pondered the meaning of history and wondered where it was headed. They loved to preserve the ancient ways. They studied languages that were no longer spoken and practiced rites that no longer retained their meaning. They treasured each small statue and brick made by their ancestors. They encouraged their scribes to preserve ancient words in dictionaries that covered almost every aspect of life.

The writers of the Old Testament saw history as the stage on which God was working out great purposes in a world-drama now nearing its climax ("the last days"). So they wanted to keep an accurate account of the past. But this sense of history was lost with the fall of Rome and the coming of the Dark Ages. Western society lost contact with its heritage. In fact, medieval art and literature had to illustrate Scripture with people who wore medieval clothing and lived in castles, because no one knew how people really lived in Bible times. The artifacts of Egypt, Mesopotamia, and the coast of Palestine have been discovered and interpreted only during the last 150 years. And even now, the ancient world puzzles us.

During most of our waking hours, we consider only what is happening to us in the present. We're wrapped up in the "now." It is exceedingly hard for us to put ourselves in the

Ancient clothing. Medieval paintings showed the people of Bible times wearing steel armor, woolen, smocks, and other clothes that were common in the Middle Ages. But relics from the Near East, such as these, prove that the people dressed much differently. These alabaster statues from Tell Asmar show the type of clothing the Sumerians wore *ca.* 2600 B.C. Both men and women wore a skirt-like garment.

shoes of those who lived in the distant past, totally out of touch with our own way of life.

We tend to misinterpret Bible passages because we assume that the events and ideas that appear in Scripture tell us all there is to know about biblical times. That just isn't so. To get a proper perspective on the events of the Bible, we need to learn more about the years when the Bible was written.

PERIODS OF HISTORY

We can't bring back the ancient past, but we have enough clues to open up great vistas of what life was like in biblical times. When we combine these insights with the narrative of Scripture itself, we begin to get a very credible picture of Bible events.

Many modern scholars say ancient society was primitive. But ancient human beings were no less creative or intelligent than we are. Their inventions (such as writing and arithmetic) laid the foundation of all civilizations, past and present. In fact, most of the characteristics of civilization—trade, money, law, warfare, and the like—were in evidence in ancient times. The names of the inventors and the political geniuses who gave us these things are unknown. But we do know the overall scheme of ancient history, and it helps us understand what happened in early times.

A. The Neolithic Revolution. Before the Neolithic or "New Stone Age," which appears to have lasted into the fourth millennium B.C., most people of Europe and the Middle East lived in small migrating bands. These were probably family groups that hunted wild game or followed semi-wild herds for their food. They made no permanent settlements, but they often returned to the same locations and used the old hunting camps for many years, even for generations. Some of them continued to do this long after permanent communities had been established. Certainly the patriarchs did (Gen. 5–9). Neolithic people domesticated wild animals and developed agriculture, with its methods of irrigation and storage. In fact, the Bible says, "Noah was the first tiller of the soil" (Gen. 9:20,

RSV). The earliest Neolithic villages have been found in the mountains of northern Iraq—the general area where the Ark is said to have landed. Neolithic relics have also been found at Jericho and other biblical locations in Israel.

So during the Neolithic Age, the roving hunters settled down to start farming the land. This meant that several generations would live together in one place. Their buildings, walls, wells, and other structures passed from one generation to another.

B. The Archaic Religious States. The archaic religious states began as local agricultural communities that had their own religious cults. Gradually the local cult and its officials would take control of a village. The whole community was dedicated to the god of the cult, and soon the cult virtually owned the community. The people worshiped agricultural gods and goddesses. Their rituals followed the agricultural cycle of the year.

As the tiny city-states grew, so did the wealth and power of their cults. Each temple extended its control, until all of the local citizens worked for the temple. We find evidence of this kind of temple-town at Sumer (biblical Shinar), Egypt and Elam.

Jericho. Some of the oldest evidence of life in the ancient world comes from the city of Jericho. Here archaeologists have unearthed a house from the early Neolithic Period, before 4000 B.C.

Kings of the ancient Near East usually served as priests for their local cults. As the political power of the temple grew, so did the power of the king. Neighboring towns that had similar religious cults started coming together. They united their beliefs under a common government. These clusters of towns built the great temple-towers of Mesopotamia, the earliest pyramids of Egypt, and massive religious buildings elsewhere. This trend is reflected in Genesis 10–11.

Early religious states achieved great things. For example, when they began keeping economic records they invented writing; the first records were probably inscribed in wax or clay. Soon the people of these cities devised arithmetic to help them compute their business deals. Then they began setting down ethics, legends, stories, laws, songs, poems, and history. So by the time of Abraham a number of civilizations around the Mediterranean Sea had put their languages into writing.

As one archaic religious state declined and another state conquered it, the local language and worship customs were mixed with others. So today we cannot tell where many of the ancient languages and beliefs came from. The people of the Near East began worshiping many gods of the same kind (a practice that we call *polytheism*). They told legends about families of older and younger gods. They added more and more gods to their religions until they had a bewildering throng of deities. As the cities of ancient Palestine traded supplies with other parts of the Near East, they also traded religious customs. They left evidence of these mixed pagan religions in the ancient cities of Jericho, Hazor, Beth-Shemesh, and others. The Old Testament describes this confused state of affairs (Josh. 24:2, 15).

C. The Establishment of Empires (ca. 2700 B.C.). As the archaic religious states grew wealthy and more secure, and as they provided more food and protection for their people, they had a population explosion. The better organized religious states spread beyond their traditional boundaries and embraced even more of the nearby city-states. They became the world's first empires. The first of these was probably Egypt; it was followed by the empires of Elam, Hatti (later Hattushash), and the Semitic cities of Mesopotamia (cf. Gen. 14:1; Deut.

7:1). The Mesopotamians installed the world's first dictator, Sargon of Agade. (He may have been the "Nimrod" of Genesis 10.) Archaeologists have found evidence of other powerful kingdoms in the middle Euphrates and along the coast of Syria and Israel. One of these kingdoms—Ebla in northern Syria—is still being investigated. In fact, it may take a generation for scholars to translate the records they're finding at Ebla.

During this time, strong sea-faring nations appeared on the islands of the eastern Mediterranean and the Aegean Sea. The two groups we should remember are the Minoans and the Akkadians, because they traded with the people of Palestine and exchanged religious ideas with them.

This was the age of Abraham and his descendants, who were Semitic wanderers. During this time, the Semitic people of the Near East took over the older non-Semitic cultures—such as the empires of the Sumerians, Hurrians, and Hittites. Abraham's people were wealthy and sophisticated. They erected great temples, traded with foreign nations, and created extensive laws and bodies of literature. The art and architecture of the Sumerians, Minoans, Akkadians, and Egyptians flourished as never before. Some of the great artistic treasures of all time have come down to us from this age.

D. The Amarna Age (1500 B.C.). Then the great empires declined and the nations of the Middle East achieved a new balance of power. The smaller states of the eastern Mediterranean and the Tigris-Euphrates Valley slipped from the grasp

Fertility goddess. This statuette of a pagan goddess came from the city of Mari on the Euphrates River, near Haran (where Abraham stopped on his way to Canaan). This figure was made in about 2500 B.C., about 400 years before Abraham. Scholars think that the goddess was of an inferior rank.

of foreign empires. For a time, they could develop and trade among themselves and with their more powerful neighbors.

The era takes its name from the capital city of the mysterious pharaoh, Akhnaton. His officials wrote many letters to the minor politicians of Syria-Palestine and the Neo-Hittites to the north, letters that we still have. The Palestinians and Hittites were supposed to be a part of the Egyptian Empire. Actually, they gave lip service to Egypt and handled their own affairs.

This was the time of the Exodus and the conquest of Canaan. It was the age of Moses and Joshua and the compiling of the Pentateuch, the first five books of the Old Testament. The wealth and grandeur of the Amarna Age has fascinated Bible students of all nations. We can see it in the treasures from King Tutankhamen's tomb. "Tut" was only a boy king, the puppet of his advisors. So the great pile of precious objects buried with him was doubtless only a sampling of the riches of the great pharaohs of the Amarna Age.

Of all the Near Eastern states of the period, we should pay special attention to Ugarit on the coast of Lebanon. Ugarit was the center of Canaanite language and religion, and the clay tablets that archaeologists have discovered there cast a great deal of light on the world of the Canaanites before the Israelites came.

During the Amarna period, the people of the Near East traded with most of the known world—all the way from northern Europe to the borders of China. The leading power was Babylon, which grew so strong that it would control the Near East in the next period of history. The Amarna Age ended during the time of the Judges of Israel. According to the Book of Judges, the Near East suffered a great deal of political strife at the end of this period, as the new empires jockeyed for control of the area.

E. The Multi-National States (from 1200 B.C.). Most kingdoms of the Amarna Age were small, and we mark the end of the Amarna Age at the time when broader kingdoms arose. Each Amarna kingdom had been limited to the people of one race, language, or religion; but the new kingdoms controlled many different groups. Among these new kingdoms were Assyria, Persia, and the early Greek cities on the coastland of Turkey.

Israel's leaders wrote the historical and prophetic books of the Old Testament during this new age, which began for Israel with the kingdom of Saul, David, and their descendants. Historians often call this the First Commonwealth of Israel. King David lived at about the same time as Homer, the legendary blind Greek poet who wrote the *Iliad* and the *Odyssey*, probably in the tenth century B.C.

King Solomon, David's son, traded with the Egyptians to the south and the Hittites to the north. He brought Israel to the height of its wealth and power. Under his son Rehoboam, the two southern tribes split with the ten northern tribes of Israel. The southern tribes rallied around Rehoboam and were called the nation of Judah; the northern tribes followed Rehoboam's rival, Jeroboam, and were called the nation of Israel. Assyria conquered Israel in 722 B.C. Later in this period, in 586 B.C., King Nebuchadnezzar II of Babylon conquered Jerusalem and carried away the people of the southern kingdom.

In the next century, Persia became the major power of inland Asia. The Persian Empire grew until it ruled Egypt, Babylon, and all of Syria-Palestine.

F. The Age of Greek Supremacy (450–325 B.C.). By this time, the people of the Greek peninsula had built a very successful system of city-states and trading colonies. They shipped goods from the shores of the Black Sea to the coasts of Europe and Africa. They built cities and ports on every shore of the Mediterranean. However, they were never able to unite behind one city or leader. As the period of the multi-national states drew to a close, the Persians tried to invade Greece, but they were repelled by Athens and its allies. Athens became a great power in the half-century that followed.

During this new age, the Jews came back to Palestine and rebuilt their nation from the ruins. Israel was still a part of the Persian Empire, but the new Persian kings allowed the Jews to govern themselves. Historians call this second period of Israel's self-government the Second Commonwealth. While the Persians lost strength in their wars with Greece, Israel expanded and took back some of its former territories.

Then a new power arose to unite the Greek states. The new conqueror was Macedonia, under the leadership of King Philip (whose tomb was recently discovered in northern Greece). Philip left his empire to his son, Alexander. The lad had been taught in the academy of Athens by the famous Greek philosopher, Aristotle. He loved Greek civilization and culture, and he set out to bring all of the world under the influence of Greek customs. In technical language, Alexander wanted to "Hellenize" the world. (The term "Hellenize" comes from the Greek word *Hellenes,* which means "Greek.") To do this, Alexander knew he must break the power of Persia, so that it would never threaten Greece again. He brought together the world's best army and marched across central Asia into India. In the process, he destroyed the last of the archaic states, along with their languages and their religious cults.

Alexander and his men used a folksy form of the classical Greek language, and they gave this dialect to the people they conquered. We call it *koiné,* or common Greek. The New Testament was written in this language, and Paul and the other early missionaries used it as they preached the gospel.

Alexander the Great was the foremost figure of the Intertestamental Period (the era between the writing of the Old and New Testaments). He died suddenly in 323 B.C., and his generals divided the conquered lands among themselves. They established what we call the Hellenistic Kingdoms, and began an era known as the Hellenistic Age. The Hellenistic kings treated the Jews harshly. Jews who had been scattered outside Palestine (a company called the *Diaspora*) became a mixture of races and cultures under the Hellenistic reigns. They neglected their traditional religious practices and picked up a secular lifestyle, which was to mark the last ancient power, Rome.

G. The Roman Era (100 B.C.–A.D. 450). Jesus Christ was born at the height of Roman political power. Beginning as a small but powerful city-state in the hills of central Italy, Rome built upon the successes of Hellenism. The Romans assembled great fleets of ships to extend their power across the whole European continent—from Spain and Britain to Arabia and North Africa. Roman roads, buildings, walls, and canals still dot the landscape of every European country from the Atlantic to the Red Sea. Christians used this amazing system of roads and sea routes to carry the gospel to every corner of the known world.

In time, the political might of the Roman Empire began to decay, and the tribes of northern Europe conquered it. But by then, the Christian church had grown so rapidly that it survived the fall of the Roman Empire. The Edict of Constantine (A.D. 313) gave the church a special place in the life of Rome a century before the empire fell apart. The Roman church became the greatest unifying force in the Middle Ages; it effectively ruled the kingdoms of Europe for a thousand years.

INFORMATION ABOUT EVERYDAY LIFE

We know the names of many kings and conquerors from ancient times. But what were the common people doing and thinking? We really don't know a great deal about everyday life in the ancient world. Yet the Bible gives us more of this kind of information than do most other sources. We pick up quite a lot of details from 1 and 2 Samuel, 1 and 2 Kings, and the prophetic books of the Old Testament.

The next-best information comes from secular sources that are widely spaced in time and location. These sources tell us many things that are important for our study of the Bible.

A. Sumero-Babylonian Texts. The Sumerians settled in the Tigris-Euphrates Valley after the Neolithic era and founded there a number of states, each with its religion. Genesis 10 mentions some of these, such as Kish (wrongly spelled *Cush* by many translations), Babel, Erech, and Akkad. In Genesis 10 and other passages, the Bible uses the Semitic word *Shinar* to refer to Sumer. But that city is the most important for our study of this period.

The people of Sumer invented an unusual writing system. They used a pointed stick to press tiny wedge-shaped characters on to clay tablets, and then baked the tablets in an oven until they were as hard as bricks. When these tablets were buried in dry ground, they lasted for thousands of years to our own day. The Sumerians kept very careful records of legal decisions, contracts, and commercial dealings. So their clay tablets give us a full and exact picture of their daily life.

The Babylonians and Assyrians studied the movement of the stars, and they used what they learned to make a very precise calendar. So now we can figure the time of many events in Sumero-Babylonian history almost to the day and the hour!

The clay tablets found so far at Sumer were written in the middle period of the early religious states (about 2000 B.C. to 1650 B.C.). Some were written at later periods, closing about 500 B.C. The tablets tell us quite a bit about how the Hebrew language changed across the centuries, and how it resembled other Semitic languages. Some clay tablets also show us how the Israelites crossed the path of the Babylonians at different times in history.

The Isaiah Scroll. This is one of the best-preserved parchment scrolls from the caves of Qumran near the Dead Sea. It contains the entire Book of Isaiah, copied about 150–50 B.C. The scroll is over 7 m. (24 ft.) long. Before this and other scrolls were discovered in 1947 the earliest available Old Testament manuscripts dated to about A.D. 900.

Sargon. This bronze mask from the ruins of Nineveh is thought to represent King Sargon of Agade (Akkad). It was fashioned in about 2500 B.C. Sargon made Agade and Nippur powerful city-states that later became the nucleus of the Babylonian Empire.

B. Deir el-Bahari. We also get a glimpse of everyday life in ancient times in the ruins of a village known as the Deir el-Bahari. Here lived the workmen who built the great tombs in Egypt's Valley of the Kings, where the pharaohs of the eighteenth dynasty had elaborate tombs carved out of a rock canyon (1580–1340 B.C.). The workmen of Deir el-Bahari jotted notes about their daily doings on broken bits of pottery. These *potsherds* were a cheap and plentiful kind of stationery. And since they were actually bits of baked clay, they've survived almost as well as the clay tablets of Sumer.

So what do these potsherds tell us? For one thing, the craftsmen had a great deal of self-esteem and independence. They worked an eight-hour day and a ten-day week on the Egyptian calendar. Their masters paid them wages and gave them rations of food. The potsherds show that these workmen worried about the metal, stone, and tools they needed to finish the project, and complained about absentees from the job. So they were much like construction workers in our own day! We know that workmen like these also mined copper in the southern Sinai and built roads in Palestine.

C. Hellenistic Towns in Egypt. In the late nineteenth century, archaeologists started digging around the ruins of old cities beside the large lakes in lower Egypt. Many people lived there in Hellenistic times, and so the archaeologists expected to find some interesting relics. They discovered stacks and stacks of *papyri* (an ancient kind of paper made from river reeds). On these papyri they found records written in Hellenistic Greek of the many minor details of daily life in the ancient cities. The papyri opened a new door to understanding the customs of New Testament times. In fact, they made the world of the Roman imperial government come alive. In addition, papyri have given us the earliest known manuscripts of many classical Greek writings—among them, Plato, Aristotle, Homer, Pindar, and Menander. Most important of all were some of the earliest scraps of the New Testament. So from the trash heaps of Egypt came some of the best records of everyday life in the ancient world.

D. The Caves of Qumran. In 1948 a shepherd discovered huge clay pots in the caves of Qumran, on the northwest shore of the Dead Sea. Inside the pots he found scrolls with very old Hebrew writing. As it turned out, they were written between 100 B.C. and A.D. 100. These scrolls were some of the most important items ever found in Palestine. After 2,000 years they were still in good condition! They contained the text of many Old Testament books, and thus confirmed that the later copies Bible translators had been using were quite accurate. This was weighty evidence for the conservative view of Scripture, which contends that God's Word has been handed down faithfully. Not all of the Qumran texts have been published, and many of the controversies about them have not yet been settled.

Archaeologists have thoroughly searched the west bank of the Jordan River and the high cliffs along the Dead Sea. But they have done little work along the east bank, which was as much settled as the west bank in ancient times. We can also expect the north shore of the Dead Sea to yield more surprises for biblical study as research continues. Already the finds from Qumran have helped us understand the times of the New Testament and the Roman control of Palestine.

E. Pompeii and Herculaneum. A violent eruption of the volcano Vesuvius destroyed two small Roman towns along the Bay of Naples in August of A.D. 79. Treasure hunters and scientists have been digging up the ruins of these cities— Pompeii and Herculaneum—for over 200 years. If you visit them today, you'll see many acres of them, just as they were 1,900 years ago.

They were typical towns, with rich and poor people living side by side. Archaeologists found a dazzling collection of art and sculpture in both cities. They also dug up some large-scale waterworks, well-planned buildings, and ingenious household tools. Unfortunately, only a few scraps of scorched papyri survived the eruption, and these are copies of Greek philosophical essays. But walk down the streets of one of these excavated ruins on the beautiful Bay of Naples, and you will see the kind of world Peter and Paul knew as they carried the message of Jesus throughout the Roman Empire.

F. Ebla. This is a city in northern Syria that archaeologists started exploring in 1964. Here an Italian team dug up thousands of clay tablets written during the time of the early religious states, about 1850 B.C. So far, the Italians have published only a few details from these texts. But even this sketchy information shows that the people of Ebla had a very sophisticated way of life. They knew the Sumerian and Akkadian cultures and languages, and they traded with other wealthy city-states throughout the Near East.

For many years, scholars wondered how Mesopotamian literature crossed over to the west Semites of Syria-Palestine. Now it seems that kingdoms such as Ebla carried the East Semite and Sumerian cultures to the rest of the Near East.

The tablets of Ebla mention names and locations that we already know from the history of the patriarchs and the Old Testament. But archaeologists will be deciphering, translating, and publishing Ebla tablets for many years. When all of the material is available, it will help us understand the ancient world described in the early chapters of Genesis.

2

OLD TESTAMENT HISTORY

Think for a moment about this remarkable volume that we call "The Bible." Three major religions—Christianity, Judaism, and Islam—claim the Bible or portions of the Bible as a holy book and Christianity claims the Bible as its *only* Holy Book. Christians believe the Bible is God's Word for every age, including our own. That is why we study it and try to understand it better in every new generation. To gain more than a casual understanding of the Bible, we must get a clear picture of the history recorded in it.

It is convenient to study Old Testament history in four sections: (1) from Creation to Abraham, (2) from Abraham to Moses, (3) from Moses to Saul, and (4) from Saul to Christ.

"There is *one* central theme which . . . runs through all the stories of the Old Testament," William Hendriksen says. "That theme is the coming Christ."[1] Keep this in mind as we look at each section of the Old Testament.

FROM CREATION TO ABRAHAM

God revealed to Moses how He created all things, and Moses described Creation in the Book of Genesis, the first book of the Bible. According to Genesis, God made the world and all that is in it within the space of six days, and He declared it all "to be very good." On the seventh day, He rested from His creating. Christian scholars disagree about how long these "days" might have been or even if they were periods of time at all.

Christians also differ on the *date* of Creation. The Bible's lists of generations might skip names, as other genealogies

15

sometimes do, so many scholars feel that we cannot safely add up the ages of the people listed to get the number of years in Old Testament history. The number thus reached could be far too small. There are other difficulties, too, in figuring the dates of creation—difficulties too complex to discuss here.

After God created man (Adam), He placed him in a garden called Eden. There, God decreed the first man and woman (Eve) to worship Him and rule the earth. (This is sometimes called our "cultural mandate.") God commanded the man and woman not to eat any fruit from the tree of knowledge of good and evil. If they did, they would know what is meant to participate in evil, and the happy life of Eden would be taken away from them!

We might think Adam and Eve would have had no trouble obeying this commandment. But someone else entered the picture: Satan, who leads the evil spirits who conspire to defeat God. Satan became a serpent; his lies seduced Eve into eating the forbidden fruit, and Adam joined her. They both sinned against God. Instead of living in harmony with God, they began a life of sin and misery and they fell from God's favor.

God promised Adam and Eve that He would send a Redeemer (also called a Savior, or a Messiah), who would destroy Satan and restore them to a right relationship with Him (Gen. 3:15). The Bible tells how God accomplished this plan of salvation. Of course, since the Bible focuses on that one aspect of world history, we can't expect it to tell us everything that happened in ancient times. It records only what we need in order to understand the history of redemption.

Several important things happened between the time of Adam and the time of Abraham, "father of all who believe" (Rom. 4:11, RSV). For example, there was the first murder. Adam and Eve had many sons and daughters (Gen. 5:4), but the Bible names only two because they are important to the history of redemption. Eve thought that her firstborn son, Cain, was the one who would destroy Satan and deliver them from the curse of sin and death (Gen. 4:1). But Cain jealously

Ziggurat of Ur. This temple at Ur was used in the pagan worship that Abraham left behind when he traveled to the Promised Land. The word *ziggurat* is an English rendering of the Assyrian *ziqquratu* ("height, pinnacle").

killed his brother Abel. God punished him by driving him out of the community of people who served God. (We know Adam and Eve continued to worship God because their sons offered burnt sacrifices to Him [Gen. 4:3-5], and the New Testament calls Abel a man of true faith [Heb. 11:4].) Yet God saved Cain from the full penalty of his crime; He marked Cain so that other people would know God did not want him killed. We are not certain what God's mark was, but it must have been clearly visible to other people.

Then God gave Adam and Eve a third son, Seth, who replaced Abel. The Redeemer of the world would come from Seth's family.

But what about Cain's family? The Bible shows that Cain's son, Lamech, inherited his father's evil ways (Gen. 4:19-24). Lamech boasted that he did not need God's protection, for he could use his sword (Gen. 4:23-24). He rejected God's holy standards of marriage and took more than one wife. In fact, he set such a low value on human life that he killed a man for striking him.

Evil spread to all mankind (Gen. 6:1-4). The Bible says human giants or "mighty men" lived during this time, but their spiritual life certainly didn't stack up to their physical stature!

God sent a great Flood to punish sinful mankind, and this was the most important event of the ancient period. However,

God preserved the lives of Noah and his family in an ark (a large wooden ship), so that He could eventually keep His promise to redeem mankind. Many Christians are now convinced that the Flood covered the entire world. According to 2 Peter 3:6, ". . . The world that then was, being overflowed with water, perished." Gleason L. Archer shows in detail that the ark was large enough to hold all the varieties of animals that exist today.[2] If that is so, it certainly could have held all the varieties of life in Noah's day. Notice that God sent the clean animals to the ark seven by seven (Gen. 7:2), and unclean animals two by two (Gen. 7:15).

After the Flood, God set the death penalty for murder and appointed human agents as executioners (Gen. 9:1-7). He also put a rainbow in the sky to remind His people that He would never destroy all mankind by water (Gen. 8:13-17).

Yet right after the Flood, Noah's son Canaan (or "Ham") sinned against God (Gen. 9:20-29). God cursed Canaan because of his disrespect for his father, Noah (Gen. 9:25).

Then God spoke through Noah to describe the course of subsequent history. He said a descendant of Shem would bring salvation into the world, and the descendants of Japheth would share in that salvation. Japheth's family moved north and became progenitors of the Gentiles of New Testament times (Gen. 10:2).

One more thing happened before Abraham appeared on the scene. Proud city-dwellers tried to get to heaven by building a tower in Babel (Gen. 11). God condemned their arrogant ways by breaking them up into different language groups, then scattering them to live in different areas (Gen. 10:4; cf. 9:1). This, it seems, is how the large language families of the world began.

So what does all this tell us? Clearly, it shows that evil continued to increase from the time of the Flood to Abraham. We know that people during this period worshiped many gods (Josh. 24:2; cf. Gen. 31:29-31), and immorality was rampant. So God, who intended to save humanity, decided to begin anew in one family . . . "through whom all the families would be blessed."

FROM ABRAHAM TO MOSES

God chose Abraham's family to bring this salvation to the rest of mankind. Abraham lived in the city of Ur (capital of the ancient kingdom of Sumer). Sometime around 2000 B.C., God called Abraham to leave his father's home and go to a new land. The Bible traces Abraham's steps from Ur to Haran (north of Palestine), through the land of Palestine, into Egypt, and back into Palestine. God promised to give Abraham a son, whose children would become a great nation. God also promised to make Abraham's descendants a blessing to all nations (Gen. 12:2-3; 17:1-6). At first, Abraham believed what God said; but later he doubted that God would do as He promised, and tried to force God's hand by his own action. Thus, when God didn't give him a son as soon as he expected, Abraham took his wife's servant girl Hagar and had a son by her. Though the ancient world accepted this means of securing an heir, it violated God's law for marriage (Gen. 2:24), and Abraham suffered sorely for his sin. His first-born son Ishmael turned against Isaac, the promised son who was born 13 years later. So Ishmael had to leave Abraham's household.

But Abraham came to trust God more completely as the years went by. Finally, God told him to offer Isaac as a burnt sacrifice to prove his love for God (Gen. 22). By this time, Abraham knew that God expected him to obey, and so, trusting God, he laid his son on the altar (cf. Heb. 11:17-19). At the last minute, God ordered him not to kill Isaac and gave him a ram for the sacrifice.

Another time, Abraham asked God to spare the sinful cities where his nephew Lot lived. But Lot failed to redeem his community (cf. 2 Pet. 2:8); God could not find even ten righteous men there. So God destroyed the cities as He had planned. Again, God was training Abraham and his family to obey Him.

Then the Bible turns our eyes to the life of Jacob, Isaac's second son. Jacob lived around 1850 B.C. God chose Jacob to inherit the promises He had given to Isaac. He named Jacob's

Making bricks. Murals from the tomb of Rekhmire, the vizier of Pharaoh Thutmose III, show how bricks were made in Egypt at the time of the Exodus (1446 B.C.) At the top left, two men are shown drawing water from a pool to make the mud. Beside them, two men work the clay. Slaves press the clay into wooden molds to form the bricks, which are left to dry in the sun. Notice that the slave kneeling in the middle of the upper panel has lighter skin than the other slaves; this indicates that he was of Semitic origin, perhaps a Hebrew. The bottom panel shows how the bricks were laid with mortar.

family as the one that would bring the Redeemer to the world.

But what an unlikely choice! Jacob grew up a self-seeking and deceitful fellow. He tricked his brother Esau and lied to his father so he could steal Esau's birthright. Then he fled to his uncle Laban's home to escape his brother's wrath. God confronted him as he ran away, and yet Jacob held his ground.

So God began a long, slow job of teaching Jacob how to trust Him. He gave Jacob a good wife and great possessions. His uncle tricked him into marrying Leah, a girl he did not want, so Jacob pressed on to marry her sister Rachel as well. Jacob grew rich, but his greed led to family trouble and he had to leave Laban's land. He returned to his father's home in Palestine. There he found that God had prepared the way for him, and his brother was no longer angry.

But Jacob's troubles were not over. Years later, ten of Jacob's sons got jealous of their youngest brother, Joseph, because Jacob obviously preferred him. Joseph had dreamed they would bow down to him someday, along with their parents. The ten brothers resented this. They trapped Joseph, sold him into slavery, and told their father that he was dead.

Slave traders carried Joseph to Egypt, where he became one of the pharaoh's servants. God used Joseph to interpret the pharaoh's dreams, and the young man rose to become second in command under the pharaoh.

Then a famine in Palestine drove Joseph's family to Egypt in search of food. His older brothers came first. When they bowed before Joseph, he immediately recognized them; but he did not tell them who he was. Eventually, Joseph forced them to bring his younger brother Benjamin to Egypt, too. Then he revealed his identity and forgave them for selling him into slavery. Joseph invited them to bring his entire family. The pharaoh received them warmly and allowed them to settle in a rich part of Egypt.

FROM MOSES TO SAUL

Now the Bible moves its spotlight to Moses (ca. 1526–1406 B.C.), who holds a vital place in the history of redemption. Jacob's descendants had so many children that the pharaohs feared they would take charge of the country. So a new pharaoh put them into slavery and ordered all of the Israelites' boy babies to be killed. Moses' mother put him in a little basket and set him afloat in the river, near the place where the pharaoh's daughter bathed. When the princess found the baby, she took him to the palace to raise as her adopted son. Moses' mother became his nursemaid and she probably took care of him well beyond the time he was weaned (Exod. 2:7-10).

As a young man, Moses began to feel burdened for his people; he wanted to bring them out of slavery (Exod. 2:11; Acts 7:24-25). When Moses was about 40 years old, he saw an Egyptian beating an Israelite; he flew into a rage and killed the Egyptian. Afraid the pharaoh would execute him, Moses fled into the Midian Desert (Exod. 2:14-15). There he married into the family of Jethro (also called "Reuel"), a pagan priest. Moses agreed to tend Jethro's flock (Exod. 2:16-21).

After about forty years, God spoke to Moses from a bush that burned but was not consumed. He ordered Moses to go back to Egypt and lead the Israelites into Palestine, the land He had promised to Abraham. Moses didn't believe he could do this, and he made excuses for not going. But God answered every one of them, and gave him power to work miracles that would induce the Israelites to follow him. God

Moses

The most crucial figure of Old Testament history was Moses, who led the people of Israel out of bondage. Some commentators believe that his name is a combination of the late Egyptian words for "water" *(mo)* and "take" *(shi)*. Thus it may be a reminder of how the pharaoh's daughter took the infant Moses from a basket on the Nile (Exod. 2).

Moses had an older brother named Aaron and a sister named Miriam. He was born just after the Egyptian pharaoh ordered his soldiers to kill all new Israelite babies to control the population of the slaves. Moses' mother made a basket of bulrushes, placed him in it, and floated it on the Nile River under the watchful eye of his sister. When the pharaoh's daughter found the baby, she adopted him into the royal family.

When Moses was a young man, he killed an Egyptian slave driver in a fit of rage (Exod. 2:11ff.). He escaped into the rugged land of Midian, where he married a priest's daughter named Zipporah. Together they had two sons—Gershom and Eliezer (Exod. 2:22; 18:4).

After Moses had lived in Midian for about forty years, the Lord appeared to him in a burning bush on the side of Mt. Sinai or Horeb (Exod. 3). He instructed Moses to lead his people out of Egypt to the Promised Land of Canaan. Moses protested that he would not be able to convince the pharaoh to let the Israelites leave, so the Lord allowed him to take Aaron as his spokesman.

Moses went back to Egypt and conveyed God's message to "let my people go." When the pharaoh demanded a sign of divine power to confirm Moses' message, Moses was pitted against the pharaoh's court magicians. (According to Jewish tradition, they were named Jannes and Jambres.) Though the pharaoh saw Moses and Aaron perform miracles more spectacular than those of his own magicians, he refused to let the people of Israel leave his land. So God sent a series of ten plagues, culminating in the death of all the firstborn of Egypt—including the pharaoh's own son—to convince the ruler who finally decided to honor Moses' request. Even so, the pharaoh changed his mind while the Israelites were leaving. He tried to stop them at the shores of the Red Sea, but God parted the waters so that the Israelites could escape.

Moses led his people to Mount Sinai, where he met with God and received a system of law to govern them in the Promised Land. God summarized this Law in the Ten Commandments, which He engraved on tablets of stone that Moses brought back to the Israelite camp. Moses found that his people had turned to pagan worship, and he angrily dashed the tablets to the ground, symbolizing the people's breaking of the covenant. After the people repented of their sin, Moses returned to the mountain and received the Ten Commandments once again.

For forty years the Israelites wandered in the wilderness between Sinai and Canaan. During this time, Moses and Aaron were their civil and religious rulers. God prevented Moses from entering the Promised Land because he had disobeyed the Lord at Meribah, where he struck a stone with his rod to receive water. Yet God allowed Moses to view the Promised Land from the top of Mount Nebo. Then Moses died.

In the 120 years of his life, Moses had led his people in their journey from bondage to freedom. He had recorded their past history by writing what are now the first five books of the Old Testament, and he had received the Law that would govern them for centuries to come.

revealed His holy name *YHWH* (sometimes translated "Jehovah") to Moses. Moses tried to beg off by saying, "I am slow of speech . . . ," perhaps because he had a speech impediment. So God sent Moses' brother Aaron along with him, to translate what Moses had to say (Exod. 7:1).

Moses and Aaron persuaded the people of Israel to follow them, but the pharaoh refused to let them leave Egypt. Then God sent ten devastating plagues on Egypt to change the pharaoh's heart (Exod. 7:17–12:36). The last plague killed the firstborn son in every home whose doors were not marked with blood. Because the people of Israel obeyed God's instructions, the death angel passed over Israel's firstborn. (God commanded the Israelites to celebrate this event with a yearly festival that is actually named "the Passover.") The death plague made the pharaoh give in; he agreed to let the Israelites go back to their native land. But as soon as they left, the pharaoh changed his mind. He sent his army to bring the Israelites back.

God led His people to the Red Sea, where He parted the waters and led them through on dry ground. Several scholars, such as Leon Wood, estimate that it happened around 1446 B.C.[3]

Moses led the people from the Red Sea to Mount Sinai. On the way, God miraculously gave them bread and quail to eat. At Mount Sinai, God revealed through Moses the laws and social plans that would mold the Israelites into a holy nation. These included the Ten Commandments.

From Sinai, God led the Israelites to Kadesh, where they sent spies into Palestine. The spies reported that the land was rich and fertile, yet full of giants. Most of the spies believed that the giants would destroy them if they tried to take the land. Only two—Caleb and Joshua—believed it was worth the fight. The Israelites accepted the skeptical advice of the majority, and turned away from Palestine. God condemned them to wander in the wilderness for 40 years because they hadn't trusted Him.

At the end of their wandering, they camped on the plains of Moab. Here Moses spoke to them for the last time, and his words were recorded in the Book of Deuteronomy. Moses turned his leadership over to Joshua. Then he gave the Israelites his final instructions and ended with a hymn of praise to God. Notice that Moses could not enter the Promised Land because he had rebelled against God at Meribah (Num. 20:12). But after Moses gave his farewell to the Israelites, God led him to the top of Mount Nebo to see the land they would enter. There he died.

Joshua had proven himself a capable leader of Israel's army in the battle of Amalek (Exod. 17:8-16). Now God used Joshua to lead the people of Israel in conquering and settling the Promised Land. He had been one of the spies who had first looked at the Promised Land. Because they trusted God to give them the land, Joshua and Caleb were the only adults of their generation that God allowed to enter it. All the others had died in the wilderness.

So Moses ordained Joshua to replace him, and he announced that God would give Palestine into Joshua's hands. After Moses died, God spoke to Joshua, encouraging him to stay true to his calling (Josh. 1:1-9).

Immediately, Joshua led Israel into the Promised Land. God rewarded Joshua's faith by helping Israel to take possession of it. First, God divided the overflowing Jordan River so they could cross over on dry land (Josh. 3:14-17). Then the angel of the Lord led the Israelites in their miraculous defeat of Jericho, the first city conquered in the Promised Land. When the people blew their trumpets as God had ordered, the walls of the city fell down (Josh. 6). Under Joshua, Israel proceeded to conquer the entire country (Josh. 21:23-45). They suffered defeat only at Ai, when one of their men disobeyed God's battle orders (Josh. 7). Having learned their lesson, the Israelites decided to follow God's orders and try again, and this time they defeated Ai. In all, they conquered 31 kings in the new territory. Joshua divided the land among the Israelite tribes according to God's directions. Just before he died, Joshua urged his people to keep trusting God and obeying His commands.

But they didn't. After Joshua died, "every man did what was right in his own eyes" (Judg. 21:25). The great leaders of this period acted much like Moses and Joshua; they were military

THE KINGS OF ISRAEL

Name	Length of Reign (Years)	Reference
Jeroboam I	22	1 Kings 11:26–14:20
Nadab	2	1 Kings 15:25-28
Baasha	24	1 Kings 15:27–16:7
Elah	2	1 Kings 16:6-14
Zimri	(7 days)	1 Kings 16:9-20
Omri	12	1 Kings 16:15-28
Ahab	21	1 Kings 16:28–22:40
Ahaziah	1	1 Kings 22:40–2 Kings 1:18
Jehoram (Joram)	11	2 Kings 3:1–9:25
Jehu	28	2 Kings 9:1–10:36
Jehoahaz	16	2 Kings 13:1-9
Jehoash (Joash)	16	2 Kings 13:10–14:16
Jeroboam II	40	2 Kings 14:23-29
Zechariah	½	2 Kings 14:29–15:12
Shallum	(1 month)	2 Kings 15:10-15
Menahem	10	2 Kings 15:14-22
Pekahiah	2	2 Kings 15:22-26
Pekah	20	2 Kings 15:27-31
Hoshea	9	2 Kings 15:30–17:6

THE KINGS OF JUDAH

Name	Length of Reign (Years)	Reference
Rehoboam	17	1 Kings 11:42–14:31
Abijam	3	1 Kings 14:31–15:8
Asa	41	1 Kings 15:8-24
Jehoshaphat	25	1 Kings 22:41-50
Jehoram	8	2 Kings 8:16-24
Ahaziah	1	2 Kings 8:24–9:29
Athaliah	6	2 Kings 11:1-20
Joash	40	2 Kings 11:1–12:21
Amaziah	29	2 Kings 14:1-20
Azariah (Uzziah)	52	2 Kings 15:1-7
Jotham	18	2 Kings 15:32-38
Ahaz	19	2 Kings 16:1-20
Hezekiah	29	2 Kings 18:1–20:21
Manasseh	55	2 Kings 21:1-18
Amon	2	2 Kings 21:19-26
Josiah	31	2 Kings 22:1–23:30
Jehoahaz	¼	2 Kings 23:31-33
Jehoiakim	11	2 Kings 23:34–24:5
Jehoiachin	¼	2 Kings 24:6-16
Zedekiah	11	2 Kings 24:17–25:30

Figure 1

heroes and chief judges in the courts of Israel, and we call them the "judges." The most noteworthy were: Othniel, Deborah (the only woman judge), Gideon, Jephthah, Samson, Eli, and Samuel. (Ruth also lived during this period.)

As you read the colorful stories of these ancient heroes, spend some extra time on the life of Samuel. He was one of the most important figures of this era.

Samuel's mother had prayed for a son, so she praised God to see him born (1 Sam. 12:1-10). Samuel's parents gave him to the chief priest Eli so that he could be trained to serve the Lord. While Samuel was still a child, he helped Eli care for the Tent of Meeting. There he heard God calling him to become the new leader of Israel, as a prophet and judge.

Before Samuel's time, the Israelites called a prophet a "seer" (1 Sam. 9:9; cf. Deut. 13:1-15; 18:15-22). But Samuel, like other later prophets, was not just a forecaster of the future. He spoke God's messages to the nation about the lives they lived, often rebuking the people for their wicked ways. He stands as the first of Israel's great prophets, and the last of the judges. At God's direction, he anointed Saul to be the first human king over Israel (1 Sam. 8:19-22; cf. Deut. 14:14-20), though he later regretted it.

THE UNITED MONARCHY

In his early years, Saul appeared as a man of humility and self-control. Over the years, however, his character changed. He became a man of self-will, disobedience to God, jealousy, hatred, and superstition. His anger turned against David, a young warrior who had killed the giant Goliath, and who served as his court musician. He often tried to murder David, being jealous of David's popularity (1 Sam. 18:5-9; 19:8-10).

But God had secretly chosen David to be the next king, and He promised the kingship to David's family forever (1 Sam. 16:1-13; 2 Sam. 7:12-16). Yet Saul continued to be king for many years.

After Saul's death, King David brought the ark of the covenant to Jerusalem (cf. Deut. 12:1-14; 2 Sam. 6:1-11). The

Ark of the Covenant.
This bas relief from the synagogue of Capernaum shows the ark of the covenant. The ark was kept in the holy of holies of the temple in Jerusalem. It disappeared when Nebuchadnezzar's armies razed the city in 586 B.C.

ark was a wooden box that held the stone tablets on which God wrote for Moses the Ten Commandments; the Israelites had carried it with them through their years of wandering in the wilderness, and they prized it as a holy object. David brought it to his capital city so that Jerusalem would become the spiritual center of the nation, as well as its political center.

David had the kind of qualities they were looking for—military skill, political savvy, and a keen sense of religious duty. He had made the nation stronger and more secure than it had ever been.

But David was only a man, with weaknesses like everyone else. He toyed with the idea of starting a harem such as other kings had, and he arranged the murder of an officer in his army so he could marry the man's wife whom he had already seduced. He took a census of the men of Israel because he no longer trusted God for military victory; he only trusted the strength of his army. God punished David and Israel with him for his sin. David was the head of the nation; so when he sinned against God, all of his people suffered the punishment.

David's son Solomon was Israel's next king. Despite Solomon's legendary wisdom, he did not always live wisely. He did carry out David's political plan, strengthening his hold on the territories conquered by his father. He was a shrewd businessman, and he made some trade agreements that brought great wealth to Israel (1 Kings 10:14-15). God also used Solomon to build the great temple in Jerusalem (cf. Deut. 12:1-14). But Solomon's lavish style of living increased the burden of taxes upon the common people. He inherited his father's desire for women, and he concluded trade agreements with foreign kings which involved "political marriages" and thus he put together a harem of brides from many foreign lands (1 Kings 11:1-8). These pagan wives enticed him to worship pagan gods, and he soon set up their rites and ceremonies in Jerusalem.

THE DIVIDED MONARCHY

After Solomon, the fortunes of Israel went downhill. The nation rebelled against God and His laws. God might have destroyed Israel; but He did not do so for He still planned to use the House of David to introduce the Redeemer who would save the world from sin. He had promised to raise this Redeemer from Abraham's family, and He intended to keep His promise.

When Solomon died, Israel stumbled into a bloody civil war as Solomon's sons and generals fought for the throne. Rehoboam had his father's blessing to be the new king; but his rival Jeroboam wielded more influence among the military chiefs of the land. In the end, Rehoboam took the southern half of the country and called it Judah. Jeroboam set up his own government in the northern half and retained the name of Israel. Each claimed to be the king God had chosen.

Look at the two charts covering this period, and you'll see the main leaders in Israel and Judah, including the major prophets. The first chart (Fig. 1) shows who ruled Israel and Judah in each generation. The other chart (Fig. 2) shows what else was happening during the time of the divided monarchy. None of Israel's kings served God, and Judah wasn't much better; only Kings Asa, Jehoshaphat, Joash (Jehoash), Amaziah, Azariah, Jotham, Hezekiah, and Josiah were faithful to God's Word. Finally, God allowed the pagan empires of

Assyria and Babylonia to destroy both kingdoms and carry the people away into exile.

Two important leaders emerged in the time of the divided monarchy. The first was the prophet Elijah. He stands out as a uniquely rugged character in the Bible story. We don't know where he came from; he just suddenly appeared before the wicked King Ahab and declared that God would bring a long drought because the people were so wicked. Elijah fled to the wilderness and stopped by the brook Cherith, where God miraculously provided food for him. When the stream dried up, God sent Elijah to help the widow Zarephath, who was suffering under the drought. She was nearly out of food when Elijah came to her door, but she fed him anyway. Because she did, the prophet decided to stay at her house and miracles

The Divided Monarchy

Biblical Events	Secular Events
The Division of the Kingdom (931) **Asa's Reformation In Judah (910)**	Pharaoh Shishak I Invades Palestine (925)
Omri Makes Samaria His Capital (879) Ahab And Jezebel Lead Israel to Idolatry (ca. 870) Elijah And Elisha (ca. 850) Jehu Pays Tribute To Shalmaneser III (841)	Assyria Begins Its Rise To Power (ca. 900) The Battle of Qarqar (853) Tyre Pays Tribute to Shalmaneser III (841)
Moabite Bands Invade Israel (795) Uzziah Is Struck Leprous (ca. 750) Beginning Of Isaiah's Ministry (ca. 739) The Fall Of Israel (723)	Assyria Destroys Damascus (732) Tyre Falls To Assyria (723) Sennacherib Invades Judah (701)
Manasseh Carried To Babylon (ca. 648) Jeremiah Begins His Ministry (ca. 627) Josiah's Reformation (621) Daniel And His Friends Carried to Babylon (605)	Esarhaddon Of Assyria Captures Sidon (677) Egypt Overthrows Its Ethiopian Rulers (663) Nabopolassar Overthrows The Assyrians (625) The Fall of Nineveh (612) Nebuchadnezzar Defeats Egypt At Carchemish (605)
The Fall of Jerusalem (597) The Fall of Judah and The Exile (586)	Nebuchadnezzar Invades Egypt (568)

Figure 2

followed; her supplies never ran out while he was there, and when her son died, Elijah raised him from the dead.

Then the prophet returned to King Ahab and told him to summon all the prophets of the pagan god Baal whom Jezebel, Ahab's wife worshiped, to meet him on Mount Carmel. There Elijah challenged the prophets to a contest to prove which god was stronger. Elijah asked God to send fire from heaven to light a water-logged sacrifice, and He did. Elijah killed all the false prophets (cf. Deut. 13:5). Then he asked God to end the drought, and God sent a cloudburst of rain. Elijah was so happy that he raced to the gates of Jezreel, outrunning the king and his chariots.

But Jezebel's threats against his life kept Elijah discouraged and frightened, and he asked God to let him die. Instead, God sent angels to minister to Elijah, and ordered him to recruit two future kings and his own successor. Elijah obeyed, appointing a farmer named Elisha to be the new prophet.

Elijah confronted Ahab again, condemning him and Jezebel for murdering their neighbor Naboth to get his vineyard. The king sent two companies of soldiers to capture the prophet, but Elijah called fire down from heaven to destroy them. Once more he declared the doom of the king.

Soon after that, Elijah and Elisha went for a walk, discussing the problems their nation faced. When they came to the Jordan River, Elijah divided the water by striking it with his mantle (a cape). They calmly walked across to the other side, as if they'd done it every day! As they stood on the river bank talking, a chariot of fire swooped down from the sky. It picked up Elijah and carried him away in a whirlwind, while his mantle fell on Elisha.

The second great personality of the divided monarchy was Elisha. He was like his teacher in many ways. Both men parted the waters of the Jordan, brought rain in times of drought, increased a widow's supply of food, raised a boy from the dead, performed miracles for Gentiles, pronounced doom upon kings, and destroyed their enemies with supernatural power. But there were also differences between them. Just before Elijah was taken into heaven, he prayed that God would give Elisha a double portion of His spirit. No doubt this had something to do with the differences between the two men. While Elijah fell under times of depression, Elisha had an attitude of triumph and confidence. He never seemed to complain or lose courage. The Scriptures show that he performed more miracles than any other prophet of the Old Testament (e.g., 2 Kings 4:38–5:19).

Isaiah, Jeremiah, Amos, Hosea, Micah, Ezekiel, and other prophets warned Israel and Judah that God would punish their wickedness. Isaiah and Ezekiel also had words of consolation for them after they went into exile. God used these men as His holy spokesmen in this crucial epoch of His people's history.

FROM THE EXILE TO THE RETURN

The Jewish people were taken into exile more than once. So when we discuss "the Exile," we should be careful to say *which* exile we mean. The Assyrians twice conquered the northern kingdom (Israel); the southern kingdom (Judah) was conquered once by Assyria and three times by the Babylonians. Each time, the conquerors carried off many captives. Most often when we talk about "the Exile," we mean the 70-year Babylonian captivity of Judah.

Religiously speaking, the Babylonian Captivity had three successive phases: one of unrealistic hopefulness (cf. Jer. 29; Ezek. 17:11-24); one of truer and humbler hopefulness, when God used Ezekiel to comfort the people (Ezek. 36–38); and one of revived hopefulness in the time of Daniel. The Jews returned from the Exile in two stages: One group was led by Sheshbazzar and Zerubbabel (Ezra 1:8–2:70). The second was led by Ezra and Nehemiah (Ezra 8:1-14). Just as Isaiah had predicted (Isa. 44:28; 45:1), God raised up a kind-hearted pagan king—Cyrus of Persia—who let the Jews return to Palestine. The people who had taken their place tried to ruin their plans; but the Jews rebuilt the Temple in Jerusalem and resettled in their land. The prophets Zechariah and Haggai encouraged the people in their work. But toward the end of this period, Malachi condemned them for slipping back into their sinful ways.

INTERTESTAMENTAL HISTORY

It is not always clear what happened in the 400 years between the writing of Malachi and the time Jesus was born. We call this the "Intertestamental Period" because it is the time between the writing of the Old and New Testaments.

We know the restored nation of Israel had serious political upsets during this time. After Alexander the Great conquered the Persian Empire, Greek princes and generals wrestled for the right to govern the Near East. The Seleucid king Antiochus III took Palestine away from Egypt in 198 B.C. and tried to make it a base for building a new empire in the East. But Antiochus III was no match for the Roman legions. They defeated his army in 190 B.C. and made him a puppet ruler in the Roman chain of command.

The Maccabee family (the offspring of the high priest Mattathias) began a civil war against the Seleucid governors and captured Jerusalem in 164 B.C. But they weren't able to push the Seleucids completely out of their affairs until 134 B.C. In that year, John Hyrcanus I of the Maccabee family set up his own dynasty, known as the Hasmoneans. They ruled until 37 B.C., when Rome established the Herodian family as the new puppet government in Palestine.

The books entitled 1 and 2 Maccabees describe the Maccabean revolt and the chaos of Palestine up to the time of the Hasmoneans. Roman Catholics include these books and other writings from the Intertestamental Period in their Bible, but Protestants do not, although translations of them are often included in Protestant versions of the Bible.

Old Testament history paints a colorful picture of God's dealings with man; but it doesn't give us the whole story of God's plan to redeem men from sin. The New Testament brings us to the climax of God's redemptive work, because it introduces us to the Messiah, Jesus Christ, and to the beginning of His church.

3

OLD TESTAMENT CHRONOLOGY

FINDING THE DATES OF BIBLE EVENTS

Scripture tells how God revealed Himself at specific points in time. To help grasp the relation of these divine revelations to other historical events, we need to know the dates of the biblical events themselves.

The word *chronology* comes from the classical Greek word *chronos,* which signifies time viewed as a flowing stream—a stream that cannot be stopped, but can be measured. *Chronology* is simply the dating of historical events within the "stream" of time. The Bible devotes quite a lot of space to matters of chronology.

For instance, the prophets dated their writings to show the background of their message. Their chronological notes help us understand why God said what He said, and why He did what He did at each particular time.

Jewish people followed their calendar with great care. Ancient Israel had a lunar calendar that pegged religious festivals to certain seasons of the year. The Israelites harvested barley in the spring during Abib, the first month of the religious year (Exod. 23:15). After the Exile, they called this month Nisan. They celebrated the Feast of Weeks during the month of Sivan, which began the summer harvest of wheat (Exod. 34:22). Their Feast of the Ingathering (or Feast of Booths) coincided with their general harvest in the autumn month of Ethanim, later called Tishri (Exod. 34:22). Generally their months were 30 days long. But since each month was counted from a new-moon day, the calendar sometimes called for a 29-day month. The lunar calendar was 11 days shorter than the solar year and yet had to match the seasons, so the Israelites sometimes had to add a thirteenth month to the year. This gave them some leap-year days. Their pattern of inserting leap-year days repeated itself in a 19-year cycle.

ESTABLISHING ABSOLUTE DATES

The Bible doesn't give its chronology according to the calendar in use today. To establish absolute dates, we need to figure out the Bible's system for recording the dates of the kings and then lay it alongside the dates for rulers of Assyria and Babylon. The Assyrians based their history on the data of astronomy, and so we can check the Assyrian dates against the movement of the stars, which our present knowledge enables us to plot accurately. Then we can use that information to pinpoint the dates of Old Testament events.

A. Assyrian Lists. The Assyrians' *eponym* lists give the dates of the Assyrian kings. An *eponym* is a person for whom a period of time has been named: for example, Queen Elizabeth I of England was the eponym of the Elizabethan Age. So the Assyrian lists put a number of important officials in sequence and name each year after a particular leader. Clay tablets from Nineveh and other Assyrian cities list the names

Jehu offers tribute. Shalmaneser III of Assyria recorded his military victories on a large black limestone obelisk near his palace at Calah. This panel from the obelisk shows King Jehu of Israel (wearing a pointed hat) bowing down to Shalmaneser. On either side of Shalmaneser are servants with parasol, fan, and scepter. The Bible does not mention Jehu's tribute.

of these leaders, along with the consecutive years of Assyrian history. These lists give us a history from 892 to 648 B.C. During that time, several Assyrian leaders made contact with the Hebrew kings.

The tablets mention Bur-Sagale, governor of Guzana. The Assyrian record says that an eclipse of the sun occurred in the month of Simanu during Bur-Sagale's term of office. Astronomers tell us that the eclipse occurred on June 15, 763 B.C. Therefore, Bur-Sagale governed in 763 B.C., and we can use this date to establish the dates of other Assyrian leaders.

A tablet about the Assyrian leader Daian-Assur says that he governed during the sixth year of Shalmaneser III. In that same year, the Assyrians fought an important battle at Qarqar against a group of kings from the Mediterranean seacoast, and the tablet lists King Ahab of Israel among them. Other information in the Assyrian lists gives the date of this battle—and of Ahab's death—at 853 B.C.

Still another eponym list says that a certain "King Ia-a-u" began paying tribute to Shalmaneser III in the eighteenth year of Shalmaneser's reign. Most likely this was King Jehu of Israel. The Assyrian list shows that the date was 841 B.C.

By comparing Assyrian and Hebrew records in this fashion, we can learn a great deal about the chronology of the kings of Israel and Judah.

B. Two Systems of Figuring Dates. How did the chroniclers of the Bible date the reigns of the kings? After the death of King Solomon and the division of the kingdom, it seems that chroniclers in the southern kingdom of Judah counted the official reign of their kings from the Hebrew month of Ethanim, or Tishri (September-October)—the beginning of the civil year. In the northern kingdom of Israel, scribes used the month of Abib, or Nisan (March-April)—the beginning of the religious year.

Compare 2 Kings 22:3-13 and 23:21-23 for proof of this. These texts tell how King Josiah's men discovered a book of the Law in the temple, and how Josiah restored the Passover observance on the traditional fourteenth day of Abib. The Bible says all of this happened in the eighteenth year of

Josiah's reign. If the writer of 2 Kings began counting the years of Josiah's reign with the month of Abib, he would be saying that the priests cleansed the temple for the Passover in a maximum of 14 days—from between the first and the fourteenth of Abib. This is not very likely. Therefore he may have figured that the eighteenth year of Josiah's reign began the previous fall, in the month of Ethanim.

No Scripture passage indicates when the reigns of Israel's kings began. However, Edwin R. Thiele has shown that if we assume Judah began her year with the month of Ethanim and Israel began her year with Abib, "the perplexing discrepancies disappear and a harmonious chronological pattern results."[1]

C. Two Systems of Elapsed Time. But knowing about these two different ways of counting years doesn't solve all the problems. Ancient historians were not consistent when they talked about a king's "first year" on the throne because each king decided for himself how his history books would handle this. A king might call the year in which his reign commenced his "first" year; scholars refer to this as *non-accession year* dating. On the other hand, he might call the first year after he took the throne his "first" year; scholars label that *accession year* dating. To accurately establish absolute dates, the method a king was using to designate the years of his reign must be established.

Suppose the kings of Israel used non-accession year dating, while the kings of Judah used accession year dating. Figure 3 shows how these systems would give different dates for the reign of a king. If this really happened, Israel's records would always give one year more for the reign of a king than Judah's records would. As each king of Israel came to the throne, the total span of the kings' reigns would seem to increase by one year. To correlate the royal chronologies of the two nations, we would therefore need to subtract one year from the reign of each king who sat upon the throne in the North.

Have we reason to think Israel's custom was to use the non-accession year system of dating? Yes, we have. We have already learned from the Assyrian list that King Jehu probably paid tribute to Shalmaneser III in 841 B.C., 12 years after King Ahab fought in the battle of Qarqar. The records of Israel (from which the relevant dates in Kings and Chronicles are presumably taken) say that Ahab was succeeded by Ahaziah, who ruled for two years (1 Kings 22:51). Then Joram (Jehoram) was king for 12 years (2 Kings 3:1), making a total of 14 years for these two kings. After Joram, Jehu came to the throne and began paying tribute the Shalmaneser III. It is possible to match the 12 years in Assyrian chronology with the period of 14 years in Israel's chronology only if Israel followed the non-accession year dating scheme. That means we should take one year from the reign of each of Israel's kings. Thus, Ahaziah actually reigned for only one year and Joram for 11

Assyrian calendar. This cuneiform tablet from Assyria ties the political events of the nation to movements of the planets and stars. Such calendars help modern scientists to figure the exact dates of key events in Assyrian history, which in turn allow us to calculate the dates of biblical events.

years. That means Ahaziah and Joram actually reigned for a total of 12 years, and this corresponds with the Assyrian chronology for Jehu. The evidence fits together only if Israel followed the non-accession year dating.

On the other hand, the scribes of Judah undoubtedly used the accession year dating scheme for their kings. They may have changed this system occasionally when the northern kingdom had a close influence on Judah. For instance, the two nations became more friendly when princess Athaliah of Israel married Jehoram, the son of Judah's King Jehoshaphat. The Bible says Jehoram "walked in the way of the kings of Israel, as did the house of Ahab" (2 Kings 8:18; 2 Chron. 21:6). Under Jehoram's reign, as we shall see, Judah adopted the non-accession method for dating her kings, and used it for a number of years.

When studying the dates of the kings, we also need to allow for overlappings of kings' reigns. This happened when a son reigned as co-regent with his father. The same years were then reckoned to both reigns. There are several instances of this, as will appear.

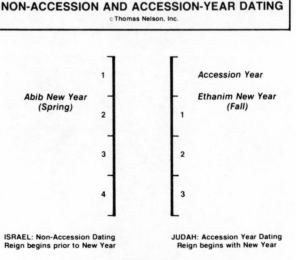

NON-ACCESSION AND ACCESSION-YEAR DATING
c Thomas Nelson, Inc.

1

Abib New Year
(Spring)

2

3

4

ISRAEL: Non-Accession Dating
Reign begins prior to New Year

Accession Year

Ethanim New Year
(Fall)

1

2

3

JUDAH: Accession Year Dating
Reign begins with New Year

Figure 3

RULERS OF THE DIVIDED KINGDOM

We are now ready to work back to the pivotal date of King Solomon's death, when the kingdom split. Figure 4 uses the biblical dates for rulers of the divided kingdom, keeping in mind the methods of dating we have already discussed.

Since we're assuming that Israel followed a non-accession dating scheme, we need to deduct one year from the reign of each king of Israel as we work our way back from the Assyrian dates of 841 B.C. (the beginning of Jehu's reign) and 853 B.C. (the death of Ahab). Use Figure 2 to compare the dating of Israel's and Judah's kings. For clarity, the name of each king of Israel is shown in bold face type while the name of each king of Judah is shown in capital letters.

Joram—2 Kings 3:1; "12 years" (11 years). Joram began his rule in the eighteenth year of Jehoshaphat (see below); since he reigned for 11 years before Jehu, his first year of sole reign was 852 B.C. (841 B.C. plus 11 years).

AHAZIAH—2 Kings 8:25; one year. Ahaziah began his rule in the eleventh year of Joram's reign (2 Kings 9:29). (The reason why 2 Kings 8:25 states that he began in the twelfth year of Joram is that Judah had adopted Israel's non-accession dating scheme at this time.) Both Joram of Israel and Ahaziah of Judah died in 841 B.C. (2 Kings 9:24, 27); so Ahaziah probably reigned for only a few months, even though Israel's records say he reigned for "one year." (Remember that Israel's non-accession dating method would have called the first months of Ahaziah's reign his "first year.")

JEHORAM—2 Kings 8:17; "8 years" (7 years). Jehoram evidently adopted Israel's non-accession dating scheme, so one year should be deducted from his reign. Apparently Jehoram reigned with his father for five years before his official reign began. We know this because, when 2 Kings 8:16 says Jehoram began ruling Judah, it also mentions Jehoshaphat as king of Judah. Compare this text with 2 Kings 3:1 and 2 Kings 1:17, which say that Joram ("Jehoram") of Israel

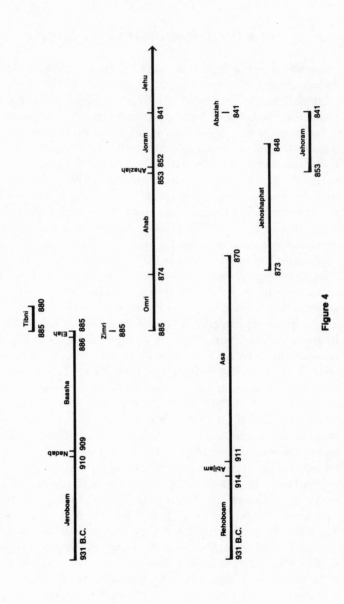

DATING SOLOMON'S REIGN
©Thomas Nelson, Inc.

Figure 4

became king in the eighteenth year of Jehoshaphat's sole reign and in the second year of Jehoram of Judah. (We have already learned that this year was 852 B.C.) This indicates that Jehoram ruled with his father for five years before his official reign began in Joram's fifth year (fourth year according to non-accession dating), or 848 B.C. (852 B.C. minus 4 years.)

Ahab—1 Kings 16:29; "22 years" (21 years). Ahab died in 853, so he must have begun his reign in 874 (853 B.C. plus 21 years).

JEHOSHAPHAT—1 Kings 22:41-42; 25 years. Settling the dates of Jehoshaphat is difficult because his reign overlapped with those of both his father and his son. He began his rule in the fourth year of Ahab, whose reign began in 874 B.C. Ahab's fourth year (the year Jehoshaphat took the throne of Judah) was 870 B.C. Since Jehoshaphat joined Ahab in the battle with the Syrians in 853 B.C., he would naturally have put his son Jehoram on the throne as co-regent at that time, in case he did not come back. We've already noted that Jehoram began his *sole* reign in the fifth year of Joram (the fourth year in the accession dating system). So if we take 852 B.C. (the first year of Joram's reign) and subtract four years, we find that Jehoram became sole ruler of Judah in 848 B.C., and we assume that was the year Jehoshaphat died. We know that Jehoshaphat reigned for 25 years (1 Kings 22:42), so we can infer that his reign began in 873 B.C. (848 B.C. plus 25 years). As we saw, his sole reign formally began in 870 B.C. He reigned with his father Asa for about three years, because Asa suffered from a disabling disease in his feet that had come on in his thirty-ninth year as king (2 Chron. 16:12).

Ahaziah—1 Kings 22:51; "2 years" (one year). Ahaziah began his rule in the seventeenth year of Jehoshaphat's sole reign, 853 B.C. (870 B.C. minus 17 years).

ASA—1 Kings 15:10; 41 years. Since we know Jehoshaphat took the throne in 870 B.C., that must have been the year Asa died. And he must have begun his reign in 911 B.C. (870 B.C. plus 41 years).

Omri—1 Kings 16:15-16, 23; "12 years" (11 years). Since we know that Ahab began his reign in 874 B.C., Omri must have died that year. That means Omri began his reign in 885 B.C. (874 B.C. plus 11 years).

Zimri—1 Kings 16:15; seven days. Zimri killed Elah, son of Baasha. In turn, Omri deposed Zimri (1 Kings 16:17-18).

Elah—1 Kings 16:8; "2 years" (one year). Elah was killed in Zimri's coup of 885, so he began his rule in 886.

Tibni—1 Kings 16:21-24. We are not told how long this rival of Omri ruled. We assume he began his rule at the same time as Omri in 885; they simply reigned in different parts of Israel. We know that Omri ruled in Tirzah for six years (actually five), until 880. Then he moved to Samaria and established his rule there, which suggests that Tibni was dead.

Baasha—1 Kings 15:33; "24 years" (23 years). Since Elah took the throne in 886, we know Baasha died that year. So he began his reign in 909 B.C. (886 B.C. plus 23 years).

Nadab—1 Kings 15:25-31; "two years" (one year). Baasha seized control of Israel by murdering Nadab, so Nadab must have reigned from 910 to 909 B.C.

Jeroboam—1 Kings 14:20; "22 years" (21 years). Jeroboam's reign began in 931 (910 B.C. plus 21 years).

ABIJAM—1 Kings 15:2; three years. Since Abijam began his reign three years before his successor Asa, this would have been in 914 B.C. (911 B.C. plus 3 years).

REHOBOAM—1 Kings 14:21; 17 years. Rehoboam started his rule in 931 B.C., 17 years before Abijam (914 B.C. plus 17 years). He began to reign over Judah in the same year as his rival Jeroboam took Israel, when the kingdom divided. This also would have been the year Solomon died.

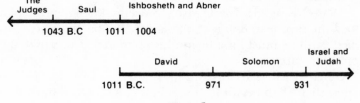

ISRAEL'S FIRST THREE KINGS

cThomas Nelson, Inc.

Figure 5

THE FIRST THREE KINGS OF ISRAEL

Having established the date of Solomon's death (931 B.C.), we can proceed backward in Israel's history even farther, using the chronology of the Bible to establish specific dates. (*See* Fig. 5).

Jeroboam I and Rehoboam divided the kingdom in 931 B.C. and Solomon died that year. The Bible says that Solomon reigned over all Israel for 40 years (1 Kings 11:42). And so in Figure 5 the start of Solomon's reign is set in 971 B.C. That would have been the year of David's death.

David was king for 40 years, which places the start of his rule in 1011 B.C. However, David ruled only Judah while Saul's son Ish-bosheth had the other tribes' allegiance. First Kings 2:11 and 2 Samuel 2:11 say that David was king in Hebron for seven years and six months. When Ishbosheth's enemies assassinated him, the tribal leaders of Israel met in Hebron and gave their allegiance to David (2 Sam. 5:3). Thus David's sole rule began in the year of 1004 B.C., and it lasted for 33 years.

Saul, who died in 1011 B.C., also had a long reign; we are told it lasted 40 years (Acts 13:21). (Something has dropped out of the Hebrew text in 1 Samuel 13:1. "Two years" could not be the complete number.) However, this figure of 40 may include both the reign of Saul and his son Ishbosheth. If so, this would leave about 33 years for the sole reign of Saul, which means that he would have begun his rule in 1043 B.C. rather than 1057 B.C.

MOSES AND THE PATRIARCHS

There are two pivotal points in the chronology of the Old Testament. The first is the date the foundations of the first temple were laid. First Kings 6:1 says that Solomon began building the temple in the fourth year of his reign over Israel, in the second month (Ziv), 480 years after the Israelites came out of Egypt. We know that Solomon began his reign in 971

B.C., and so his first year on Israel's dating scheme would have begun in the fall of 970 B.C. The fourth year would be 967/66 B.C., reckoned on a fall-to-fall basis. Since *Ziv* was the second month on the religious calendar, we conclude that Solomon began the temple in the spring of 966 B.C. On this basis, Israel's Exodus from Egypt would have begun in 1446 B.C., and Canaan would have been conquered around 1406 B.C.

The other pivotal date in the Old Testament is that of Jacob's move to Egypt, which was 430 years before the Exodus (Exod. 12:40-41). This brings us to 1876 B.C. (1446 B.C. plus 430 years).

With these numbers as a start, we can fill in dates for events in the period from the time of Abraham until Israel's first king, Saul.

A. The Date of the Exodus. Many Bible students still question the date of the Exodus. They have developed two dating schemes for the Exodus—an early date that takes 1 Kings 6:1 as a precise note of time, and an alternate suggestion that we call "the late date." Here are the arguments for both sides:

1. The Early Date. This argument insists that the ancients knew how to construct a calendar and keep accurate records of time, and that they stated the length of epochs with chronological exactness. So it accepts the 480 years of 1 Kings 6:1 and the statement of Jephthah, a judge who declared that Israel had occupied the land of Canaan for about 300 years (Judg. 11:26). Since we have already calculated that Israel's Exodus began in 1446 B.C., we can deduct 40 years for their wilderness wanderings to place them entering Canaan in 1406 B.C. If we subtract the 300 years mentioned in this verse, we see that Jephthah would have lived in 1106 B.C. This provides ample time for the period of the Judges, who ruled various sections of Israel prior to Saul's monarchy.

Bible students who support the early date of the Exodus on these grounds also point to the Amarna tablets, dated at about 1400 B.C. These tablets, discovered in Egypt, contain international correspondence during Egypt's eighteenth dynasty under Pharaoh Amenhotep III (1410–1377 B.C.). They contain numerous requests from the Canaanite city-states begging the Egyptians to help them drive out the *Habiru*, or nomadic invaders; but there is little evidence that this group included the Israelites. If we accept the early date of the Exodus (1446 B.C.) then allow 40 years for the Israelites' sojourn in the wilderness, they would have invaded Canaan in 1406 B.C. and would have been the *Habiru*.

2. The Late Date. Students who hold this view believe Moses led the Israelites out of bondage during Egypt's nineteenth dynasty, which began in 1318 B.C. The chief line of evidence for the late date is the appearance of new cultural forms in Palestine, specifically the destruction of Jericho by outside invaders at about this date. Scholars who advocate this date point out that the pharaoh of the time was Rameses II (*ca.* 1304–1238 B.C.), and they believe Hebrew slaves built the Egyptian store cities of Pithom and Ramses during his reign (Exod. 1:11; 12:37; Num. 33:3). Rameses II mentions using slave labor of the *Apiru*—perhaps the Egyptian word for "Hebrew"—to build his grain cities. Other scholars believe an earlier pharaoh first built these cities, but in that case Rameses II certainly rebuilt and named one of them for himself. Archaeological evidence seems to indicate this. If we assume that the Hebrews built these cities for Rameses II, they would have left Egypt some years later, about 1275 B.C., and conquered Canaan after 1235—a date that these scholars believe is confirmed by archaeological evidence that Canaanite cities were destroyed.

But we should note that the pharaohs of Rameses' time used the very names employed by the Hyksos kings of Egypt (1730–1570 B.C.; *see* "Egyptians"). Rameses worshiped the same gods that the Hyksos kings worshiped. So the Hebrew slaves could have worked on these cities under the Hyksos. In fact, the Hyksos would have had good reason to oppress the Israelites, since they were also of Semitic origin and considered the Israelites bitter rivals.[2] In that case, Exodus 1:13 ff. may describe events under the eighteenth dynasty, which drove out the Hyksos.

We run into many difficulties if we suppose the Exodus

took place in the thirteenth century. If the Exodus is dated at about 1275 B.C., and the conquest after 1235 B.C., and if Saul came to the throne in about 1043 B.C., only about 230 years would have elapsed from the Exodus until Saul, and only 190 from the conquest to Saul.

B. The Life of Moses. Figure 6 shows Egypt's eighteenth dynasty and the events of Israel from the birth of Moses until the time of Saul's reign. We have divided Moses' life into three parts:

1. Early Life. Since Moses was 120 years old when the Israelites were ready to enter Canaan in 1406 B.C. (Deut. 34:7), he must have been born in 1526 B.C. near the beginning of Egypt's eighteenth dynasty. Until he reached 40 years of age, he lived in the royal palace as the adopted son of Hatshepsut, the daughter of Thutmose I. In 1486 B.C. (1526 B.C. minus 40 years) he fled into the wilderness (cf. Acts 7:23).

2. Confrontation with the Pharaoh. Moses spent 40 years in the wilderness, caring for the flocks of his father-in-law, Jethro. Then God called Moses to lead Israel from Egypt to be a free people, in 1446 B.C. (cf. Acts 7:30).

3. Life in the Desert. Until 1406 B.C., Moses led the Israelites on a wayward course to the Promised Land.

Amenhotep III (1410–1377 B.C.). Clay tablets from Amarna show that the princes of Canaan appealed to Pharaoh Amenhotep III for help in fighting invaders known as the *Habiru.* The Israelites fleeing from Egypt may have been part of this wave of invaders.

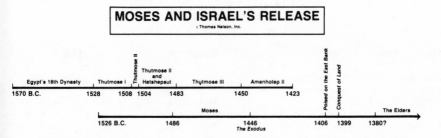

Figure 6

God chose Joshua to lead Israel in the conquest of Canaan, which took six years—to about 1400 B.C. (Josh. 14:7, 10). We know this because Caleb was 40 years old when he spied on Canaan in the second year of the Exodus, 1444 B.C., and he was 85 years old when the Israelites divided the territory of Canaan in 1400 B.C. (1445 B.C. minus 45 years).

Joshua lived to be 110 years of age (Josh. 24:29), but we do not know exactly when he died. The elders ruled Israel for a time after Joshua's leadership (Josh. 24:31). We can assume a period of 15 to 20 years from the end of the conquest (1400 B.C.) until the elders who served with Joshua died (about 1380 B.C.).

The Book of Judges covers a period of about 337 years, from 1380 to 1043 B.C. The judges' terms of service and the periods of oppression total about 410 consecutive years. Since Paul says the judges ruled "about the space of 450 years" (Acts 13:20), many of the judges' careers may have overlapped. In Figure 7, we attempt to reconstruct this period. However, these are approximate figures because we do not know exactly when Joshua and his elders died, nor how long certain tribes of Israel rebelled against God. But Jephthah's statement in Judges 11:26 that the Israelites conquered Canaan about 300 years before his time gives a reference point. If he is speaking in 1106 B.C. (1406 B.C. minus 300 years), it is very close to the date of 1089 B.C. that we have estimated for the raids by the Ammonites.

However, we will use the 1106 B.C. date for Jephthah to

The Judges

Description	Reference	Date
Assume 5 years of apostasy		1380–1375 B.C.
Oppression, 8 years	Judg. 3:8	1375–1367 B.C.
Deliverance by Othniel; 40 years' rest	Judg. 3:11	1367–1327 B.C.
Assume 5 years of apostasy		1327–1322 B.C.
Oppression by Moab, 18 years	Judg. 3:14	1322–1304 B.C.
Deliverance by Ehud; 80 years' rest	Judg. 3:31	1304–1224 B.C.
Deliverance by Deborah; 40 years' rest	Judg. 5:31	1224–1184 B.C.
Oppression by Midian, 7 years	Judg. 6:1	1184–1177 B.C.
Deliverance by Gideon; 40 years' rest	Judg. 8:28	1177–1137 B.C.
Abimelech's reign, 3 years	Judg. 9:22	1137–1134 B.C.
Tolah and Jair, 45 years	Judg. 10:2-3	1134–1089 B.C.
Jephthah, 6 years	Judg. 12:7	1089–1083 B.C.
Ibzan, Elon, and Abdon, 25 years	Judg. 12:9, 11, 14	1083–1058 B.C.

Figure 7

reconstruct the dates of the later judges. This new chart brings us down to the days of Samuel, the battles of Israel and the Philistines in the West and Southwest, and Saul's appointment as king in 1043 B.C.

C. The Patriarchs and the Move to Egypt. Having accepted the Exodus date of 1446 B.C., we can work our way back into the history of the patriarchs. Figure 8 shows the layout of this chronology.

1. Israel's Stay in Egypt. We have already seen that the Israelites lived in Egypt about 400 years (Gen. 15:13). Exodus 12:40 tells us that Jacob's family arrived in Egypt 430 years before the Exodus, or about 1876 B.C. (cf. Gal. 3:17). This means that Jacob's family entered Egypt at a time when Egypt was not a particularly strong nation.

Some scholars insist that the family of Jacob must have entered Egypt after the time of the Hyksos, because the Israelites would have found easier access to Egypt after their time. However, the Hyksos did not leave Egypt until 1570 B.C. That would push the Exodus down to 1270 B.C., the "late date," which we saw to be doubtful on other grounds.

The Scriptures say Jacob was 130 years old when he entered Egypt (Gen. 47:9, 28). Joseph was 39 years old (age 30 plus 7 years plus 2 years, Gen. 41:46-47; 45:6). With the date of 1876 B.C. for Jacob's move to Egypt, we can plot out the dates of these men.

2. Joseph. Joseph's birth date would be 1915 B.C. (1876 B.C. plus 39 years). According to Genesis 50:26, he would have died in 1805 B.C. (1915 B.C. minus 110 years).

3. Jacob. Jacob was 130 years old when he entered Egypt and lived there 17 years. So he was 147 years old when he died in 1859 B.C. (1876 B.C. minus 17 years). Working the other way, we find that he was born in 2006 B.C. (1876 B.C. plus 130 years).

4. Isaac. Jacob's father, Isaac, was 60 years old when Jacob

Foreign captives. The pharaohs used foreign slaves to erect their massive temples and tombs. This relief from the tomb of Rameses III shows (from left to right) Libyan, Semitic, Hittite, Philistine, and Semitic captives being led to the pharaoh's compound.

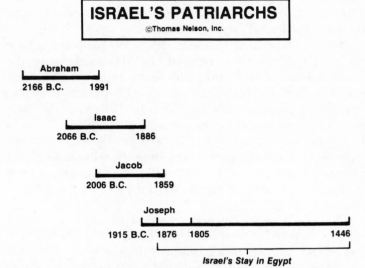

Figure 8

was born (Gen. 25:26), and so Isaac himself was born in 2066 B.C. (2006 B.C. plus 60 years). He lived to the age of 180, which means that he died in 1886 B.C., about 10 years before Jacob took his family into Egypt.

5. Abraham. The Bible says Abraham was 100 years old when Isaac was born (Gen. 21:5), and so Abraham himself was born in 2166 B.C. in Ur of the Chaldees. He entered Canaan at age 75 (Gen. 12:4) in 2091 B.C. He died at 175 years of age in 1991 B.C. (Gen. 25:7).

DATING PRIOR TO ABRAHAM

Our study of the chronology prior to Abraham is divided into two sections: (1) from the Flood until Abraham and (2) from the Creation to the Flood. Needless to say, this span of time poses the greatest problems because we can no longer compare biblical dates with historical records of the nations surrounding Israel. The ancient histories of these other

nations are very sketchy and poorly understood. Even different versions of the Old Testament disagree sharply about the
events of history before the patriarchs. We will generally
follow the Masoretic (Hebrew) text, but we will compare its
account with the other ancient versions at specific points.

A. From the Flood to Abraham. Abraham's family list
(Gen. 11:10-26) provides the information we need for this
period. Figure 9 charts the lives of Abraham's ancestors. First,
notice that Abraham has a birth date of 2166 B.C. and a death
date of 1991 B.C. These figures are based on the calculations
we have already done.

1. Abraham's Father, Terah. Abraham's father, Terah, had
worshiped idols for several years (Josh. 24:2) when he moved
his family from Ur to Haran. Terah lived there until he died
at the age of 205 (Gen. 11:32).

God called Abraham to go to Canaan at the age of 75 (Gen.
12:4). It appears that this was immediately after Terah's death.
This would fix Terah's death at 2091 B.C. (2166 B.C. minus 75
years), making him 130 years old when Abraham was born
(age 205 minus 75 years). Thus we find that Terah was born in
2296 B.C. (2166 B.C. plus 130 years or 2091 B.C. plus 205
years).

2. Nahor. Terah was born when his father, Nahor, was 29
years of age (Gen. 11:24). Nahor lived for 119 more years
(Gen. 11:25), so he must have been born in 2325 B.C. (2296
B.C. plus 29 years).

3. Serug. Nahor's father, Serug, was 30 years old when
Nahor was born, and he lived 200 years afterward (Gen.
11:22-23). Therefore, Serug's birth date was 2355 B.C. (2325
B.C. plus 30 years) and he died in 2125 B.C. (2325 B.C. minus
200 years).

4. Reu. Serug's father, Reu, was 32 years old when Serug
was born, and he lived 207 years afterward (Gen. 11:20-21).
So the date of birth for Reu was 2387 B.C. (2355 B.C. plus 32
years), and he died in 2148 B.C. (2355 B.C. minus 207 years).

5. Peleg. Reu's father, Peleg was 30 years old at the birth of
Reu, and he lived 209 years afterward. So Peleg's birth date
was 2417 B.C. (2387 B.C. plus 30 years) and his date of death
was 2178 B.C. (2387 B.C. minus 209 years).

6. Eber. Eber was 34 years old when he became the father of Peleg, and he lived 430 years after Peleg's birth (Gen. 11:16-17). So we calculate that Eber was born in 2451 B.C. (2417 B.C. plus 34 years) and died in 1987 B.C. (2417 B.C. minus 430 years). This means that Eber lived beyond the time Abraham entered the land of Canaan. If the evidence from the tablets excavated at Ebla is correct, the term *Hebrew* may be derived from this man's name.

7. Salah. Eber's father, Salah, was 30 years old when Eber

Figure 9

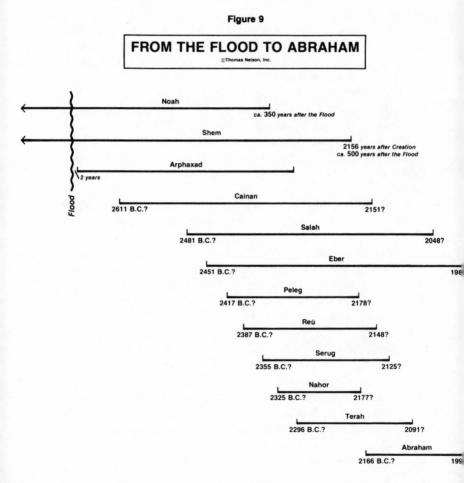

FROM THE FLOOD TO ABRAHAM

©Thomas Nelson, Inc.

Noah
ca. 350 years after the Flood

Shem
2156 years after Creation
ca. 500 years after the Flood

Arphaxad

2 years

Flood

Cainan
2611 B.C.?   2151?

Salah
2481 B.C.?   2048?

Eber
2451 B.C.?   198

Peleg
2417 B.C.?   2178?

Reú
2387 B.C.?   2148?

Serug
2355 B.C.?   2125?

Nahor
2325 B.C.?   2177?

Terah
2296 B.C.?   2091?

Abraham
2166 B.C.?   199

was born; he lived for 403 years more (Gen. 11:14-15). So Salah's birth date was 2481 B.C. (2451 B.C. plus 30 years) and the date of his death was 2048 B.C. (2451 B.C. minus 403 years).

8. Cainan. The Hebrew text of Scripture does not mention Cainan's life, but there is a statement about him in the Septuagint version of Genesis 10:24 and 11:12-13, as well as 1 Chronicles 1:18. Luke 3:36 also mentions him. The Septuagint indicates that Cainan was 130 years old at the birth of Salah and lived 330 years beyond Salah's birth. This would mean that Cainan was born in 2611 B.C. (2481 B.C. plus 130 years) and died in 2151 B.C. (2481 B.C. minus 330 years).

9. Arphaxad. The Hebrew text says Arphaxad was the father of Salah, but the Septuagint states that Arphaxad was the father of Cainan. In view of these conflicting statements, we will not try to date Arphaxad's birth or death. We do know that he was born two years after the Flood (Gen. 11:10) and he lived about 400 years after the birth of either Salah or Cainan.

10. Shem. Shem was 100 years old when his son Arphaxad was born, and he had a total lifespan of about 600 years (Gen. 11:10-11).

These figures confront us with some very distinct problems. In view of the great length of life ascribed to the earlier patriarchs, should the years always be understood as full calendar years? Why does the Septuagint include Cainan in the list, while the Hebrew text does not? Could there be gaps in the genealogical lists? In fact, it appears that the lists of Genesis 5 and 11 are not complete records, but selections of outstanding men.

In addition, note that the time span from Cainan (in 2611 B.C.) to the entrance of Abraham into Canaan (in 2091 B.C.) is about 520 years. We might have to add about 60 years to allow for whether Arphaxad is the father of Cainan or Salah.

And what about Eber? If we take the Masoretic text at face value, Eber lived beyond the time Abraham entered Canaan. Was this really so? Not necessarily. If there are gaps in the list, Eber may have died long before Abraham was in Canaan.

Here's another problem: The 520-year span from Cainan to Abraham's entrance into Canaan does not square with the figures given by other versions of the Old Testament. The Septuagint says 1,232 years elapsed from the Flood to Abraham's journey into Canaan, while the Samaritan Pentateuch says it was 942 years. We have no way of testing either of these figures. But ever since the discovery of the Qumran scrolls, the Masoretic text has been viewed as probably authentic. Still, the Masoretic text disagrees with the records of early Egyptian and Mesopotamian history. Accounts of Egyptian and Mesopotamian history for these regions begin at about 3000 B.C. The Flood must have occurred prior to that time, and at an earlier time than what we see in Figure 9.

The best conclusion is that the list in Genesis 11 is not strictly genealogical so much as *epochal*. In other words, it gives the names of certain outstanding individuals in the correct genealogical line, but not always in a father-to-son sequence. Thus the length of time covered is longer than it might appear.

The Bible offers us several other examples of epochal lists, as in Matthew 1:8, where Jehoram appears to be the father of Uzziah. Actually, Jehoram was the great-great-grandfather of Uzziah. Matthew could not have expected this omission to go unnoticed by his readers, nor did he seem to expect them to find fault with it. However strange it is to us, this method of epochal genealogy was well understood in the ancient world.

B. From Creation to the Flood. Since we cannot establish a specific date for the Flood, we will have trouble proceeding backward to the date of Adam and Eve. All we can do is trace the family line of Adam to the time of the Flood, using the chronologies found in Genesis 5 and 7:11. Refer to Figure 10 as we explore this pre-Flood history.

1. Adam to Enoch. Adam was 130 years old when Seth was born (Gen. 5:3). We can ignore the family of Cain, since Genesis gives us no specific dates for his descendants. And the Bible mentions no descendants of Abel when he was murdered. So the genealogy must begin with Seth. Adam lived for 800 years after Seth's birth (Gen. 5:4).

Seth was 105 years old when he became the father of Enos. He lived 807 years after Enos was born (Gen. 5:6-7).

Enos was 90 years old when his son Cainan was born, and he lived 815 years after that (Gen. 5:9-10). Cainan was 70 years old when Mahalaleel was born, and he lived 840 years more (Gen. 5:12-13).

Mahalaleel was 65 years old when his son Jared was born, and he continued to live for 830 years (Gen. 5:15-16). Jared was 162 years old when he fathered Enoch, and he lived beyond Enoch's birth for 800 years (Gen. 5:18-19).

Enoch was 65 years old when Methuselah was born, and then he lived for 300 years. Enoch "walked with God" and God took him up into heaven (Gen. 5:21-24).

Sumerian king list. An historian in ancient Sumer recorded the reigns of the Sumerian kings on this prism sometime between 2250–2000 B.C. The list mentions a great flood that destroyed the world, just as the Book of Genesis does.

2. Methuselah to Noah. Methuselah was 187 years old when his son Lamech was born, and the Bible tells us that he lived beyond Lamech for 782 years (Gen. 5:25-26). The length of Methuselah's age would put his death in the year of the Flood, according to the Bible's account. Does this mean that Methuselah died during the Flood? Perhaps. The Bible doesn't say.

Lamech was 182 years old at the birth of Noah and lived another 595 years (Gen. 5:28-31).

Noah was 500 years old when his three sons were born (Gen. 5:32). Noah built a ship to carry himself and his family, along with certain animals, through the Flood that God sent to destroy the wicked life of the earth in Noah's six hundredth year (Gen. 7:6). Noah lived 350 years after the Flood, dying at the age of 950 years (Gen. 9:28-29).

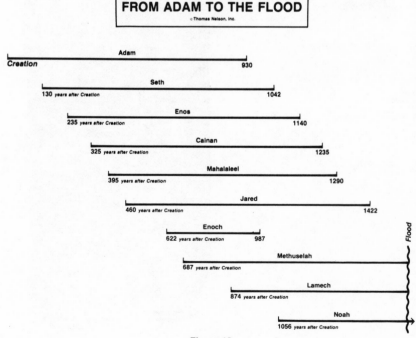

FROM ADAM TO THE FLOOD
©Thomas Nelson, Inc.

Figure 10

Sennacherib Prism. King Sennacherib of Assyria instructed his scribes to record his victories on this massive clay prism. The prism tells of Sennacherib's seige against Jerusalem in 701 B.C., during the reign of Hezekiah. The narrative says, "Hezekiah himself I shut up like a caged bird in Jerusalem, his royal city. I erected fortifications against him and blocked the exits from the gate of his city. . . ."

If we add up the ages of each of these men (from Adam to Noah), we get a total of 1,656 years from the time of Adam to the Flood. But other versions of the Old Testament give us different figures. The Septuagint puts 2,242 years between Adam and the Flood, the Samaritan version 1,307 years. These differences, all else apart, would make it impossible to fix a definite date for Adam. According to this chronology, Noah was born 1,056 years after Creation (1,656 years minus 600 years).

We have no reliable secular records from this period. The Sumerian king lists show six to eight kings ruling for about 30,000 years before the Flood! Obviously these are legends. We can't give an exact answer to the question of how long man had lived on the earth, but we would not favor the suggestion of millions of years. We only venture to say that many generations passed between Adam and the Flood, and the Flood occurred sometime before 2611 B.C. (Cainan's birth).

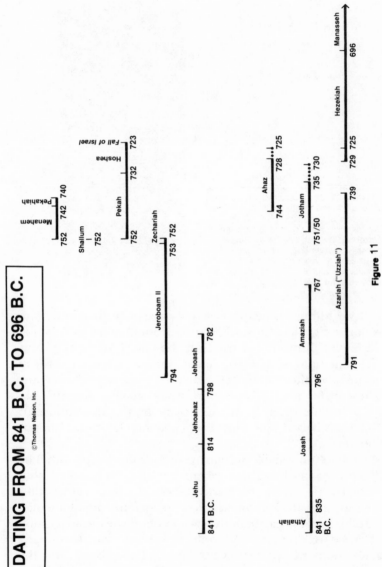

DATING FROM 841 B.C. TO 696 B.C.

©Thomas Nelson, Inc.

Figure 11

DATING FOR ISRAEL AND JUDAH FROM 841 B.C.

In Figure 4 we established two dates: 853 B.C. (the battle of Qarqar) and 841 B.C. (Shalmaneser's tribute from King "Ia-a-u," or Jehu). We have worked our way back in Israel's history from these dates. Now let us work forward to the fall of Israel and Judah. This is more difficult than one might suppose. Figure 11 lays out the history of these two kingdoms, with the bottom half referring to kings of Judah and the top half to the kings of Israel. In this text the name of each king of Judah will be shown in capital letters and the name of each king of Israel will be shown in boldface type.

Once again, we need to remember that Israel followed the non-accession dating scheme, and so one year must be subtracted from the reign of each king. Because Israel influenced Judah from the time of Jehoram, Judah followed a non-accession scheme at that time also. But both nations switched to an accession scheme during this period.

Jehu—2 Kings 10:36, "28 years" (27 years). This king killed his predecessor in Israel, Joram, and also the king of Judah, Ahaziah. Since we're assuming that Jehu began his reign in 841, his reign would have ended in 814 B.C. (841 B.C. minus 27 years).

ATHALIAH—2 Kings 11:4, 21; "seven years" (six years). This was the wife of Jehoram and daughter of Jezebel of Israel. When she saw that Jehu had killed her son, Ahaziah, she executed all the royal offspring so she could take the throne. (However, some loyal followers of Ahaziah spirited the king's son, Joash, away into hiding.) Athaliah came to the throne in 841 B.C. and ruled for seven non-accession years or six actual years. Her reign was completed in 835 B.C. (841 B.C. minus 6 years).

JOASH ("Jehoash")—2 Kings 12:1; "40 years" (39 years). Joash began his reign as the boy king in 835 B.C. and reigned for 40 non-accession years or 39 actual years. This means he was assassinated in 796 B.C. (835 B.C. minus 39 years).

Jehoahaz—2 Kings 13:1; "17 years" (16 years). Jehoahaz

began his reign upon the death of Jehu in 814 B.C., and he ruled for 17 non-accession years or 16 actual years, until 798 B.C. (814 B.C. minus 16 years).

Jehoash—2 Kings 13:10; 16 years. It appears that Israel now adopted an accession dating until the end of the kingdom. Jehoash began his reign in 798 B.C. and ruled until 782 B.C. (798 B.C. minus 16 years).

AMAZIAH—2 Kings 14:1-2; 29 years. By this time, Judah had evidently returned to the accession system of dating. Amaziah took the throne from Joash in 796 B.C. and reigned for 29 years, until 767 B.C. The Bible also says that Amaziah lived 15 years after the death of Jehoash of Israel—782 B.C. minus 15 years, or 767 B.C. (2 Kings 14:17).

Jeroboam II—2 Kings 13:10; 2 Kings 14:23; 41 years. While Jeroboam's total reign was 41 years, he seems to have reigned with Jehoash for a time. He officially became king in the fifteenth year of Amaziah, 781 B.C. (796 B.C. minus 15 years). Azariah ("Uzziah") followed his father Amaziah on the throne of Judah 14 years later (29 years minus 15 years), yet he became king in the twenty-seventh year of Jeroboam's reign (2 Kings 15:1-2), 794 B.C. (767 B.C. plus 27 years). So there must have been a 13-year overlap between Jeroboam and his father, Jehoash. This means that Jeroboam's joint reign with Jehoash began in 794 B.C., and his sole reign began in 781 B.C. (Apparently his official rule began with the new year, since the calendar says Jehoash died in 782 B.C.) He ruled until 753 B.C. (794 B.C. minus 41 years). Perhaps Jehoash set up joint rule with Jeroboam to protect the throne of Israel while he fought Amaziah of Judah (2 Kings 14:8-11).

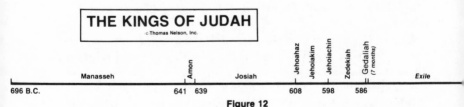

THE KINGS OF JUDAH
© Thomas Nelson, Inc.

| 696 B.C. | Manasseh | Amon | 641 | 639 | Josiah | Jehoahaz | Jehoiakim 608 | Jehoiachin 598 | Zedekiah | Gedaliah (7 months) 586 | Exile |

Figure 12

Zechariah—2 Kings 15:8; six months. Zechariah's rule spanned 753–752 B.C., and then he was assassinated.

AZARIAH ("Uzziah")—2 Kings 15:1-2, 8; 52 years. We know that Zechariah became the king of Judah in the thirty-eighth year of Uzziah, so Uzziah became king in 791 B.C. (753 B.C. plus 38 years). But the Bible also says that Uzziah became king in the twenty-seventh year of Jeroboam II, in 767 B.C. Therefore, Uzziah must have had a dual reign of 24 years with Amaziah, and his sole reign began in 767 B.C., when Amaziah died. Since Uzziah's total reign began in 791 B.C., he ruled until 739 B.C. (791 B.C. minus 52 years). Uzziah's joint reign with Amaziah probably began on account of the battle between Amaziah and Jehoash of Israel, in which Amaziah was captured and taken to Israel (2 Kings 14:8-11). He remained there until Jehoash died. Then Amaziah returned to Judah, where he lived for 15 years beyond the death of Jehoash.

Shallum—2 Kings 15:13; one month. Shallum ruled in the thirty-ninth year of Uzziah, so he ruled and died in 752 B.C. (791 B.C. minus 39 years).

Menahem—2 Kings 15:17; ten years. He also began his reign in the thirty-ninth year of Uzziah, 752 B.C., and ruled for ten years, until 742 B.C.

Pekahiah—2 Kings 15:23; two years. Becoming king in 742, he reigned until 740 B.C. (Second Kings 15:23 tells us Pekahiah began his reign in the fiftieth year of Uzziah, or 741 B.C. Evidently this is another case where the new king took the throne at the beginning of the new year.)

Pekah—2 Kings 15:27; 20 years. This appears to be a real problem. Second Kings 15:27 tells us that Pekah became king in the fifty-second year of Uzziah, which would be in 739 B.C. (791 B.C. minus 52 years). If we take that at face value, we would begin Pekah's reign in 739 and terminate it in 719 B.C. Then we would need to add the nine-year reign of Hoshea, placing the end of Hoshea's reign in 710 B.C. But this does not correspond with Assyrian records of the fall of Israel.

It is often suggested that the reigns of Jotham and Ahaz paralleled the reign of Pekah, which began in 752 B.C. In other words, Pekah began ruling Israel simultaneously with

Menahem. On this assumption, Pekah would have ruled from 752 to 732 B.C. The reference to the fifty-second year of Uzziah's reign indicates the year Pekah became the sole ruler in the North, and the statement about his reign lasting 20 years refers to the total reign of Pekah, beginning in 752 B.C.

JOTHAM—2 Kings 15:32-33; 16 years. Jotham began his reign in the second year of Pekah—751 or 750 B.C. (depending on the month when Pekah began his reign). We have seen already that Uzziah reigned until 739 B.C., so Jotham and Uzziah must have reigned together for several years. Indeed, the Bible says that Uzziah became leprous at the end of his life (2 Chron. 26:21); this would have made a co-regency necessary, since lepers had to be isolated. Second Kings 16:1 says that Ahaz succeeded Jotham in the seventeenth year of Pekah, or 735 B.C. (752 B.C. minus 17 years). So Jotham must have reigned from 750 to 735 B.C. While the Bible says Jotham reigned 16 years, it also indicates that he lived to what would have been the twentieth year of his reign, 730 B.C. Hoshea of Israel plotted Pekah's assassination in Jotham's twentieth year (2 Kings 15:30). So we show the end of Jotham's life at about 730 B.C. on Figure 11. Scripture says that the Ammonites paid tribute to Jotham until the third year of his official reign (2 Chron. 27:5). That would be about 736 B.C. (739 B.C. minus three years).

Hoshea—2 Kings 17:1; nine years. Beginning his rule at the death of Pekah in 732 B.C., Hoshea saw his reign end in 723 B.C. when the Assyrians carried off the northern kingdom. Here again, the official records of Assyria help to confirm the chronology of the Bible. They tell us that Shalmaneser V died in 722 B.C., just after capturing an important city in Palestine (cf. 2 Kings 17:3-6). Shalmaneser's successor, Sargon II, boasted of capturing Israel in the year he came to the throne of Assyria; apparently the government of Assyria changed hands during this conquest.

AHAZ—2 Kings 16:1-2; 16 years. Second Kings 17:1 says King Hoshea of Israel came to the throne in the twelfth year of Ahaz, so Ahaz's rule began in 744 B.C. (732 B.C. plus 12 years) and ended in 728 B.C. (744 B.C. minus 16 years). This means that Ahaz overlapped the reign of his father, Jotham, by nine years.

HEZEKIAH—2 Kings 18:1-2, 13; 29 years. Second Kings 18:1 says that Hezekiah came to power in Hoshea's third year, or 729 B.C. (732 B.C. minus three years).

Second Kings 18:3 says that Sennacherib attacked Jerusalem in the fourteenth year of Hezekiah's reign, which would be 715 B.C.; but Assyrian records show that this attack came in 701 B.C. Perhaps a scribe copied 2 Kings 18:13 incorrectly, and should have written 24 instead of 14. (It's easy to confuse these numbers in the Hebrew script.) In that case, Hezekiah's sole "reign" began in 725 B.C. (701 B.C. plus 24 years) and ended in 696 B.C. (725 B.C. minus 29 years).

Let us suppose that Hezekiah set up a rival government against his father, Ahaz. Let us also suppose that Ahaz left his throne but lived for a few more years, exerting a powerful influence in the country. If this was the case, we can understand why 2 Kings 18:1 says Hezekiah became king in 729 B.C., when 2 Kings 18:13 suggests that he became king in 725 B.C.—both would be right because of the way Ahaz's abdication muddied the political waters in Judah.

Of course, this still leaves unanswered questions. Why would the same book date a king's reign two different ways? How could Uzziah, Jotham, and Ahaz rule Judah at the same time (744–739 B.C.)? What power struggles were going on in Judah? Frankly, we don't know. But it is better to live with some of these questions and continue to investigate, than to reject one section of Scripture in favor of another. That course cannot be right.

DATING FOR JUDAH FROM 696 B.C. TO 587/86 B.C.

By this time, the northern kingdom of Israel had ceased to exist, and so we can no longer compare dates for the kings of Israel and Judah. We will begin at 696 B.C. (the end of Hezekiah's reign) and lay out the reigns of the remaining kings of Judah. Figure 12 does this.

MANASSEH—2 Kings 21:1; 55 years. Manasseh began his reign in 696 B.C. and reigned for 55 years, until 641 B.C.

AMON—2 Kings 21:19; 2 years. Amon began his reign in 641 and ruled until 639 B.C.

JOSIAH—2 Kings 22:1; 31 years. Josiah began his reign in 639 B.C. and ruled until 608 B.C., when he lost his life on the battlefield trying to stop Pharaoh Necho and the Egyptians on their way to join the Assyrians in their battle against the Babylonians (2 Kings 23:29).

JEHOAHAZ—2 Kings 23:31; 3 months. The people chose the first son of Josiah, Jehoahaz, to be their new king. But Pharaoh Necho did not want him and placed another son of Josiah on the throne, Jehoiakim.

JEHOIAKIM—2 Kings 23:36; 11 years. During this king's reign Nebuchadnezzar came to Jerusalem for the first time and brought Judah under the domination of Babylon. Jehoiakim was confirmed as king in the year 605 B.C. We can fix this year without any doubt, because two eclipses established 605 B.C. as the date when Nebuchadnezzar began his reign. One of these eclipses took place in the fifth year of Nabopolassar, father of Nebuchadnezzar. We also know that Nebuchadnezzar came to the throne in his father's twenty-first year. The other eclipse took place on July 4, 568, when Nebuchadnezzar had ruled for 37 years. This places Nebuchadnezzar's accession to the throne in 605 B.C. Also, Daniel was taken to Babylon and the 70-year Judean exile began in 605 B.C. (cf. Jer. 25:9-12; Dan. 9:2). Jehoiakim began his rule in 608 B.C. and reigned for 11 years, until 597 B.C. (608 B.C. minus 11 years), when he died.

JEHOIACHIN—2 Kings 24:8; 3 months. Jehoiachin became king after Jehoiakim, but Nebuchadnezzar attacked Judah a second time and deported Jehoiachin to Babylon. Nebuchadnezzar then placed another son of Josiah, Zedekiah, on the throne.

ZEDEKIAH—2 Kings 24:18; 11 years. This was the last king of Judah's first commonwealth. He ruled from 597 until 586 B.C., when Nebuchadnezzar came a third time, destroying the temple and ending the Judean kingdom.

GEDALIAH—2 Kings 25:22-26; seven months. Gedaliah became governor in the nineteenth year of Nebuchadnezzar, which confirms Gedaliah came to power in 586 B.C. (2 Kings 25:22). Apparently Nebuchadnezzar had to quell another rebellion in Judah, since some of the people did not accept the fact that the first commonwealth had come to an end. This happened in the twenty-third year of Nebuchadnezzar, or 582 B.C. (cf. Jer. 52:30).

EXILIC AND POST-EXILIC DATING

The Bible provides some dates for the period of the Exile. Jehoiachin was released in the thirty-seventh year of his exile (2 Kings 25:27). This would place it at about 560 B.C. (597 B.C. minus 37 years). Ezekiel also gives us specific dates for the events of his ministry, from the time of Jehoiachin's captivity (Ezek. 1:1-2; 29:17). Ezekiel heard that Jerusalem had fallen in the twelfth year of his exile, which would place it at about 586 B.C. (Ezek. 33:21).

Babylon fell to Cyrus and the Persians in 539 B.C., and Cyrus immediately decreed that all refugees could return to their homelands (2 Chron. 36:22; Ezra 1:1). Again we see God working in history to accomplish His purpose for His people Israel. The Jewish people took about a year to return to their homeland and settle down to begin the second commonwealth. The Persian calendar system was different from the Jewish calendar, but we can calculate that the Jews began to lay the foundations for the second temple in 536 B.C. It is interesting to note that the Exile indeed ended 70 years after the Babylonians seized Judah in 606 B.C., as God had foretold (Jer. 25:11). The building of the temple came to a halt not too long after the start of construction. It began again in the second year of Darius I, in 520 B.C., under the preaching ministry of Haggai and Zechariah (Ezra 4:24; 5:1-2; Haggai 1:1-15; 2:1-9). It was completed in the sixth year of Darius (Ezra 6:15), which would be about 516 B.C. This is another

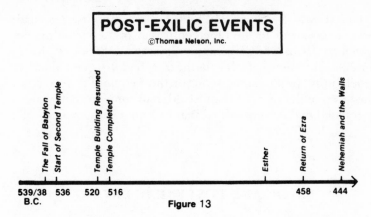

POST-EXILIC EVENTS
©Thomas Nelson, Inc.

The Fall of Babylon | Start of Second Temple | Temple Building Resumed | Temple Completed | Esther | Return of Ezra | Nehemiah and the Walls

539/38   536   520   516   458   444
B.C.   **Figure** 13

way to mark the 70-year interval of Exile—from the destruction of the first temple in 586 B.C. to the completion of the second temple in 516 B.C.

Esther lived in the days of Ahasuerus or Xerxes (486–464 B.C.); and she is dated at about 483 and 479 B.C. (Esther 1:3; 2:16).

The closing historical events of the Old Testament occurred within the reign of Artaxerxes I (464–423 B.C.). Ezra took a contingent of Jews to Jerusalem in the seventh year of Artaxerxes (Ezra 7:7-9), about 458 B.C. To help Ezra and the Jewish community, Nehemiah arranged for an appointment as governor of the land. He was permitted to return in the twentieth year of Artaxerxes (Neh. 1:1), which would be about 444 B.C. There appears to be an interval between this first journey to Jerusalem (Neh. 2:1-11) and a second journey in the thirty-second year of Artaxerxes (Neh. 13:6), which would have been about 432 B.C.

Daniel predicts that the Messiah will redeem His people after 70 sets of 7 years ("weeks"), beginning with Nehemiah's return to Jerusalem in 444 B.C. (Dan. 9:24). The Messiah is to be "cut off" at the end of 69 sets of sevens (Dan. 9:25-26), or 483 years starting with the proclamation of Artaxerxes in 444 B.C. This turns out to be the very week Jesus was crucified, taking into account all the necessary calculations.[3]

4

ARCHAEOLOGY

The English word *archaeology* comes from two Greek words, *archaios*, meaning "ancient," and *logos*, meaning "word," "matter," "account," or "discourse." *Archaeology* literally means "account (or discourse) of ancient matters," and people occasionally use the word to refer to ancient history in general. Usually, however, the word *archaeology* is applied to the *sources* of history that were unknown until excavations brought them to light.

Archaeologists are students of the past who dig up important historical sites and study what they find in relation to each site. In the Near East archaeologists depend on these historical objects for their knowledge much more than they do when they excavate cities in Italy or Greece because very little literature survives from the ancient Near East. If the archaeologist finds written texts, he turns them over to a specialist in the language or culture, who translates them and compares them with other bits of literature from that time.

BIBLICAL ARCHAEOLOGY

Scholars disagree about whether we can speak of *"biblical* archaeology." Some say that archaeology is archaeology—that is, its methods and goals are essentially the same everywhere, whether the Bible is involved or not. They also have valid concerns about the unscientific (occasionally even fraudulent) claims that have been perpetrated in the name of "biblical" archaeology. They believe we should use another term, such as *"Palestinian* archaeology," or speak of "archaeology and the Bible."

Perhaps the term *biblical archaeology* has fallen into disfavor because scientists today are simply not very interested in biblical matters. Scholars with a professional interest in the Bible are not as actively engaged in archaeological work as they once were. Today, professional archaeologists study a broad spectrum of cultural and anthropological interests that may not be immediately relevant for the student of the Bible. The long-standing alliance between biblical studies and archaeology is not as firm as it once was.

The major funding and staffing of archaeological projects in Bible lands has never come from church organizations or institutions. It has come from universities, museums, or other private sources. This trend will probably become even stronger in the future because of inflation, the increasing specialization in archaeology, and archaeology's growing skepticism toward traditional Christianity. Nevertheless, churches and their institutions should seek to be involved to the maximum practical extent.

Does archaeology "prove the Bible true"? Not exactly. It is true that archaeology has enhanced our confidence in the broad outlines of the biblical report. Archaeological finds have supported many, many specific statements in the text. Archaeology has often been useful in refuting the attacks of skeptics. But much of the Bible has to do with relatively private, personal matters which archaeology cannot verify. And the farther back we go into history, the less evidence we have.

A. Its Limitations. The "truth" of the Bible is not only a matter of facts, but of their interpretation. Even if we could demonstrate the factuality of the entire Bible, that would not prove its redemptive significance. Because the Christian faith is based on historical events, Christians welcome any evidence that archaeology can provide—but they do not anchor their faith to it. No lack of evidence nor critical skepticism can disprove God's Word. It is better to emphasize how archaeology helps us *understand* the Bible than to insist that it proves the Bible true. In fact, it cannot do so much, nor is there need that it should.

B. Its Value. Archaeology can provide background information thousands of years after the Bible was written. Although archaeology deals primarily with concrete, material objects, it can help us comprehend the spiritual message of the biblical writers—especially their illustrations and figures of speech. There must be a "dialogue" between the biblical text and archaeological finds, because each can help us understand and interpret the other. The Bible helps us understand the archaeologists' new discoveries, while archaeology helps us "read between the lines" of the inspired record.

For example, the historical records of ancient Babylon do not mention Belshazzar, even though the Bible says he succeeded Nebuchadnezzar as king (Dan. 4–5). For a time, some Bible scholars doubted the Bible at this point. But in 1853 archaeologists found an inscription in Ur, which showed that Belshazzar reigned with his father, Nabonidus.

C. Its Reliability. How objective or truly scientific is the archaeological method, and to what extent can its results be trusted? Fortunately, we are past the day when we think that even the "hard" or physical sciences (physics, chemistry, and so on) are absolutely objective. We know that the scientists' attitudes and notions of truth will affect the way they interpret the facts. On the other hand, the degree of personal opinion in the "soft" or social sciences (history, sociology, psychology) is not so great that we should refuse to call them "scientific." Archaeology occupies a middle ground between the "hard" and the "soft" sciences. Archaeologists are more objective when unearthing the facts than when interpreting them. But their human preoccupations will affect the methods they use in making the "dig," too. They cannot help destroying their evidence as they dig down through the layers of earth, so they can never test their "experiment" by repeating it. This makes archaeology unique among the sciences. Moreover, it makes archaeological reporting a most demanding and pitfall-ridden task.

Yet archaeology does overlap with other scientific disciplines, such as history, geography, and cultural anthropology (the study of man's ways of thinking and living). Specialists in physics or chemistry often join excavation teams in order to analyze seeds, bones, pollen, soil, and the like. The study of comparative religion or the "history of religions" often plays a prominent part in interpreting the finds, because so many finds are cult-related. Geology deals with natural layers or strata of earth, in contrast to the man-made layers that claim the archaeologists' attention; yet archaeologists often consult geologists to learn more about the nature of the sites they are excavating.

D. Its Geography. Which geographical areas attract the interest in biblical archaeology? For the New Testament period, that area largely coincides with the Roman Empire. For Old Testament times the area is somewhat smaller, and the center shifts eastward to include the Mesopotamian valley and Persia (modern Iran).

It is simplest, however, to begin at the hub—Palestine or Israel (Canaan)—and fan out from there. The great empires in the Nile and Mesopotamian valleys are almost as interesting as Palestine itself. The culture of Phoenicia (modern Lebanon) had much in common with that of Canaan to the south. Syria to the east is also of prime concern—its history often intertwined with that of Israel and it was always the major corridor for invaders of Palestine. Still farther north, Asia Minor was the homeland of the Hittites and other important peoples.

THE RISE OF MODERN ARCHAEOLOGY

The history of modern Near Eastern archaeology begins at about the same time as did other modern sciences, during the eighteenth century. Before that, there had always been collectors of antiquities (usually museums or rich individuals). The resulting "excavations" were little more than treasure hunts that destroyed most information of value to the scientific archaeologist. Unfortunately, some people still have these attitudes, and every Near Eastern country must wage a difficult battle against diggers who are trying to meet the black-market demand for artifacts.

Biblical archaeology probably began with the discovery of the Rosetta Stone (named after a nearby village in the Nile Delta) when Napoleon invaded Egypt in August 1799. Written in three columns (Greek, Egyptian hieroglyphics, and a later Egyptian script), the stone was soon deciphered by Jean François Champollion. More relics of the past remained visible above ground in Egypt than anywhere else in the ancient Near East, and Napoleon's discovery of these ancient writings spurred further exploration of that country.

A similar breakthrough was made in Mesopotamia in 1811, when Claude J. Rich found dozens of baked clay tablets at Babylon with *cuneiform* ("wedge-shaped") writing. In 1835, Sir Henry Creswicke Rawlinson deciphered an inscription in three languages (old Persian, Elamite, and Akkadian), which Darius the Great had made on a cliff near Behistun in western Persia. A decade later, Sir Austen Henry Layard and other pioneer archaeologists opened mounds containing the remains of great Assyrian cities such as Ninevah, Ashur, and Calah. In these mounds they discovered more cuneiform

Grave pottery. Buried for centuries under layers of gravel and dirt, this pottery was found in a grave at Tell el-Farah (ancient Tirzah). The articles are shown as they were excavated. Archaeologists must carefully catalog their find and begin the tedious job of reassembling the shattered objects.

tablets. Since they had already learned how to read cuneiform, the tablets allowed them to review the entire history, culture and religion of ancient Assyria and Babylon. They found many parallels to the history of the Bible.

A. Petrie's Contribution. But scientific archaeology was nearly another half-century in coming to Palestine. In 1890, Sir W. M. Flinders Petrie turned his attention to the mound of Tell-el-Hesi (now considered to be the biblical city of Eglon, although Petrie thought it was Lachish). Petrie was not the first to dig in Palestine, but he was the first to recognize the real significance of *stratigraphy*—the study of the various layers of occupation in a mound, and of the pottery belonging to each *stratum* (Latin, "layer"). But even Petrie's first step was a faltering one. Petrie's method of *sequence dating* simply made "stratigraphical" divisions every foot down into the dig, instead of following the irregular lines of occupation itself.

It is not possible to mention all of the scientists who built upon Petrie's achievements. However, the next major step was taken by W. F. Albright at Tell Beit Mirsim, west of Hebron, in a series of "digs" from 1926 to 1932. (Albright identified the site with biblical Debir or Kirjath-sepher, but this has been seriously challenged.) By his meticulous methods, Albright established once and for all the correct sequence of Palestinian pottery. Albright and his successors (especially G. E. Wright) recommended and practiced the most painstaking procedures. Other improvements in excavation technique were made by G. A. Reisner and Clarence S. Fisher at Samaria (1931–1935), and by Kathleen Kenyon at Jericho and elsewhere beginning in 1952. Specialists still debate the best procedures. Different methods must be used simply because of the varying requirements of the sites. For example, present-day Israeli archaeology is often forced to forego more desirable procedures in order to beat the bulldozers of new construction.

As noted earlier, modern archaeologists tend to have a much broader concept of their task than is signaled by the term *biblical archaeology*. They want to explore the entire spectrum of human experience in connection with a site's

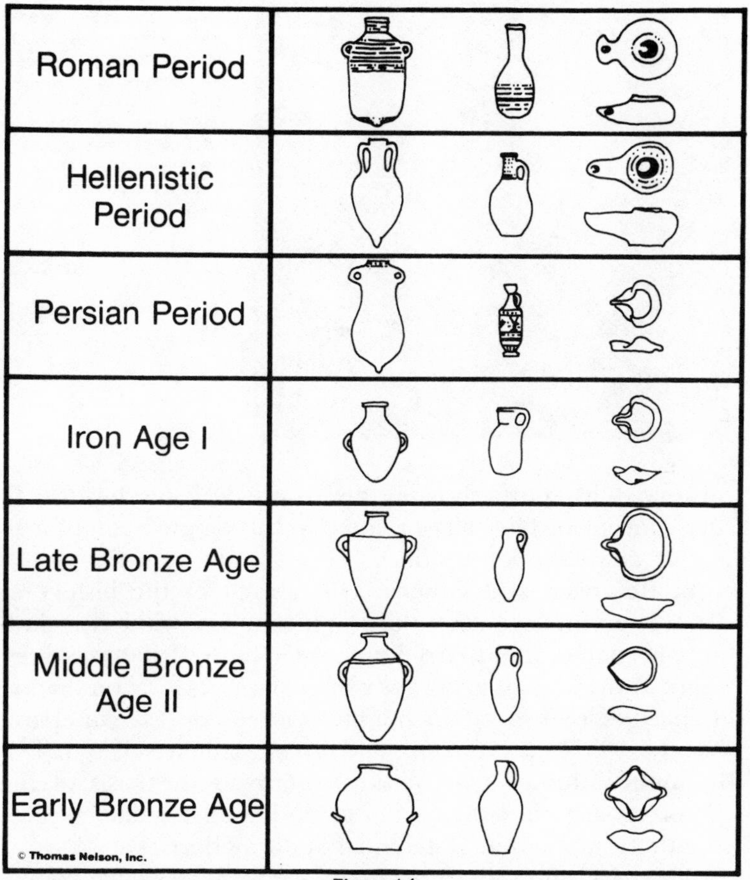

Figure 14

This chart shows several pottery types characteristic of Palestine in Bible times. They are arranged from the most recent (top) to the oldest (bottom), as they would be found in the progressively deeper layers of a tell.

Dr. W. M. Flinders Petrie developed a method for finding the approximate date of artifacts in a tell by observing the depth and physical context of each layer (*stratum*) of dirt. By using this method, called *stratigraphy,* archaeologists have learned which type of pottery was common to each period of the ancient past.

The left row shows the development of large two-handled water pots. Women used such pots to carry drinking water from the town well, these pots could also be used to store water, wine, or other liquids. The middle row shows the development of simple clay pitchers, used for household meals. The row on the right shows the evolving design of oil lamps; each section of this row gives a top view and a side view of the lamp.

Notice that the earlier designs (e.g., those of the Bronze Age) tended to be quite simple and functional. Later designs, which show the influence of Persian and Greek art, were more delicate and often had ornamental painting.

Skull with beads. Objects buried with the dead, such as this beaded headdress, help archaeologists determine the age of the skeletal remains. They also reveal something of the artistic values and skills of the people who made them.

history. This approach is not necessarily at loggerheads with the concept of biblically oriented archaeology. But unfortunately, conflict often results.

B. Robinson and Glueck. Our sketch of the history of Palestinian archaeology would be incomplete without including the name of Edward Robinson. His contributions were more in the area of geography or surface exploration than in archaeological excavation, but the two endeavors are inseparable. In 1838 and 1852 he and a companion succeeded in locating scores of biblical sites, often on the basis of the similarity between their biblical and modern names (e.g., Anathoth, the home of Jeremiah, and modern Anata).

Almost a century later, Nelson Glueck made similar contributions by his treks over the barren areas of Transjordan, the Jordan Valley, and the Negev (the semi-arid region around Beer-sheba). Still later, the Palestinian Exploration Fund brought those pioneering labors to fruition.

C. Recent Developments. Archaeologists have made great advances in two areas related to biblical archaeology; underwater archaeology and "prehistoric" studies. Underwater methods affect biblical archaeology only at the sea-coast city of Caesarea Maritima. "Prehistoric" studies, dealing with periods before 3000 B.C., depend largely on comparing the styles of flint tools. Archaeologists have made important discoveries from the "prehistoric" period at many points in Palestine, and they are focusing more of their energies in that direction.

THE ARCHAEOLOGIST'S METHOD

Archaeological methods are, in essence, very simple. In fact, they might be reduced to only two procedures—*stratigraphy* and *typology*.

A. Stratigraphy. Stratigraphy makes a careful distinction of the various levels (or *strata*) at which people lived. These are simply numbered consecutively (usually by Roman numerals) from top to bottom, the top *stratum*—the most recent one—being "Stratum I" and so on. The total number of strata at a given site may vary considerably, as well as the depth of the individual strata. A *tell* (mound of debris from an ancient city) may well reach 15 to 22 m. (50 to 75 ft.) above virgin soil, and in Mesopotamia they frequently exceed that height. Occasionally a mound has been occupied almost continuously for thousands of years; and if it is still occupied, excavation will be very difficult or impossible. At other times, there will be long gaps in the occupational history of the site. One can know this only after thorough excavation, although a study of the *sherds* (broken pieces of pottery) that have washed down the slopes of the mound will give the archaeologist a good advance picture of the civilizations to be uncovered within the tell. Sometimes the various strata will be distinguished by thick layers of ash or other destruction debris; at other times only by differences in soil color or compactness. If a mound lay uninhabited for a long time, erosion and robbing of the site may completely disrupt a stratum. Later inhabitants often dig trenches, cisterns, and pits deep into earlier strata, adding to the modern excavator's problems.

B. Pottery Typology. Identifying the strata enables the scientist to determine a relative sequence of layers, not absolute dates. For dates, he must use pottery *typology* (i.e., the study of different types of pottery). Over the course of time, archaeologists have developed a very detailed knowledge of the characteristic pottery of each period. By relating each stratum to the pottery fragments in it, the archaeologist is usually able to date the stratum within a relatively narrow period of time.

When they were introduced, the scientific community was reluctant to adopt the methods of stratigraphy and typology. At Troy, Heinrich Schliemann concluded in the nineteenth century that tells or mounds concealed the layers of more than one ancient city. This earned him the ridicule of learned circles all over Europe until he proved his point. There was similar initial rejection of pottery typology.

Typologies of other ancient objects are also useful. For example, the development of the lamp helps the archaeologist in identifying broader periods. From a simple saucer with a wick, the lamp eventually developed a lip on one side to hold the wick, then four lips at right angles to one another. Finally the top was covered over to leave only a spout for the wick. By Byzantine and Christian times, the covered top was crowned with a variety of artistic symbols. Tools, weapons, and architectural styles changed through the centuries, as did the design of pagan idols.

Jug and coins from Schechem. This small pottery jug filled with 35 silver coins probably was the private bank of some resident of Schechem, a town of Ephraim, in the second century B.C. Because they are easily dated, coins can help archaeologists determine the age of the sites in which they are found.

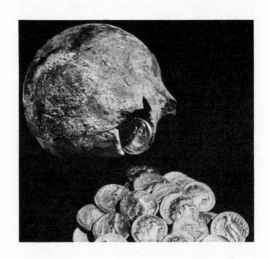

On those rare occasions when writing is found in Palestine, we have another important test for historical dates, and paleography (the study of the history of writing) has become quite a precise science.

Coins did not appear in Palestine until the very end of the Old Testament period (*ca.* 300 B.C.). Since the people sometimes hoarded coins or kept them as heirlooms, this evidence may mislead the archaeologist. The same is true of imported objects, where a time-lag of 25 to 50 years will often have to be taken into consideration.

C. Other Techniques for Dating. Pottery typology is the most basic way of dating archaeological sites. All the other methods are supplementary. In recent years, scientists have developed new procedures for dating ancient objects. But none of these threatens to replace the analysis of pottery types. Specialists are able to date pottery to within at least half a century; the margin of error is considerably greater with other procedures, and it generally grows larger the farther back in time we go. Only in a few "dark ages," for which we have no pottery clues, have the newer techniques proved to be worth the time and expense.

Of the newer procedures, the best established and most important is that of *radiocarbon* dating. Carbon isotope 14 is a form of carbon with a half-life of about 5,600 years. It "decays" to form carbon-12, the most common form of carbon. By measuring the proportion of carbon-14 to carbon-12 in an object, scientists can determine the age of the object. Although carbon-14 is supposed to disintegrate at a constant rate, some scientists still question its accuracy and reliability. It can be found only in organic substances (wood, cloth, and so on), which are rare in Palestinian excavations. A sizeable piece of the sample is destroyed in the process of testing, which makes archaeologists reluctant to use this method. Nevertheless, it has been useful, especially in quieting the skepticism of people who are not yet convinced of the archaeologists' ability to date pottery.

Some other techniques are more promising for biblical archaeology. *Thermoluminescence* measures pottery to determine when it was first fired. *Spectographic analysis* bombards a piece of pottery with electrons in order to measure the chemical spectrum of the minerals within it. Somewhat similarly, in *neutron activation* ceramic material is placed in a nuclear reactor and the chemical composition of the clay is determined from the radioactivity it can give off. The latter two methods are more helpful in determining the source of the clay from which the pottery was manufactured than its date; but often the two investigations go together. (The naked eye of a skilled pottery expert can often detect much about the original source of clay without these scientific helps.)

Scientific techniques may also help in the search for sites. So many ancient tells remain untouched by modern excavation that there has been little demand for these helps. But in the lesser populated areas of Transjordan and the Negev, infrared aerial photography has been able to isolate ancient cities by picking out differences in vegetation. An object gives off heat in the form of infrared rays; the hotter the object is, the more infrared rays it gives off. Thus infrared photographs reveal differences in the temperature of the plants that grow over ancient walls and floors. In Italy, archaeologists used the *proton magnetometer* (comparable to the Geiger counter) to locate the city of Sybaris.

D. Supervising the Work. In addition to stratigraphy and typology, careful recording and publication of the data is a third major principle of scientific archaeology. Unlike other sciences, archaeology cannot repeat its "experiments" to verify them. So the concern for careful records lies at the heart of a successful "dig."

Initially, archaeologists will plot a site on a "grid system," paralleling the latitude and longitude of the area. They usually divide the mound into "fields." Within each field, they measure certain "areas" and stake them off for excavation. The fields may be of varying sizes depending on the situation, but customarily the areas are 6 m. (19 ft.) square. Archaeologists will further subdivide each area into four squares, leaving dividers ("balks") a meter wide between each quadrant. These balks provide catwalks for observation and inspec-

Archaeologist at work. Archaeological finds are remarkably fragile, requiring great care and patience for their preservation. Here Dr. Gustav Jeeninga unearths an ancient skeleton at Caesarea Maritima. This entails the painstaking removal of centuries-old deposits, which must be cleaned away without disrupting the site where the remains are found.

tion while the work is in progress, and make points of reference if questions arise later on. Not even an entire quadrant is dug uniformly; the workers will sink "probe trenches" at right angles to other trenches, in an effort to anticipate what they may uncover as they proceed.

Each area has an area supervisor, who in turn is supervised by the director of the excavation. The area supervisor has two tasks: (1) to supervise and direct the actual digging in his area, and (2) to carefully record everything as it appears.

The laborers are basically of three types: (1) *pickmen,* who carefully break up the compacted soil (a very skilled procedure, to be distinguished from ordinary ditch-digging); (2) *hoemen,* who work over the newly loosened soil, watching for anything of significance; and (3) *basketmen,* who carry off the dirt after inspection. Sometimes the baseketmen also use sieves, as well as trowels and brushes for scraping and cleaning.

The area supervisor keeps careful notes in a field notebook, a diary of everything that his workers do. He assigns an arbitrary location number to each subdivision of his area, both vertically and horizontally. The workers collect all pottery in special baskets and tag them to indicate the date, area, and location. Then the pottery is washed and "read" by experts, who save and register pieces of special interest. They photograph or sketch anything of special interest before they take it apart. At the end of each day (or before a new phase of the excavation continues), the area supervisor must make scale drawings of both the vertical walls and the floor of his area. At the end of the season, he must write a detailed report of all that happened in his area. The director of the entire excavation pulls all these reports together into his own preliminary report, and then into a detailed publication. However, many a project director has failed to follow through on these final steps, depriving the scholarly world of the fruit of his labors.

PERIODS OF ANCIENT HISTORY

Archaeologists arrange the earliest historical and cultural evidence according to a three-period system, consisting of the Stone, Bronze, and Iron Ages (each with various subdivisions). We inherited this scheme from the early nineteenth century, and it is now antiquated. But it has become so much a part of archaeology that it seems impossible to change it. Archaeologists have attempted to substitute something more satisfactory, but these new systems have had only limited success and often they have introduced more confusion. The most successful of these new proposals have used sociological or political labels, while the traditional scheme is based on the most vital metal of those periods. After the Iron Age (that is, beginning with the Persian period) political or cultural names have always been standard for the archaeological periods.

The dates are approximate, of course, because cultural changes always come gradually. In later periods, where we usually know the history more precisely, some exact dates can be given.

When assigning dates to archaeological finds, the biggest problems occur in the earlier periods. Not until the patriarchal period (generally the Middle Bronze Age, after 2300 B.C.) do we begin to reach firm ground. And not until a millennium later (at the time of David and Solomon) do we find it easier to determine the dates of Bible events. The extremely early dates that some scientists offer for the Paleolithic or Old Stone Age are based more on theories of evolution and geology than archaeology. Such dates clash with the Bible—not only on the surface, but on the level of underlying concepts.

However, it is not easy to say precisely where to draw the line. It is difficult to interpret the chronologies of the Bible itself, and so conservative interpreters sometimes reach different conclusions.

A. The Stone Age. The earliest archaeological time period—the Stone Age—is divided into the Paleolithic Period, the Mesolithic Period, and several Neolithic Periods.

1. The Paleolithic Period. The Paleolithic or "Old Stone Age" may be described as an age of hunting and food-gathering. People lived in caves or temporary shelters. They made implements of flint or chipped stone, and subsisted from what they could gather from nature itself.

2. The Mesolithic Period. The Mesolithic or "Middle Stone Age" was a transitional stage to a food-producing economy, in which real settlements first appeared; it was a revolution that matured in the Neolithic era. We can say there was an evolution of the arts of civilization during this period, but not an evolution of man or his native capacities.

3. The Neolithic Periods. The invention of pottery around 5000 B.C. ushered in a new era of antiquity, the Neolithic or "New Stone Age."

The most spectacular Palestinian site illustrating these developments is Jericho. In the eighth millennium B.C., Mesolithic hunters built a sanctuary near a spring at Jericho. Gradually they developed their homes from nomadic shelters into mud-brick houses, and began irrigation farming. Four Neolithic Periods are distinguished at Jericho after this: two pre-pottery, and two in which pottery was known. While the first period apparently began in peace, this was certainly not the case with the other three. In fact, the first Neolithic Period was characterized by the construction of massive defensive walls—the earliest known in the history of man. After the wall was destroyed, an entirely new culture moved in at Jericho. Pottery was still unknown, but a high degree of artistic ability was evident otherwise. The people of Jericho molded mud around human skulls to make realistic portraits with shells inset for eyes, probably for some kind of ancestor worship.

The next wave of invaders into Palestine was culturally

retarded in many respects. But there was one major exception: they knew how to make pottery. After one more wave of settlers, Jericho went into temporary eclipse around 4000 B.C. During the Chalcolithic Period the city of Ghassul on the other side of the Jordan River assumed the power Jericho had known.

B. The Chalcolithic Period. The Chalcolithic (Copper-Stone) Period, covering most of the fourth millennium B.C., saw a transition to a significant use of copper. (Chalcolithic people did not use bronze, an alloy that was not yet known.)

Until this period, Palestine had kept pace with the two great river cultures of Egypt and Mesopotamia. Beginning around 4000 B.C., however, those two legs of the Fertile Crescent began to forge ahead, and Palestine began to assume the geopolitical role it played throughout most of the biblical period. It became a cultural and political backwater, but a strategic bridge for trade and communication for much of the ancient Near East. The two great rivers helped the other regions become more dominant by unifying the vast territory and opening it up to commerce. By the end of this era, these regions had developed patterns they would follow for thousands of years.

1. Ghassulian Culture. In Palestine, as we noted, Jericho appears to have been replaced by Ghassul (we know only this modern Arabic name), to the east of Jericho. The absence of fortifications indicates that it was a peaceful period. Ghassul was most famous for its sophisticated art, particularly for its multicolored frescoes containing geometric motifs, stars, masks, and other images (probably having religious or mythological significance).

Ghassul flourished during the latter half of the fourth millennium. Since it was the first known Palestinian culture of the period, the era has been given its name, "Ghassulian." Increasingly, however, archaeologists are finding that other cultures were also strong during this period. They are also finding that other Chalcolithic cultures had customs that resembled the practices of Ghassul. For example, archaeologists have documented the Ghassulian custom of burying the dead in *ossuaries* (ceramic receptacles for bones) in many other areas, particularly the coastal cities near modern Tel Aviv. These ossuaries were usually shaped like animals or houses, in imitation of those used in daily life. After the body was cremated, mourners buried the ossuary in a stone cist together with provisions for the afterlife.

Two sites near Beer-sheba (Tel Abu Matar and Bir es-Safadi) illustrate the use of copper during the Chalcolithic Period. Some of the dwellings at both of these sites were underground, entered by shafts from the surface and connected by tunnels. Copper working was found in the many pits, ovens, and fireplaces in the area, indicating the dominance of copper in the two villages' economy. The ore had to come from mines in the southern Negev, a considerable distance away, which indicates that the villages had a sophisticated social and economic organization.

Probably the most spectacular Chalcolithic site in Palestine is near En-gedi, the oasis on the western shores of the Dead Sea. High above the spring (where the Israelite city was later excavated) was a walled complex. Inside its largest structure was an open-air temple with an altar. We know nothing of the rites of the shrine, but archaeologists commonly assume that the large collection of copper objects (mace heads, scepters, processional standards) discovered in a cave nearby were used in this temple. Presumably they were hidden in the cave when the temple was threatened, and no one was able to return and save them.

2. Megalithic Culture. The Megalithic remains of Palestine straddle the Chalcolithic and Early Bronze Periods. The term *Megalithic* simply means "large-stoned," referring to the boulders that people employed in these early constructions. In Europe such structures seem to be characteristic of the Neolithic Period, but in the Near East they appear later. However, any pottery or other remains that were originally buried with them have long since disappeared, and only quite recently have their dates been established more firmly.

The Palestinian "megaliths" are usually very simple: one or more horizontal blocks were laid over a few vertical ones averaging a meter (39 in.) or less in height, with a low entrance on one side. These may have been monuments to the dead, designed as imitations of everyday dwellings. More technically, this type of structure is called a *dolmen* (meaning literally, "stone table"). Originally, they were probably covered with small stones and earth, which has been washed away. Occasionally one or two circles of small stones surrounded them. Nearly always they are clustered in "fields" or groups, mostly in northwestern Jordan on the slopes above the east bank of the Jordan River, or in upper Galilee, especially around Chorazin.

C. The Bronze Age. Archaeologists have found many artifacts from the Bronze Age—so many that they have been able to discern several distinct cultural periods within the Bronze Age.

1. Early Bronze Age. With the Early Bronze Age and the third millennium B.C., we leave "prehistory" and enter the "historical" period—if we define *history* as the presence of written records. The cultures of the two great river valleys (Nile and Tigris-Euphrates) gained many advantages over Palestine, especially as they developed the art of writing in the latter half of the fourth millennium. The Mesopotamians (proto-Sumerians?) pioneered writing, but Egypt was quick to recognize the benefits of it.

The evolution of writing can be traced in considerable detail, from its origins in business dockets through pictographs (picture-writing) into more abstract symbols. Mesopotamia developed *cuneiform* writing—that is, using a stylus to impress wedges into soft clay tablets, which were then baked. Originally the non-Semitic Sumerians devised cuneiform for themselves, but it was soon adopted by their Semitic successors, and even by various Indo-European language groups (that is, the family of languages scattered from India to Western Europe). It became a virtually universal script until the Aramaic alphabet replaced it under the Persian Empire.

The roots of the modern alphabet are in Egypt. In one sense, the Egyptians did not develop writing beyond the earlier pictographic stage, resulting in the familiar Egyptian *hieroglyphs* (literally "sacred carvings"). Although the Egyptian symbols represented syllables (just like the Mesopotamian ones) they also contained an early alphabetic significance; each symbol stood for a letter instead of a syllable.[1]

Even though the Canaanites could not match the cultures of the great river valleys, the Early Bronze Period was a period of great urbanization here, too. In fact, virtually all of the great Canaanite cities were founded in this period. In Palestine, these cities remained independent, and never coalesced into larger empires. We find essentially the same city-state political system over 1,000 years later at the time of Joshua's invasion. The empire of King David was probably the first to supersede it completely.

Despite tradition, it is not accurate to call this period the Early Bronze Age in Palestine. "Bronze" implies an alloy of copper and tin, which was not available until at least a thousand years later. If a metal term were satisfactory at all, "copper" would be much better. Alternative names for the period have never caught on widely. However, two types of suggestions have some merit.

Kathleen Kenyon wanted to call this the Urban Period, because the people tended to build great cities. However, Israeli scholars prefer to call it the Canaanite Period (followed by the Israelite Period and the Persian Period); these labels identify the political power of each period.

The problem of terminology is even more acute for the third millennium B.C. The question is, which terminology will best indicate the continuity as well as the contrast between the periods?

a. Mysterious Invaders. No one denies the abrupt contrast between the Chalcolithic and the Early Bronze Periods. Several tells from this era indicate that the cities that stood on these sites were destroyed between the Chalcolithic and Early Bronze periods. The only evidence about the nature of the people who destroyed these cities is their new burial customs. They practiced communal burials in single chambers, pushing the bones of previous generations against the wall as the newly deceased were "gathered to their fathers."

It seems obvious that the invaders brought a new way of life. They were not nomads who gradually settled down (as we noted many times in Neolithic Jericho). This seems evident from their tendency to prefer the plains instead of the hill country, and brick instead of stone (even in the hill country where stone was so abundant). This pattern of sparse occupation of the hill country continued through the subsequent Middle Bronze Age until well into the Israelite settlement.

Who were these invaders? Without written records we cannot be sure. By calling them "Canaanites," the Israeli archaeologists are suggesting that they were related to the people who lived in Canaan at the time of the Israelite invasion. That may well be true, but not everyone agrees. And how much of these invaders' cultural influence remained after the Amorite and Hurrian invasions of the Middle Bronze eras? The geographical names of the land are quite uniformly Semitic, which indicates that the Semitic languages were certainly dominant from hoary antiquity. But what was that date? And what was the origin or identity of the people who first introduced it? Some of these invaders lived along the Mediterranean coast in the fourth millennium B.C., and archaeologists usually assume that the invasion moved southward along the coast. Perhaps this was the beginning of a pattern that prevailed throughout much of the biblical period—namely, that the term *Canaanite* referred to a southern extension or subdivision of a general Phoenician culture all along the coast. At any rate, many aspects of the Canaanite culture took shape at this time.

Among these aspects was the Canaanite pattern of city planning. Most structures within the Canaanite city walls were public buildings; for the most part, the masses lived in hovels outside the walls, perhaps working or trading within the gates and fleeing to their security in times of war. Among the most prominent of the Canaanite public buildings were temples or related structures, which proves that the Canaanites had highly developed rituals and priesthoods from antiquity. Many clues from this period indicate Palestine's trade relations with Egypt and Mesopotamia. We do not know whether

Egypt's cultural influence at this early date was accompanied by some measure of political control. During this period the Canaanites began to plant forests from the Palestinian hills. Also, lamps appeared in this period.

b. Biblical Sites. Archaeologists have found several Early Bronze sites with biblical significance. These sites include Ai, Arad, Jericho, Megiddo, and Tirzah. John Garstang identified the double walls of Jericho (which were destroyed toward the end of the Early Bronze Age) with those miraculously

Diagram of a tell. Before excavating a tell, archaeologists make a limited excavation to determine whether the site will justify the very expensive process of excavation. This photograph shows an experimental trench on Tell Judeideh in northern Syria. Each stair marks a different archaeological level.

overwhelmed by Joshua. In later excavations, Kathleen Kenyon found only scant remains of the Late Bronze city.

The site of Ai lay vacant throughout the Middle and Late Bronze periods after the Early Bronze metropolis was destroyed. Apparently the Ai of Joshua 7–8 was located elsewhere in the vicinity, but archaeologists do not agree where it was. We are interested in the Early Bronze site of Ai because its sanctuary was divided into three parts, much like Solomon's temple about 1,500 years later. An altar was found in Ai's holy of holies and many animal bones throughout. Archaeologists unearthed a simpler temple with only two chambers (no outer court) at Tirzah, later one of the capitals of the northern kingdom. At Megiddo they uncovered no temple, but they did find an open-air shrine with walls enclosing an altar—apparently the type of idolatrous installation that the Bible calls a *bamah* or "high place" (cf. Num. 22:41; 33:52). The altar was round, about 70 feet in diameter and five feet high, ascended by seven steps. The Bible prohibited altar steps because the priests became guilty of "indecent exposure" when they climbed them (Exod. 20:26).

Archaeologists also uncovered temples at the Bronze Age city of Arad (near, but not identical to the Iron Age city of Arad that is frequently mentioned in the Bible). The main significance of the settlement was the well-planned nature of the city.

We should mention two other Early Bronze sites that the Bible does not name (probably because they were uninhabited throughout that period). Beth-Yerah (Arabic name: *Khirbet el-Kerak*), on the southwestern shores of the Sea of Galilee, was another major urban center. It lent its name to some typical pottery of the period, characterized by a beautiful red burnish. Another site near the southeastern corner of the Dead Sea (known only by its Arabic name, *Bab edh-Dhra*) has an odd reputation. It was also a major city, but its major "industry" was burial. There archaeologists found a vast number of burials of various types, in various cemeteries and charnel houses. It must have been a favorite burial ground for a wide area. Because of the present arid and desolate nature of the area, it may have served the "Cities of the Plain" (Sodom and Gomorrah, and others) on the other side of the Dead Sea before they were destroyed.

c. Ebla (Tell Mardikh). One very important Early Bronze site outside of Canaan is the recently discovered city of Ebla (Ibla) in northern Syria. Also known by its modern name of Tell Mardikh, this site has already revolutionized our knowledge of the period. During the third quarter of the third millennium B.C., Ebla was the capital of a vast empire. For a time it even eclipsed the empire of Akkad in Mesopotamia. Thus, Syria cannot have been quite the backwater that it was assumed to be in this period. We are not sure of its political ties with Canaan, to the south, but there certainly were trade centers.

Ebla's business records mention a large number of Canaanite sites for the first time, among them Jerusalem—and even Sodom and Gomorrah, whose existence some scholars had previously doubted. Ebla's records also mention many personal names similar to biblical ones. One of Ebla's major kings was Eber, the same name as that of one of the "Hebrew" ancestors (Gen. 10:25; 11:14; the names are very similar in the Hebrew language).

Although Ebla's religion was polytheistic, one of its deities may have been named the same as the "Jehovah" of the Old Testament. If so, the Ebla tablets provide interesting evidence for the antiquity of the personal name of the true God.

2. Middle Bronze I. Toward the end of the third millennium (beginning around 2300 B.C.) the flourishing urban culture of the Early Bronze Period began to crumble in the face of nomadic invaders, who brought upon Palestine one of the most violent devastations of its history. Not a single Early Bronze city escaped total destruction, and all lay unoccupied for at least a couple of centuries. Transjordan did not get back on its feet for nearly a thousand years (just in time to resist the Israelites!). Some sites were never resettled. In Palestine, a "dark age" ensued (although new discoveries are filling out the picture). In many respects, the invaders were culturally "backward." They lived mostly in caves or in camps atop city ruins. But plainly they brought some highly developed traditions of their own. Their pottery differed from that of Early Bronze inhabitants in shape as well as decoration; often it was poorly fired and brittle.

But the invaders distinguished themselves by their prolific tomb building. Archaeologists have found their large burial grounds, especially near Jericho and Hebron. In contrast to the multiple burials of the preceding Early Bronze Period and the rest of the Middle Bronze era, these nomads generally made only one burial per tomb. Usually the tomb was of a "shaft" type—i.e. with a vertical shaft sunk to the horizontal entrance to the tomb. Most of the bones found were disorganized, indicating that mourners carried their dead back to the tribal burial grounds when the seasonal migration was over (cf. Jacob and Joseph, Gen. 50). Near Jericho archaeologists discovered an unwalled open-air shrine that the migrants dedicated by child sacrifice (cf. Psa. 106:37-38, which tells how the Israelites adopted this practice).

Who were these invaders? We have no written records, of course. But most scholars think that they were at least a part of that general group labeled *Amorite*. The term originally means "Westerner" and the Mesopotamians applied it to invaders who entered their country from the West. Other members of this group may have invaded Egypt at about the same time (Egypt's so-called First Intermediate Period).

The Bible uses the term *Amorite* in a slightly more general and popular sense, referring to the pre-Israelite native population of the land. This makes it essentially synonymous with *Canaanite*. By the time of the Israelite invasion, the two terms had become interchangeable. But what was the original relationship between the two groups? Archaeologists who believe that the Amorites lived in Palestine during Middle Bronze I assume that the "Canaanites" were the invaders of Middle Bronze II A, who moved down along the Mediterranean coast from Phoenicia. But the literature of the Near East does not mention Canaan until much later. Then it is referred to as a geographical location, from which the adjective *Canaanite* appears to be derived. So most modern archaeologists believe that "Canaanites" was simply a later name for the

Amorites. Unfortunately, scholars do not agree on this point. It is an urgent question for the Bible believer, however, because it would help to identify the date of the patriarchs.

For a long time Albright, Glueck, and many other archaeologists suspected that the patriarchs were somehow connected with the Amorites. After all, the Amorites settled the semi-arid region of the Negev where the patriarchs wandered. However, the patriarchs also settled in various cities (Shechem, Bethel, and Hebron), and there were no such urban centers in Palestine during Middle Bronze I. In addition, the patriarchs practiced multiple burials (Gen. 23:7-20), in contrast to the Middle Bronze I custom of individual burials. So we are reluctant to identify the patriarchs with the "Amorites"; it just doesn't seem to fit with events in Palestine, nor with the events in neighboring countries. Current archaeologists do not even attempt to identify the Middle Bronze I invaders, and they date the patriarchs sometime after 1900 B.C.

Some evidence from outside of Palestine indicates that the patriarchs lived in desert areas close to the urban centers of this era. The Mesopotamian cities of Mari and Nuzi resemble the culture of the patriarchs in many ways. Mari dates back to the eighteenth century B.C., and Nuzi to the sixteenth century B.C. This suggests that the patriarchs lived in Middle Bronze II A, instead of Middle Bronze I (the time of the new invaders).

But some of the secular records from outside Palestine do *not* confirm that they lived in this period. In fact, the new information from Ebla suggests that the patriarchs may have lived well before 2000 B.C.

Sifting dirt. To archaeologists, every fragment of history is precious. These scientists at an excavation of Caesarea Maritima (A.D. 100–500) sift dirt through a screen box to search for small relics.

3. Middle Bronze II. We have noted that another wave of northern invaders entered Palestine during Middle Bronze II A (*ca.* 1900 B.C.). Colin McEvedy observes that "presumably this was another facet of the Amorite migration."[2]

The Middle Bronze II B period was ushered in by still another invasion from the north. These invaders pushed down through Palestine into Egypt, beginning that country's Second Intermediate Period. In Egypt the new invaders came to be known as the *Hyksos* ("foreign invaders"). They centered their activities around the cities of Tanis and Avaris in the northeastern part of Egypt, which was nearer to their homeland. The Bible refers to Avaris as *Zoan,* and Numbers 13:22 dates its founding after the time of Abraham. Because the Hyksos may have been relatives or descendants of the Amorites, they probably would have felt the Israelites were rivals to the throne. Many scholars believe the Hyksos ruled Egypt during the years the Israelites lived in bondage.

Multiple burials again became common in the Hyksos period. In fact, tombs were reopened many times. Hyksos cavalrymen were sometimes buried with their horses and weapons, along with pottery, jewelry, and other articles of daily living. Near Jericho, Dr. Kenyon discovered several well-preserved Middle Bronze II tombs of this type.[3]

The Hyksos period probably lasted from 1750 to 1550 B.C. The later half of that period (after 1650 B.C.) is usually called Middle Bronze II C. An "Indo-Aryan" tribe (a group of non-Semitic people originally from the plateau of Iran) rose to power in the Near East at this time. They were probably the Hurrians (or as the Bible calls them, "Horites"). About a century later, they established the empire of Mitanni, which for a time was equal in power to Egypt. The Hurrians intermarried with the Amorites. This probably explains why the Hurrian city of Nuzi shows close similarities with the culture of the patriarchs.

Archaeologists have found that the Indo-Aryans exerted a strong influence upon Palestine. Apparently they introduced many new weapons and tools. They brought horsedrawn chariots, the composite bow, and new types of city fortifications. They outfitted nearly every major city from central Syria to the Nile Delta with a defensive wall called a *glacis*. The glacis contained alternating layers of pounded earth, clay, and gravel, covered with plaster. It sloped down from the rock city walls to a dry moat below. Perhaps it was designed to frustrate cavalrymen and battering rams. The Indo-Aryan cities also had huge cyclopean walls—a row of boulders leaning against a massive earthen fill. The people often built rectangular enclosures next to the walled city, surrounded by high ramparts. These enclosures may have been used for army camps or horse parks; but soon private homes were built inside them, and they became suburbs of the walled citadels. Hazor in the Holy Land provides a superb example of this.

Middle Bronze II (probably the time the patriarchs entered Canaan) was one of Palestine's most prosperous periods. Archaeologists have unearthed many massive fortress-temples that were built during this period. However, we have very few manuscripts from this time, and so we know little about its politics or secular history. The Bible says little about the secular world.

4. Late Bronze Age. The Late Bronze Period began about 1550 B.C. The Egyptians regained their throne and drove the Hyksos from their country about this time. Moses was born during this troubled time. By 1500 B.C., most Hyksos cities in Palestine had been destroyed.

In 1468 B.C., Thutmose III defeated the Hyksos in a famous battle at the Megiddo Pass. The Pharaoh left many accounts of this battle in his inscriptions. Egyptian troops pressed north, eventually reaching the Euphrates. However, Egypt's full political control did not extend quite that far.

a. Palestine: The Amarna Age. Canaan did not prosper during this period, on the eve of the Israelite conquest. It appears that the Egyptian pharaohs gave poor leadership to their puppet governments in Palestine; their time was consumed by military adventures to the north. So the land of Canaan gradually fell into a disconnected group of petty, quarreling city-states. These quarrelsome tendencies peaked in the fourteenth century, the so-called Amarna Age. That title comes from our modern name for the ruins of the capital of Egypt's heretic king, Amenhotep IV or Akhnaton. He spurned Egypt's traditional capitals and priesthoods to found his own capital on the middle Nile. Moreover, Akhnaton disliked politics and the business of administering the Egyptian empire, such as it was, in Palestine.

Out of this situation came the so-called Amarna letters, which the petty princelets of Palestine sent to the pharaoh. Apparently he simply discarded them where they awaited modern archaeologists. Ostensibly written in Akkadian cuneiform (the language of international diplomacy at that time), the Amarna letters are heavily influenced by the local Canaanite dialect. They give us much information on the local language shortly before the Israelite invasion. The rulers of these city-states professed their loyalty to the pharaoh, but it is obvious that many of them were simply trying to promote their own careers at the expense of their neighbors.

Of special interest are the many letters that appeal to the pharaoh for aid against the incursions of the *Habiru.* One prince wrote, "The *Habiru* are plundering all the lands of the king. If no troops come in this very year, then all the lands of the king are lost."[4] Linguistically, this word is very similar to "Hebrew," but they have nothing to do with one another. The term *Habiru* could be found all over western Asia from the end of the third millennium until the end of the second. The term was not basically ethnic or political, but sociological. It signified landless people of almost any sort, usually semi-nomads who sold their services to city-dwellers in times of peace, but who threatened their stability when the cities became weak. The leaders of the Canaanite city-states may well have reckoned with the Israelites among the *Habiru,* but the term referred to many other groups of people as well. Note that the Israelites did not refer to themselves as "Hebrews" until much later; instead, they called themselves "children (sons) of Israel."

Some scholars believe that the "Israelite invasion" was actually an internal rebellion of oppressed serfs against the landed aristocracy in the cities, abetted by newcomers from across the Jordan. While the Canaanite peasants may have indeed rebelled against the land owners, the Bible clearly shows that these serfs had only a secondary role in the invasion, if they were involved in it at all.

b. Egypt: The Nineteenth Dynasty. After Akhnaton's neglect brought Egypt to the brink of collapse, the nineteenth or Rameside dynasty brought a brief revival of Egypt's power in the thirteenth century, or Late Bronze II. But it turned out to be Egypt's last gasp. The gargantuan statues and temples of the Rameses, especially Rameses II, could not conceal the fact. Although Egypt continued to meddle in Canaanite affairs throughout biblical history, never again was she able to become much more than a "broken reed of a staff, which will pierce the hand of any man who leans on it" (Isa. 36:6, RSV). Powerful nations were contending for the Near East, and Egypt was scarcely able to survive.

A major barbarian force moved down from the Balkan and Black Sea regions, engulfing and obliterating every civilization in its path: the Myceneans in southern Greece, the Hittites in Asia Minor, and Canaanite settlers along the Mediterranean coast to the gates of Egypt. In a last-ditch stand at Medinet Habu, Rameses III stopped the barbarian horde, but the effort drained the last of Egypt's resources. The Egyptian inscriptions call these would-be invaders the "Sea-Peoples," but there is little doubt that these are the people that the Bible calls "Philistines." Ironically, this area was ultimately named after them—*Palestine.* After their defeat, the "Sea-Peoples" agreed to become a buffer state against further invasion of Egypt. That may still have been their status when they collided with the Israelites, streaming in from the southeast.

Archaeological evidence suggests that the Israelites arrived before the Philistines, were pushed back by the Philistine invaders, and then conquered the Philistines under Joshua. The biblical accounts that say Joshua swept all the way to the Mediterranean coast (Josh. 10:40-41) are not simple boasting. They are supported by the first mention of Israel in extrabiblical history by Pharaoh Merneptah (*ca.* 1224–1211), who led a raid into Canaan *before* Rameses III's confrontation with the Philistines. Upon his return, Merneptah boasted that "Israel is laid waste, his seed is not." His report characterizes Israel only as a people, not as a nation. That certainly would have been their status shortly after entering Canaan under Joshua.

Archaeological evidence does not support the biblical account of the conquest as firmly as we might wish. At best, of course, archaeology can only "prove" the destruction of certain cities at a certain time; it cannot tell us why the cities were destroyed, or by whom. However, the lack of evidence does not entitle us to contradict the Bible; that would be an argument from silence.

There are many good explanations for the scarcity of evidence from cities of this period. For example, the severe erosion of the Jericho site during the centuries it lay unoccupied accounts for our lack of Late Bronze evidence there. A similar explanation may apply to Gibeon; but it may also be that the city was located at a different place in Joshua's time. (It was not all that unusual for Near Eastern people to relocate their cities when they were destroyed by war or natural disaster.) The lack of destruction evidence at Shechem agrees with the Bible account that no destruction was necessary there—probably because an "advanced guard" of Israelites was already in control (cf. Gen. 34). And the Bible's report of destruction is beautifully corroborated by finds at Hazor, Lachish, and Debir (cf. Josh. 10:11, 30-31, 38-39).

D. The Iron Age. We are not surprised that the remains of Iron Age I are of relatively poor quality. The Israelites were not experienced in the arts of civilization, and they really did not establish their culture in Canaan until the days of David and Solomon. As the Book of Judges shows, a protracted and troubled period of consolidation followed Joshua's initial lightning victories. Recent excavations at Ashdod have illustrated, by way of contrast, the high level of Philistine culture at the same time. Often the relics from the Philistine cities show clear evidence of the people's Aegean backgrounds. A highwater mark of Philistine imperialism came with their capture of the ark of the covenant and the destruction of Shiloh (1 Sam. 4:1-10). Archaeological research at Shiloh has now confirmed this defeat. Saul's citadel at Gibeah, just north of Jerusalem, is another excellent example of the crude architecture of Iron Age I. It is just the rustic fortress one might have expected. As W. H. Morton says, "The unpretentiousness of its structure and the simplicity of its furnishings . . . are suggested by the smallness of its rooms and the common quality of its artifacts."[5]

With the rise of David's empire, we have more secular histories to confirm the Bible record, and so we depend much less upon archaeology than we did for information about earlier periods. The records of the great empires of the period, especially those of Assyria, often parallel and give more detail to the biblical testimony.

Only recently have archaeologists found some remains of the Jebusite city of Jerusalem (Ophel), which David and Joab captured. The nearly vertical shaft to the water supply was discovered early, as well as Hezekiah's later replacement, bringing water from the Gihon spring to the pool of Siloam within the walls. A new round of excavations just beginning may uncover even more of the early history of this pivotal spot.

Because the Israelis are creating many new buildings, archaeologists have uncovered more of Solomon's efforts in the past decade. Among them are his massive fortifications throughout the land, including standard-size gateways at many sites (e.g., Gezer, Megiddo, and Hazor).

Israeli archaeologists have just begun to publish their newest discoveries at Solomon's temple. We know of many parallels to its floor plan and some details of its structure.

Early archaeological literature touted the importance of "Solomon's stables" at Megiddo; but now scholars debate whether they are really either stables or Solomon's. They almost certainly must be redated to the time of Ahab.

Shortly after the time of Solomon, someone prepared the clay tablet that we know as the famous "Gezer calendar." Apparently, it was only a schoolboy's exercise for memorizing the agricultural activity for each month of the year; but until recently it was our oldest known specimen of Hebrew writing.[6]

We can trace archaeologically Baasha's first attempts to construct a capital at Tirzah (1 Kings 15:33) and Omri's founding of Samaria (1 Kings 16:24). Among the many magnificent finds at Samaria, two stand out: the ivory plaques and the *ostraca*. The former were apparently inlays in the "ivory house" of Ahab (1 Kings 22:39) and other kings very similar to those popular in Phoenicia and Assyria at the time. The *ostraca* (inscribed potsherds) probably came from the reign of Jeroboam II. They contain commonplace records of taxes or contributions to the throne but they are important for the work of linguistic scholars.

Beginning about the time of Omri and Ahab, the Assyrians increased their pressure on Israel and Judah. The archaeological record of that conflict is too plentiful to detail here. The famous Lachish *ostraca* (discovered in the guardhouse of one of that city's gates) are nearly contemporary with the fall of Jerusalem to Babylon in 587 B.C. Recent excavations at Jerusalem have uncovered some of the walls toppled by the Babylonians, and even some of the arrowheads that the attackers fired.

We know as little about some periods after the Exile (such as the Persian Period) as we do about the patriarchal age. Archaeological finds for these periods are correspondingly meager. But archaeologists have found Nehemiah's rebuilt walls around Jerusalem, as well as inscriptions naming his three enemies—Sanballat, Tobiah, and Geshem (cf. Neh. 6:1).

E. The Hellenistic Period. Archaeology gives us no direct information concerning Alexander the Great's invasion of Palestine (330 B.C.) and the beginning of the Hellenistic Period. However, we have ample written records from this period, especially from Greek and Roman sources. This lessens our dependence on archaeology. The most important archaeological material from the time of the Maccabean struggles is the renowned Qumran scrolls, found in caves along the northern shores of the Dead Sea in 1947. These scrolls had been stored in huge clay jars by members of a hermit Jewish sect, probably the Essenes. However, the scrolls' importance for the Old Testament is largely limited to the area of textual criticism. For the New Testament scholar, they help to illuminate the religious and political ferment of the times.

F. The Roman Period. Generally, biblical archaeology deals far less with the New Testament than with the Old. There are good reasons for this. The wealth of literary information about the New Testament period makes us much less dependent on archaeological sources. Also the history of the New Testament is largely that of a small, private group that affected external history only occasionally. Christianity left no architecture of its own until after it became a state religion in the fourth century.

Many excavations have been made at the traditional sites of New Testament events. Much of this work has been done by Franciscan monks, who traditionally have had custody of Palestinian "holy places." However, they generally discover only the remains of the churches or shrines erected at these spots shortly after the early fourth century. Many of these shrines were probably erected at the behest of Helena, mother of the Emperor Constantine. The archaeologist can rarely prove (or disprove!) the authenticity of these sites or discover evidence to clearly associate them with New Testament times.

However, there are some notable exceptions in which the evidence clearly does reach back to New Testament times. The most important of these have been sites in or around Jerusalem itself, where modern habitation generally makes excavation very difficult. Archaeologists made several probes in connection with the renovation of the Church of the Holy Sepulchre, covering the traditional site of Calvary and Joseph's tomb. (There are competing claims for these sites, especially "Gordon's Calvary" and the "Garden Tomb" outside the present walled city. But these sites are discounted by virtually all scientific scholarship.)

Other significant finds have emerged in the course of Israeli excavations around the Temple Mount. It has long been known that the so-called "Wailing Wall" represents part of the western wall that Herod's builders erected in connection with rebuilding the temple.

At the back of St. Anne's Church on the northern edge of the Temple Mount grounds, archaeologists have found the probable site of Jesus' cure of the paralytic (John 5:1-9). Underneath a fifth-century basilica on the site, the researchers found remains of various pools and baths. Jesus' miracle apparently took place at a small pool near the entrance to a cave at the site.

Many details of the surrounding city are unclear, however. For example, it has been demonstrated that "Robinson's Arch," jutting out from the western wall of the temple, was *not* the beginning of a bridge across the Tyropean Valley, as previously thought. Rather it was the last link in a grandiose

Basalt bowls. These basalt bowls, a pestle, and grindstones, were discovered at the site of Ghassul, to the east of Jericho. The city flourished during the Chalcolithic Period and was famous for its sophisticated art and advanced culture.

stair system that led up from the main street to the temple precincts themselves. South of the Temple Mount archaeologists have uncovered a magnificent plaza and broad steps leading up to the "Hulda Gates," the main entrance to the temple courtyards at the time of Christ. (They proved that Josephus' descriptions of this and of other nearby structures were phenomenally accurate.)

Across the valley on the western hill of Jerusalem, archaeologists have found luxurious residences of the Herodian period. They have also established that this area had already been inhabited and enclosed in a wall when Solomon's Temple was built. This section of town was probably the "Second Quarter" mentioned in 2 Kings 22:14 and Zephaniah 1:10.

Other Herodian sites have been cleared recently. Probably the most famous is Herod's resort at Masada, overlooking the southern end of the Dead Sea. After Titus' destruction of Jerusalem (A.D. 70), Masada became a refuge for fanatical zealots fleeing from the Roman armies. The Romans finally captured the site after a long siege, only to find nearly all the defenders dead in a suicide pact.

The "Herodium," which dominates the skyline a few miles southeast of Bethlehem, has also been cleared recently. It may be called Herod's "mausoleum," although it is debated whether he was actually buried in this luxurious structure at the top of the hill or somewhere on its lower slopes. Finally, we should mention the "digs" at the site of New Testament Jericho (about a mile west of the Old Testament site, at the foot of the mountains). It was one of Herod's most luxurious retreats, replete with palaces, baths, pools, sunken gardens, and the like. Undoubtedly it was the scene of some of his most infamous debaucheries.

Nearby is Qumran, excavated by the Dominican scholar, Roland de Vaux. Most of our knowledge of the important site is based on the famous scrolls found there. However, de Vaux's excavation illuminated the community's life. For example, he found elaborate devices for catching and storing the sparse rainfall. De Vaux also uncovered the "scriptorium," where the famous scrolls had originally been copied.

On the Mediterranean sea coast to the west, at Caesarea Maritima, continuing excavations have exposed much of the layout of that great Roman and Byzantine city. In many respects, Caesarea was quite typical of urban construction in those days. The relics of Caesarea illustrate how Jews, Christians, and pagans lived and worked side by side in such metropolitan centers.

The relatively well-preserved synagogue of Capernaum can hardly be the very one in which Jesus taught (Mark 1:21). The existing synagogue was built in the third or fourth century. But it may well be the successor of the synagogue Jesus knew, and perhaps it is of very similar design. Archaeologists think they may have discovered Peter's house at the same site (Matt. 8:14ff.). Graffiti on the plastered walls of this second-century house clearly link it with Peter. Later it was replaced by a succession of octagonal churches.

Atop Mount Gerizim, excavations have uncovered the foundations of the Samaritan temple that competed with the temple of Jerusalem in New Testament times. Visitors can now see traces of a massive staircase down the mountainside to the city below. Near the bottom of this staircase is the traditional site of "Jacob's Well" (cf. John 4:1-42), which may well be genuine.

The search for the scenes of the Gospel narratives has been going on for centuries. A few traditions report very early sites. Justin Martyr was told the location of a cave in Bethlehem where Jesus was born. (This would have been before A.D. 130.) The supposed location of Golgotha at the end of the Via Dolorosa was first mentioned by A.D. 135 and was officially recognized by the Emperor Constantine after A.D. 325. Both sites (that of Jesus' birth and death) have been continually venerated to modern times. The excavations in and around Jerusalem are beginning to provide a much better idea of how that city looked in the days of the New Testament.

5

PAGAN RELIGIONS AND CULTURES

The Israelites of Old Testament times came into contact with Canaanites, Egyptians, Babylonians, and other people who worshiped false gods. God warned His people not to imitate their pagan neighbors, yet the Israelites disobeyed Him. They slipped into paganism again and again.

What did these pagan nations worship? And how did it pull the Israelites away from the true God?

By studying these pagan cultures we learn how man attempted to answer the ultimate questions of life before he found the light of God's truth. Also, we come to understand the world in which Israel lived—a world from which she was called to be radically different, both ethnically and ideologically.

Before beginning such a study, we should note some cautions. First, we need to remember that we stand at least two millennia from the pagan cultures we are about to describe. The evidence (texts, buildings, artifacts) is often very sketchy. So we need to be cautious in drawing conclusions.

Secondly, we should realize that we live in a pluralistic society in which every person is free to believe or disbelieve as he chooses; but ancient peoples felt that some sort of religion was necessary. An agnostic or "free thinker" would have had a hard time living among the Egyptians, the Hittites, or even the Greeks and Romans. Religion was everywhere. It was the heart of ancient society. A person worshiped the deities of his town, city, or civilization. If he moved to a new home or traveled through a foreign land, he was duty-bound to show respect to the deities there.

COMMON FEATURES OF PAGAN RELIGIONS

Certain features were common to most of these pagan religions. They all partook of the same world view, which was centered on the locality and its prestige. The differences between Sumerian and Assyro-Babylonian religions or between Greek and Roman religions were marginal.

A. Many Gods. Most of these religions were *polytheistic*, which means that they acknowledged many gods and demons. Once admitted to the *pantheon* (a culture's collection of deities), a god could not be eliminated from it. He or she had gained "divine tenure."

Each polytheistic culture inherited religious ideas from its predecessors or acquired them in war. For example, what Nanna was to the Sumerians (the moon god), Sin was to the Babylonians. What Inanna was to the Sumerians (the fertility goddess and queen of heaven), Ishtar was to the Babylonians. The Romans simply took over the Greek gods and gave them Roman names. Thus the Roman god Jupiter was equal to Zeus as sky god; Minerva equaled Athena as goddess of widsom; Neptune equaled Poseidon as god of the sea; and so forth. In other words, the idea of the god was the same; just the cultural wrapping was different. So one ancient culture could absorb the religion of another without changing stride or breaking step. Each culture not only claimed gods of a previous civilization; it laid claim to their myths and made them its own, with only minor changes.

The chief gods were often associated with some phenomenon in nature. Thus, Utu/Shamash is both the sun and the sun god; Enki/Ea is both the sea and the sea god; Nanna/Sin is both the moon and the moon god. The pagan cultures made no distinction between an element of nature and any force behind that element. Ancient man struggled against forces in nature that he couldn't control, forces that could be either beneficent or malevolent. Enough rain guaranteed a bumper crop at harvest, but too much rain would destroy that crop. Life was quite unpredictable, especially since the gods were thought to be capricious and whimsical, capable of either good or evil. Human beings and gods participated in the same kind of life; the gods had the same sort of problems and frustrations that human beings had. This concept is called *monism*. Thus when Psalm 19:1 says, "The heavens declare the glory of God, and the firmament showeth his handiwork," it mocks the beliefs of the Egyptians and Babylonians. These pagan people could not imagine that the universe fulfilled an all-embracing divine plan.

The Egyptians also associated their gods with phenomena of nature; Shu (air), Re/Horus (sun), Khonsu (moon), Nut (sky), and so on. The same tendency appears in the Hittite worship of Wurusemu (sun goddess), Taru (storm), Telipinu (vegetation), and several mountain gods. Among the Canaanites, El was the high god in heaven, Baal was the storm god, Yam was the sea god, and Shemesh and Yareah were the sun and moon gods respectively. Because of this bewildering array of nature deities the pagan could never speak of a *"uni*verse." He did not conceive of one central force that holds all together, and by which all things exist. The pagan believed he lived in a *"multi*verse."

B. Worship of Images. Another common trait of pagan religion was religious *iconography* (the making of images or totems to worship). All of these religions worshiped idols, Israel alone was officially *aniconic* (i.e., it had no images, no pictorial representations of God). Images of Jehovah, such as Aaron's and Jeroboam's bull-calves (Exod. 32; 1 Kings 12:26ff.) were forbidden in the second commandment.

But aniconic religion was not always the whole story. The Israelites worshiped pagan idols while they lived under Egypt's bondage (Josh. 24:14); and even though God banished their idols (Exod. 20:1-5), the Moabites lured them into idolatry again (Num. 25:1-2). Idolatry was the downfall of Israel's leaders in different periods of her history, and God finally allowed the nation to be defeated "because of their sacrifices" to pagan idols (Hos. 12:19).

Most pagan religions pictured their gods *anthropomorphically* (i.e., as human beings). In fact, only an expert can look at a picture of Babylonian gods and mortals and tell which is which. Egyptian artists usually represented their gods as men or women with animal heads. Horus was a falcon-headed man, Sekhmet was a lioness-headed woman, Anubis was a jackal, Hathor a cow, and so forth. Hittite gods can be recognized by the drawing of a weapon they place on their shoulder, or by some other distinctive object such as a helmet with a pair of horns. The Greek gods also are pictured as humans, but without the harsh characteristics of the Semite deities.

C. Self-Salvation. What is the significance of portraying the gods like human beings? The opening chapters of Genesis say that God made man in His image (Gen. 1:27), but the pagans attempted to make gods in their own image. That is to say, the pagan gods were merely amplified human beings. The myths of the ancient world assumed that the gods had the same needs as humans, the same foibles and the same imperfections. If there was a difference between the pagan gods and men, it was only a difference of degree. The gods were humans made "bigger than life." Often they were the projections of the city or township.

D. Sacrifice. Most pagan religions sacrificed animals to soothe their temperamental gods; some even sacrificed

Pagan gods. This illustration from a vase depicts the Greek gods watching over Darius I of Persia (in the bottom row, with scepter in right hand and sword in left), who attempted to conquer Greece in the fifth century B.C. Zeus, the central figure among the gods in the top row, is shown with the scepter and thunderbolt that symbolize his status as ruler of the gods.

human beings. Because the heathen worshipers believed their gods had human desires, they also offered food and drink offerings to them (cf. Isa. 57:5-6; Jer. 7:18).

The Canaanites believed sacrifices had magical powers that brought the worshiper into sympathy and rhythm with the physical world. However, the gods were capricious, so worshipers sometimes offered sacrifices to secure a victory over their enemies (cf. 2 Kings 3:26-27). Perhaps this is why the decadent kings of Israel and Judah indulged in pagan sacrifice (cf. 1 Kings 21:25-26; 2 Kings 16:23). They wanted magical aid in fighting their enemies, the Babylonians and Assyrians—preferably the aid of the same gods that had made their enemies victorious.

OFFICIAL RELIGION VS. POPULAR RELIGION

Ancient polytheistic religions operated at two levels: the official religion of the archaic religious state and popular religion, which was little more than superstition.

A. Categories of Gods. Each ancient religious system had a chief god who was more powerful than the rest. For the Egyptians, this might be Re, Horus, or Osiris; for the Sumerians and Akkadians, it might be Enlil, Enki/Ea, or Marduk; for the Canaanites, it would be El; and for the Greeks, Zeus. In most instances, the pagans built temples and recited liturgies in honor of these high gods. Usually the king presided over this worship, acting as the god's representative in a ritual meal, marriage, or combat. This was the official religion.

"The temple was the home of the god, and the priests were his domestic staff. . . . Every day it was the duty of the staff of the temple to attend to the god's 'bodily needs' according to a fixed routine. . . .

"But the god was not merely the householder of the temple, he was also the lord and master of his people, and as such entitled to offerings and tributes of many kinds. . . ."[1]

The gods of the official state religion were too far removed from the local man to be of any practical value.

Ancient Egypt was divided into districts called *nomes*. In the early days of Egypt there were 22 of these in Upper Egypt (the southern part) and 20 in the northern delta area. Each *nome* had a key or capital city and a local god who was worshiped in that territory: Ptah in Memphis, Amen-Re in Thebes, Thoth in Hermopolis, and so on. In Mesopotamia too, each city was sacred to one god or goddess: Nanna/Sin in Ur (Abraham's birthplace), Utu/Shamash in Larsa, Enlil in Nippur, and Marduk in Babylon. The Canaanites worshiped "the Baal" (the local fertility deity) but the people of each community had their own *baal*, as we can tell by place names like Baal-zephon, Baal-peor, and Baal-hermon (all mentioned in the Old Testament—e.g., Exod. 14:2; Num. 25:5; Judg. 3:3). In the ancient Near East, official religion was oriented to the state, while popular religion was oriented to the geographical locale. Ancient man saw no inconsistency between believing in gods "up there" and another god "right here"—all competing for his attention and servitude. This was a partial recognition of the ultimate problem of immanence and transcendence.

B. Abstract Philosophy. The ancients began to move away from pure superstition and deified various abstract ideals under the names of ancient gods.

In Mesopotamia, "Justice" and "Righteousness" appear as minor deities in the retinue of Utu/Shamash, the sun god; they were called Nig-gina and Nig-sisa, respectively. Their "boss" was Shamash, the Mesopotamian god of law. Ancient thinkers conceived of these abstract ideas as gods, rather than dealing with the ideas themselves.

The Egyptians did this more than anyone else. Some of the major Egyptian gods fell into this category. For example, Atum expresses the concept of universality. The name *Amon* means "hidden"—the Egyptians thought he was a formless, unseen being who might be anywhere, and anyone could worship him. For that reason, they later grafted the idea of Amon on to Re, and the god became Amen-Re, "the king of eternity and guardian of the dead."[2] The most massive temples of Egyptian history were built in honor of Amen-Re at Karnak. The goddess Maat was another Egyptian idea-become-god. She was supposed to personify truth and justice, and was the cosmic force of harmony and stability.

The Canaanites represented truth and justice with gods Sedeq and Mishor, who were supposed to serve under the god Shemesh. But even though pagan thinkers could deal with these ideas more easily this way, few of the gods lived up to their ideals, according to legend. Canaanite religion continued the ancient desire for sexual harmony with nature, and it encouraged particularly obscene rituals.

C. Akhnaton's Belief. The pagan religions of Mesopotamia never broke out of their polytheistic mold. One scholar of ancient religions, W. W. Hallo, speaks of the Mesopotamians' "unsurmountable antipathy to an exclusive monotheism."[3] The same can be said for other people of antiquity: Hittites, Persians, Canaanites, Greeks, and Romans.

There is perhaps one exception. Typically Egypt was polytheistic; but during her eighteenth dynasty she produced the famous pharaoh Amenhotep IV (1387–1366 B.C.). He outlawed the worship of all gods except Aton (the "sun disk"), and then changed his own name to Akhnaton. Prior to Akhnaton, the Egyptian deities had often been merged or coalesced into a single god-concept (usually Re); this, however, is not monotheism. But the Egyptians called the god Aton "the sole god, like whom there is no other." This had far-reaching political effects and could not have been accomplished without the support of the army and the priests. But Akhnaton's religion fell far short of saying anything like, "Hear, O Israel, the LORD our God is one" (Deut. 6:4). Akhnaton's "reform" was short-lived, however, and his successors purged Egypt of this "heresy." The old political priesthood returned to power and supported their own pharaoh.

In the ancient world, only Israel was fully monotheistic. But let us be sure we understand what this means. Monotheism is not simply a matter of arithmetic. Perhaps the most succinct statement is that of W. F. Albright, who says that monotheism is "the belief in the existence of only one God, who is the Creator of the world and the giver of all life, . . . [Who is] so far superior to all created beings . . . that He remains absolutely unique." This made Israel radically different from her pagan neighbors.

PAGAN RELIGION IN LITERATURE

When we turn to the literature of the ancient world we get the clearest picture of pagan religions. Almost all ancient literature reflects the religion of its culture: hymns, prayers, royal inscriptions, incantations, historical texts, and epics. The beliefs of a people are seen most clearly when they address themselves to questions such as: Who am I? Where did I come from? What is this world? How does one explain pleasure and pain? We find their answers to most of these questions in ancient creation stories (technically called *cosmogonies*), and hardly any group of people is without some tradition at this point.

A. Egyptian Creation Stories. Egypt had at least five different stories that explained the origin of the world, the gods, and man. Two of these five will be enough to illustrate what the Egyptians believed.

The city of Heliopolis hands down the story that Amen-Re came forth from the watery mass (Num) by his own power. He then reproduced from himself the first divine couple, Shu and Tefnut (air and moisture, male and female). This couple mated and produced another generation of gods, Geb (earth) and his wife Nut (sky). And so the process of life started.

In another story (this one from the city of Hermopolis), creation began with four couples of gods. These four couples created an egg from which the sun (Re) was born. Re then created the world.

Egyptians told these creation stories to try to prove that their city was the place of creation. Memphis, Thebes, Heliopolis, and Hermopolis claimed to be the territory where it all started.

B. Babylon's Creation Story. The most complete creation account from Babylon is usually called the *Enuma Elish*. These are the first two words of the narrative, and they translate into English as "When on high. . . ."

In the beginning there were two gods, Apsu and Tiamat, who represented the fresh waters (male) and marine waters (female). They cohabited and produced a second generation

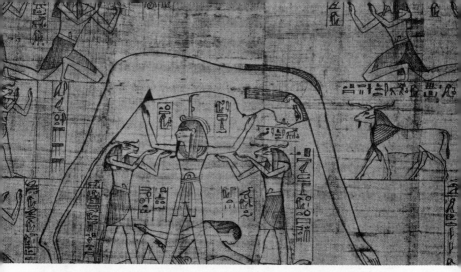

Egyptian gods. This papyrus from the tenth century B.C. depicts the Egyptian universe. The sky goddess Nut, arched as the heavens, is supported by the upstretched arms of the air god Shu. At Shu's feet, the earth god Geb stretches his left arm along the ground. Other gods look on from the sides.

of divine beings. Soon Apsu was suffering from insomnia because the young deities were making so much noise; he just could not get to sleep. He wanted to kill the noisy upstarts, despite the protests of his spouse, Tiamat. But before he managed to do that, Ea, the god of wisdom and magic, put Apsu to sleep under a magic spell and killed him.

Not to be outdone, wife Tiamat plotted revenge on her husband's killer and those who aided the killing. Her first move was to take a second husband, whose name was Kingu. Then she raised an army for her retaliation plans.

At this point the gods appealed to the god Marduk to save them. He happily accepted the challenge, on the condition that if he was victorious over Tiamat, they would make him chief of all gods.

The confrontation between Tiamat and Marduk ended in a blazing victory for Marduk. He captured Tiamat's followers and made them his slaves. Then he cut the corpse of Tiamat in half, creating heaven from one half of it and the earth from the other half. He ordered the earlier supporters of Tiamat to take care of the world.

Shortly thereafter, Marduk conceived another plan. He had Kingu killed and arranged for Ea to make man out of his blood. In the words of the story, man's lot is to be "burdened with the toil of the gods." To demonstrate their gratitude to Marduk, the gods then helped him to build the great city of Babylon and its imposing temple. The story ends by describing the gods' great feast in Marduk's honor and by listing Marduk's fifty names, each of which is supposed to indicate some power or accomplishment that characterizes him.

Note some of the emphases of this story. It says that in the beginning there were two gods, Apsu and Tiamat, male and female. This is markedly different from the creation account of Genesis 1–2, which states that in the beginning there was one God, not two. Why is it important to know that God had no spouse or consort, and was alone? Because it shows that God finds fulfillment in himself, and needs no resources outside himself. The opening chapters of Genesis refer to nothing else that finds fulfillment in itself. All of God's creatures find fulfillment in something or someone outside themselves.

The pagan Babylonian had no problem believing that there were two gods in the beginning. As far as he was concerned, there could be no future with only one god. How could there be creation or procreation if there was only one god? When the pagan talked about his gods, he talked only in human categories. He could not imagine a god who was any different.

It seems strange that the Babylonian god Apsu complains that he wants to sleep. But when the Psalmist said that our God "shall neither slumber nor sleep" (Psa. 121:4), he was stating something that was not obvious in his day. It underscores the fact that Israel's belief in God was radically unique among the people of the ancient world.

Apsu was ready to kill because his children kept him awake. He had no clear-cut moral motive. The god is angry—not because man has filled the earth with violence or corruption, but because it is so noisy he cannot sleep! It seems strange that a god like Apsu could act out of such selfish motives. But the pagan mind reasoned that if mortal man conducts himself this way, why not the gods, too?

The real purpose of the *Enuma Elish* is not to tell about the creation of the world. The story is intended to answer the question: How did the god Marduk become chief god of the mighty city, Babylon? More than likely, the Babylonians read this particular composition at the New Year's festival, in the hopes of guaranteeing a good year ahead. Marduk represented the forces of order and Tiamat the forces of chaos. This line of thinking concludes that, if a person says the right words at the right time, his chances of success will increase. It sees celebration or invocation of the gods as a kind of magic charm.

Pagan myths view the creation of man as an afterthought. They say that man was created to be a servant of the gods, to do their "dirty work." The Babylonians believed that man was evil because Marduk had created him from the blood of the rebellious god, Kingu. Certainly this account has none of the majesty that we find surrounding the creation of man in Genesis.

The Bible says God created man in His own image, distinct from all else that God had made (Gen. 1:26ff.). And the Bible alone, of all ancient literature, has a separate account of the creation of woman (Gen. 2:21-25).

C. Pagan Flood Myths. In the Bible, the creation story is soon followed by the Flood, God's response to man's repeated iniquities (Gen. 6–9). In both Egypt and Canaan we find narratives about angry gods who unleashed their fury on mankind, sometimes accompanied by a great flood.

In Egyptian mythology the goddess Sekhmet intended to wipe out the human race. She was thwarted only when others flooded the world with beer, which had been dyed blood-red. Bloodthirsty as she was, Sekhmet drank all she could and was put to sleep by the beer.

Canaanite literature tells a similar story about the goddess Anath (wife of Baal), who went on a rampage against man. No gory detail is omitted from the story as she wades into battle with a club and bow: "Under Anath (flew) heads like vultures/ Over her (flew) hands like locusts . . . She plunges knee-deep in the blood of heroes/Neck-high in the gore of troops . . . Anath swells her liver with laughter/Her heart is filled with joy/For in the hand of Anath is victory."[4]

The literature of Mesopotamia includes a crucial text that

describes a flood as divine punishment. This particular text is called the Gilgamesh Epic. The main character is himself a combination of history and legend. He was in fact the fifth king of the Uruk (around 2600 B.C.), and appears in legend as a Samson-like individual. Two things stand out in the traditions about Gilgamesh. First, the story says he was one-third human and two-thirds divine. Second, he supposedly was of mixed human and divine parentage; his mother was the goddess Ninsun and his father was Lugal-banda, an earlier king of Uruk.

The Gilgamesh Epic tells how Gilgamesh brutalized his subjects. To tone him down, the people of Uruk persuaded the goddess Aruru to create a man named Enkidu. Enkidu eventually met Gilgamesh and the two became the best of friends. Subsequently, they waged war against all types of monsters, such as the evil dragon Humbaba. Gilgamesh is handsome—so handsome that the goddess Ishtar proposes marriage. Gilgamesh rejects her proposal because she is a promiscuous wife and lover. Fuming, Ishtar obtains permission from her father, Anu, to destroy Gilgamesh with the Bull of Heaven. Ferocious fighting follows, and again Gilgamesh and Enkidu are victorious.

Amen-Re. Egypt's sun god, Amen-Re, was considered the king of the gods. Egyptians believed he traveled across the sky in his boat by day, then continued his journey at night into the underworld, using a second boat. Egyptian mythology also pictured him as a falcon soaring through the skies or as a young hero in a constant struggle with the powers of darkness. In his right hand, Amen-Re carries the ankh, a religious symbol of life.

But then Enkidu becomes ill and dies. Brooding over the death of his companion, Gilgamesh determines to find a man called Utnapishtim, the only mortal who had ever become immortal by surviving the flood, because Gilgamesh wants to learn how to do the same. After much hair-raising adventure through the underworld, Gilgamesh finally meets Utnapishtim.

Utnapishtim tells Gilgamesh how the gods secretly decided to send a flood on the earth, principally through the storm god Enlil. One of their own, Ea, divulged the plan to Utnapishtim and urged him to build a boat to save himself, his family, some precious metals, and various species of animals. Utnapishtim took all of these aboard, along with several skilled crewmen. The rains fell for seven days and nights, after which Utnapishtim's boat landed on a mountain. Utnapishtim sent out various birds to determine whether or not the waters had receded. When he finally left the ship he made a sacrifice to the gods, who "gathered like flies" around it. Enraged that two humans had escaped his catastrophic blow, Enlil at first threatened but then conferred divinity upon Utnapishtim and his wife—not as a reward, but as an alternative to destroying humanity.

But all this means nothing for Gilgamesh. Utnapishtim's rescue was an exception, not a precedent. As a consolation, Utnapishtim offers Gilgamesh the Plant of Life; but even this is stolen by a serpent. Frustration upon frustration! Drearily Gilgamesh trudges home to Uruk. He knows he must die, but at least he will be remembered for his building accomplishments—his immortality being in the work of his own hands. This is one of the great poetic epics of the Akkadian language.

Woven into this myth is a Mesopotamian flood story, with fascinating parallels to Scripture. But in no way does the Mesopotamian myth cast doubt on the authenticity of Genesis.

There are many ideological differences between the two flood stories. The Gilgamesh Epic gives no clear-cut reason for Enlil to send the flood. Certainly he was not moved by the moral degeneracy of mankind. How could he be? These pagan gods were not paragons of virtue nor did they champion it. One modern scholar, C. H. Gordon, says, "The modern student must not make the mistake of thinking that the ancient Easterner had any difficulty in reconciling the notion of divinity, with carryings-on that included chicanery, bribery, indecent exposure for a laugh, and homosexual buffoonery."[5]

Also, note that the Gilgamesh Epic emphasizes Utnapishtim's use of human skill in saving himself from the flood. That's why there were navigators on board; it is a match of human wits and divine wits. There is nothing like this in the Genesis account; there were neither navigational equipment nor professional sailors on board. If Noah, his wife, and family were to be saved, it would happen by God's grace, not human expertise or ingenuity.

Third, the Gilgamesh story is basically without educational and long-range moral value. Scripture explains the significance of the Flood for subsequent generations by the words of a covenant from God: "And I will establish my covenant with you; . . . neither shall there any more be a flood to destroy the earth" (Gen. 9:11).

Fourthly, the Bible shows that God saved Noah to preserve the human race. The myth of Utnapishtim does not reflect any such divine plan. He was saved by accident, because one of the gods tattled to him about Enlil's intentions.

D. Divination Texts. Texts dealing with divination represent the second largest single category of the cuneiform literature of Mesopotamia (after economic texts). At its most elementary level, *divination* is an attempt to decipher the will of the gods through the use of magical techniques. The pagans believed they could use human skill and ingenuity to acquire from the gods knowledge about certain situations. In the words of Yehezkel Kaufmann, a diviner is "a scientist who can dispense with divine revelation."[6]

Divination usually followed either the inductive or intuitive method. In the former, the diviner observes events and then draws conclusions from them. The most common method was to observe the inner parts of slaughtered sheep or goats. Diviners usually studied the liver (a technique called *hepatos-*

Enuma Elish. These cuneiform tablets contain the Enuma Elish, the Babylonian creation epic. Although the story bears similarities to the biblical story of creation, there are striking differences. The Babylonians perceived their gods in human terms and believed that there must be two gods, a male and a female, for creation to take place. This is in sharp contrast to the monotheistic view of Creation in the Bible.

copy). A typical divination formula might run something like this: "If the liver has the shape X, then the outcome of the battle/sickness/journey will be as follows. . . ."

This particular system was fine for the king and the wealthy, but for the average citizens a variety of cheaper techniques was needed. There were at least half a dozen of these, such as *lecanomancy* (letting drops of oil fall into a cup of water and observing the patterns that appear) or *libanomancy* (watching the various shapes from the smoke of incense).

In the intuitive type of divination, the diviner is less active; he is more of an observer and interpreter. The best-known type of intuitive divination was dream interpretation *(oneiro-mancy).* This method produced a body of dream interpretation literature that said, "If you dream such and such, it means. . . ." Other means of divination were the texts known as *menologies* and *hemerologies.* The first type listed the months of the year and told which months were favorable for certain

Akhnaton. A king of Egypt in the fourteenth century B.C., Akhnaton believed exclusively in Aton, the sun god. For this reason, his polytheistic countrymen considered him a heretic. This relief shows him with Queen Nefertiti and their three daughters. The sun god is depicted by the shining orb at the upper center of the picture.

kinds of tasks. The latter listed activities that a person should engage in or avoid for each day of the month. From all of this, astrology was born.

The Old Testament forbids all techniques of divination (cf. Deut. 18:10; Lev. 20:6; Ezek. 13:6-8). The Bible calls divination an "abomination"; for that reason, there were no professional diviners in Israel. The confidence that divination put in human wisdom was an insult to God, for it reflected unwillingness to trust His revelation of truth.

E. Ritual Literature. The vast majority of the texts that tell of pagan temples, offerings, sacrifices, and clergy are describing the religion of the king. They are not usually applicable to the commoner's religion. Leo Oppenheim has said correctly, "The common man . . . remains unknown, the most important unknown element in Mesopotamian religion."[7] The same could certainly be said for Egypt. It was unthinkable that "the man on the street" could receive revelations from the gods. This was a prerogative of the kings.

The chasm between Christian Scripture and pagan religions is enormous here. In the Old Testament, God speaks not only to leaders like Moses and David, but also to harlots, outcasts, sinners, and others. For example, note that the first person of whom Scripture says, "He was filled with God's Spirit," was a man named Bezalel (Exod. 31:3), the foreman in charge of building the tabernacle.

Whether in Egypt or Mesopotamia, pagans believed that their gods lived in the temples they built for them. As such, they considered the temple to be sacrosanct. Hymns to temples are quite common in pagan literature.

In this respect, Solomon's prayer of dedication at the Jerusalem temple reveals a clear anti-pagan emphasis. Consider this verse: "But will God indeed dwell on the earth? Behold, heaven and the highest heaven cannot contain thee; how much less this house which I have built!" (1 Kings 8:27, RSV).

The pagan king administered the temple and performed the priestly services for his gods. He was thought to be the mediator between man and the gods. He reigned for gods (as in Mesopotamia) or as god (as in Egypt).

Incidentally, here we meet one of the most distinctive characteristics of biblical faith. The pagan religions never produced spokesmen who ventured to contradict the king, as the biblical prophets did. The pagans had no concept of "prophetic immunity." Only in Israel could a king be reproached by a prophet with the words, "Thou art the man!" (2 Sam. 12:7). After all, if the king is sovereign, divine, and the head clergyman, who can tell him that he is out of line? This is why Jezebel, being of Phoenician background, could not understand why her Israelite husband cowered before the prophet Elijah (cf. 1 Kings 16:31; 21:6, 20-27).

HOLY DAYS

The Israelites celebrated a number of religious festivals during the year. Their pagan neighbors had holy days of their own, and these observances give us further insight into their spiritual outlook.

The Babylonians observed moon festivals on fixed days of the month: the first, seventh, fifteenth, and twenty-eighth. In addition, they had special "seventh" days—the seventh, fourteenth, twenty-first, and twenty-eighth of each month. They took special precautions to avoid bad luck on these "seventh" days. And they did not work at all on the fifteenth day of the month, because they believed there was no chance for good fortune on that day; this day of rest was called *shappatu.* On the *shappatu,* the Babylonians tried to pacify the gods and appease their anger with a day of penitence and prayer.

In pagan religions a sacrifice was a meal for the god, the source of his nutrition. "Like flies" the gods converged on the sacrifice of Utnapishtim after he got off his boat. It is hard to believe that anyone really believed the idol ate a morsel when no one was looking. Probably the dishes were brought to the king for consumption after being presented to the image. The food, having an aura of the holy, was supposed to sanctify the consumer—in this case, the king. When very large amounts of food were presented for sacrifice, as in Egypt or Persia, the food would go to temple personnel. The apocryphal story of Bel and the Dragon describes this practice.

In addition to the lucky and unlucky days we discussed earlier, the greatest festival in Babylon was the *akitu* (i.e., the New Year Feast). The Babylonians celebrated *akitu* in March and April, when nature began to revive. They spent the first four days making prayers to Marduk, the chief god of Babylon. In the evening of the fourth day they recited the creation story (the *Enuma Elish*). By recounting the original victory of order (Marduk) over chaos (Tiamat), the Babylonians hoped that the same victory would be evident in the new year. The Babylonians believed that the spoken word had power. And so on the fifth day, the king appeared before Marduk's statue and declared his innocence from faults and his fulfillment of his obligations. We are not sure what the people did for the next few days, but on the ninth and tenth days they held a banquet. On the eleventh day soothsayers divined the destinies of the following year.

VIEWS OF THE AFTERLIFE

Two radically different concepts of the afterlife appeared in the pagan Near East. In Mesopotamia, very few people believed there was life after death. The Gilgamesh Epic had this to say: "Gilgamesh, whither runnest thou? Life, which thou seekest, thou wilt not find. When the gods created mankind, they allotted to mankind Death, but Life they withheld in their hands."[8]

At the other end of the spectrum were the Egyptians. Their religion was saturated with a belief in the afterlife. The Egyptians believed the dead go to a territory ruled by Osiris, where a person must give an account of his good and bad deeds. Behind this was the Osiris legend, which tells how the benevolent ruler Osiris was killed by his wicked brother Seth, who cut his body into pieces. His wife, Isis, searched for his dismembered body and restored it to life. Eventually Osiris

Altar. This domestic altar illustrates the meaning of the biblical phrase, "four horns of the altar"— as when Adonijah clung to the horns of the altar, for fear of Solomon (1 Kings 1:50-51). This tenth-century limestone altar from Megiddo served an undetermined function in religious ceremonies.

descended into the underworld as the judge of the dead. His son, Horus, avenged his father's death by killing Seth. Subsequently the myth of Osiris' death and resurrection stimulated the Egyptians' hope for immortality. For Osiris, life won out over death; good won over evil. So the Egyptian reasoned the same could happen to him.

At this point, however, we meet another basic contrast between Egyptian religion and biblical faith. The Old Testament affirms that, at least for the righteous, life continues after physical death (cf. Psa. 49:15; Prov. 14:32; Isa. 57:2). So in the biblical faith there is an afterlife for everyone who is faithful to God, whether that person is king or slave. The Egyptian religion was obsessed with the afterlife; but this afterlife was only for the pharaoh and his high-ranking officials. The Bible teaches that no man has a special claim on the presence of God, and no man is exempt from God's moral law. In essence, the difference boils down to a religion for the king (pagan) versus a faith for all believers (biblical).

6
THE EGYPTIANS

Many barriers seemed to separate Egypt from the Promised Land. It was on a different continent, separated from Palestine by the rocky Sinai Peninsula and the marshes and lakes between the Mediterranean and the Red Sea. Egypt was rich in crops, livestock, and precious metals, while Palestine could offer few goods in exchange. The culture of Egypt was radically different from that of the Canaanites and Israelites, and its people came from a different race. Yet some unexpected turns of history brought the Egyptians and the Israelites together, and the Old Testament refers to Egypt more than 550 times. For centuries, Egypt ruled the coastland of Palestine; its culture and religion was dominant from Gaza to Suez.

THE EGYPTIAN PEOPLE AND THEIR LANGUAGE

We do not know the exact racial origin of the Egyptian people, but their statues and temple paintings give us a detailed picture of them during biblical times, and the embalmed bodies of Egyptian kings give us further evidence of how they looked.

Most Egyptians were fairly short, brown-skinned, with the stiff brown hair that was typical of people on the southern Mediterranean coasts. Negroes from the hinterlands of the Nile did not move down the river and mingle with the Egyptians until around 1500 B.C. (However, we do not know whether the "Ethiopian woman" that Moses married was a Negro—cf. Num. 12:1.)

By contrast, the Israelites originally came from the roving

bands of shepherds who lived along the northern edges of the Arabian desert. So Abraham and his descendants were probably about the same height as the Egyptians, but they had a light olive-colored complexion and dark brown or black hair.

Egyptians referred to the people of other lands according to their geographical location: "the Libyans," "the Nubians," and so on. But they simply called themselves "the people."[1]

Their language came from a Hamito-Semitic background. In other words, it carried some traits of languages from Northern Africa ("Hamitic," supposedly from Ham's family—Gen. 10:6-20) and from southern Asia Minor ("Semitic," supposedly from Shem's family—(Gen. 10:21-31). Although the basic structure of the Egyptian language (such as the construction of verb forms) resembled the Semitic languages such as Hebrew, it was much more like the Hamitic languages of Egypt's African neighbors along the Mediterranean coast.

Captain Bouchard of Napoleon Bonaparte's army discovered the Rosetta Stone in the western Nile Delta in 1799. It bore one inscription in three languages—Greek and two forms of Egyptian—honoring Ptolemy V Epiphanes, a Hellenistic ruler of Egypt who lived 200 years before Christ. An English physicist named Thomas Young and a French linguist named Jean François Champollion used the Greek portion of the stone to decipher the two Egyptian scripts.

Champollion and Young found that one of the Egyptian texts on the Rosetta Stone was written in the *demotic* script (from the Greek *demotikos*, "pertaining to the people"); this was a simple form of writing that Egyptians began using

The Book of the Dead. This papyrus manuscript contains the Book of the Dead, a vast collection of Egyptian incantations to aid the journey of the soul through the netherworld. In this illustration, two gods carry the dead man's soul on a silver boat across a mystical sea. The three figures at left are glorified ancestors of the deceased, awaiting his arrival.

around 500 B.C. The other text was written in the classic Egyptian script called *heiroglyphics* (from the Greek *heiroglyphikos,* "sacred carvings"). Champollion and Young deciphered both of the Egyptian texts by 1822, and their work opened the way for further study of ancient Egyptian literature.[2]

GEOGRAPHY AND AGRICULTURE

Egypt's territory covered the northeast shoulder of Africa, bordered by the Sahara Desert to the west, the tropical forests of Nubia to the south, the Red Sea to the east, and the Mediterranean to the north. The Nile River was like the bloodstream of ancient Egypt. The waters of the Nile brought life to the parched plains that the Egyptian people cultivated in Bible times. Yet the Nile was unpredictable; in the flood season, it became a ferocious, destructive tyrant that flattened peasant homes and ruined vital crops. The river was both a blessing and a curse to the Egyptian farmers *(fellahin)*.

The Nile River watered a green valley that varied from one to twenty miles in width. Egyptians called the rich soil of this valley "Black Land," and the surrounding desert the "Red Land."

Every June, the rains of central Africa and the melting snows of Abyssinia raised the river waters more than fifteen feet over their banks. The flood reached Syene (modern Aswan) in the middle of June, and the river remained at flood stage for more than a week. Normally, the fellahin were glad to see the Nile cover their land with its sluggish waters, for they knew it would leave behind a deep layer of silt that would give them an abundant harvest that fall. If the Nile did not rise as much as usual, they would have a "lean year" (cf. Gen. 41:30 ff.). But if the river rose too swiftly, it destroyed everything in its path. So the peasants and herdsmen were at the mercy of the river.

At the city of Heliopolis, the Nile River split into the Rosetta and Damietta Branches, then broke into the many arteries of

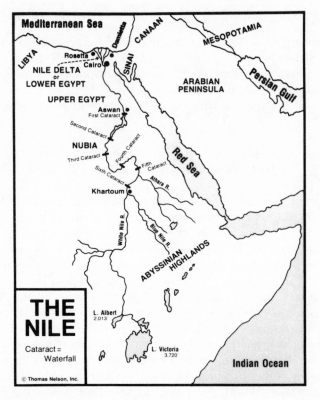

Mediterranean Sea

LIBYA

CANAAN

MESOPOTAMIA

Rosetta

Damietta

Cairo

NILE DELTA
or
LOWER EGYPT

SINAI

ARABIAN
PENINSULA

Persian Gulf

UPPER EGYPT

Aswan
First Cataract

Second Cataract

NUBIA

Third Cataract

Fourth Cataract

Fifth Cataract

Sixth Cataract

Khartoum

Atbara R.

Red Sea

White Nile R.

Blue Nile R.

ABYSSINIAN HIGHLANDS

THE
NILE

Cataract =
Waterfall

© Thomas Nelson, Inc.

L. Albert
2,013'

L. Victoria
3,720'

Indian Ocean

the Nile Delta. The small branches of the river crisscrossed
the Delta, irrigating the land even during the dry winter
months. For this reason, the Delta became the "bread basket"
of Egypt.

The Nile was Egypt's most important trade route. Because
the prevailing winds blew south, boats could sail upstream on
the Nile. The waters were smooth for about six hundred miles
from the Mediterranean coast to Syene. There caravans from
the Upper Nile unloaded their cargo for shipment to the
outside world. (Egyptians called the land upstream [south]
from Syene "Upper Egypt," while the land downstream
[north] was "Lower Egypt." Just above Syene was the first of
seven *cataracts*—rapids and waterfalls that blocked navigation.
So the port city naturally became an important landmark for
the Egyptians.)

". . . From prehistoric times on, the Egyptians were a river-faring people, and by [3000 B.C.] they had taken their boats out into the open sea. . . . On the Red Sea the Egyptian vessel was dominant in the trade southward to the land of incense, myrrh, gums, and ivory. . . ."[3]

As Egypt expanded her trade and became a prosperous nation, she had to develop better agricultural methods. Food crops and textile fibers were the mainstays of her economy, so the farmers had to devise more efficient methods for irrigating their fields, making the most of their narrow strip of soil along the Nile. They built dikes to protect their crops from the river in years of severe flood; they drained the marshes of the Delta region; they installed crude wooden irrigation devices to lift water from the river; and they abandoned the hand-held hoe in favor of ox-drawn wooden plows.

Compared to the lush river valley of the Nile, the eastern coastal region was bleak and hostile. "Along the coast there appear to have always been a number of lagoons, separated from the sea by low bars of sand, and used as salt-pans. In Greek and Roman times the largest of these was known as the Serbonian [Sirbonian] Bog or Marsh. It had a very evil repute. The dry sand blowing across gave it the appearance of solid ground, which was sufficient to bear those who ventured on it, only until they were beyond flight or rescue, and it swallowed up more than one unfortunate army."[4]

The Delta and coastal regions had high temperatures and high humidity in the summer and heavy rain in the winter. A hot, scorching wind known as the *Khamsin* blew across the Delta between March and May, leaving the people fatigued and irritable. The *Sobaa* wind generated blinding dust storms that could bury a merchant caravan in minutes.

This variable climate brought many diseases to the Egyptian people. In fact, Moses warned the Israelites that if they were not faithful to God, He would afflict them with "the diseases of Egypt" (Deut. 7:15; 28:60). Men of Napoleon's army suffered from boils and fever when they camped in Lower Egypt; even modern visitors find it difficult to adapt to the climate there.

Yet the climate of Egypt benefited her people in other ways. The warm Mediterranean breezes gave Egypt a year-round growing season, which the *fellahin* exploited to the limits of their technical abilities. At the same time, the dryness of arid wastelands along the edge of the Nile Valley preserved the pharaohs' embalmed bodies *(mummies)* and other relics. And the desolate lands surrounding Egypt made natural borders that were fairly easy to defend.

RELIGION AND HISTORY

When the Egyptian priest Manetho (*ca.* 305–285 B.C.) wrote a history of Egypt in Greek, he divided the history of the kings into 30 (later expanded to 31) periods known as "dynasties." The dynasties were then grouped into kingdoms: the Old Kingdom (*ca.* 2800–2250 B.C.; dynasties 3–6), the Middle Kingdom (*ca.* 2000 B.C.–1786 B.C.; dynasties 11–12), and the New Kingdom (1575–1085 B.C.; dynasties 18–20). Manetho labeled the time of the last pharaohs the Late Period (*ca.* 663 B.C.–332 B.C.; dynasties 26–31). The first two dynasties belonged to the Early Dynastic Period (3100–2800 B.C.). Between the Old and Middle Kingdom and between the Middle and New Kingdom were tumultuous times, known respectively as the First and the Second Intermediate Period. The period between the New Kingdom and the Late Period was known as the Third Intermediate Period (1085–661 B.C.).

The conquest of Alexander the Great introduced a new period in Egypt's history, known as the Ptolemaic Period (332–30 B.C.). With the victory over Cleopatra VII, Augustus incorporated Egypt into a Roman province (30 B.C.–A.D. 395).

The development of Egyptian religion is reviewed in the chapter "Pagan Religions and Cultures," but here we should note the allegiance of different pharaohs to different Egyptian gods. A pharaoh's religious beliefs often revealed something of his personal character and political ambitions.

A. Early Dynastic Period and Old Kingdom. Before Menes united Egypt (*ca.* 3200 B.C.), the land was divided into two kingdoms that roughly corresponded to Upper and Lower Egypt. Seth, the patron god of the city Ombos, had become the god of Lower Egypt while Horus, the patron god of the city Behdet, had become the god of Upper Egypt. When Menes of Thinis united the two Egypts (*ca.* 3200 B.C.), he made the sky god, Horus, the national god and claimed that he was the incarnation of Horus. Most pharaohs of the Old Kingdom (2800–2250 B.C.) did the same, and the Egyptians built up a large collection of myths about Horus.

B. First Intermediate Period. The First Intermediate Period followed the Old Kingdom. This time of social upheaval saw the total collapse of the central government. Local princes and barons gained power during the sixth dynasty; at last they became completely independent. Rulers of Thebes restored order to the troubled nation during the eleventh dynasty, but they were not able to reunite Egypt. During this time Abraham came to Egypt for relief from the famine in Palestine (Gen. 12:12-20). The "pharaoh" that Abraham tried to deceive may have been a king of Thebes, but most likely it was a ruler of the region of Upper Egypt.

C. The Middle Kingdom. The Middle Kingdom began around 2000 B.C. when Amenemhet I of Thebes forced the princes of the land to give their grudging allegiance to him.

Egyptian wall painting. This wall painting from the fourth dynasty (*ca.* 2700 B.C.) depicts the Egyptians as a brown-skinned people with stiff, dark hair.

Amenemhet made Amun, the god of Thebes, the national god of his new Middle Kingdom. By setting up Amun as the spiritual symbol of his new dynasty, Amenemhet tested the political allegiance of his subjects. Loyal Egyptians worshiped Amun in obedience to their new pharaoh, much as in later days the patriots of a country would rally around its flag. For more than two hundred years (2000–1780 B.C.) the Amenemhet and Senwosret pharaohs used Thebes as their central seat of power and worshiped Amun as the "king of the gods."

Joseph was brought to Egypt as a slave around 1876 B.C. (cf. Gen. 37:5-28). Several years later he became the *vizier* (an officer second only to the pharaoh) in a united, powerful Egypt (cf. Gen. 41:38-46). During this Middle Kingdom period Egypt was awakening to the world. It traded commercial goods with Crete, Palestine, Syria, and other lands. Art and literature blossomed and peaceful conditions generally prevailed. When Jacob and his family migrated to Egypt, they no doubt felt secure from attack and persecution.

D. Second Intermediate Period. Shortly before 1700 B.C., the Hyksos ("foreign rulers") seized control of Egypt and made Heliopolis their new capital. They adopted the local god of Heliopolis, Re, as the national god of their new kingdom. Re was another sun god; artists portrayed him as a falcon-man with a solar disk over his head. The Hyksos used Re to emphasize that Heliopolis dominated all of Egypt. Actually, the Hyksos controlled only Lower Egypt, while the kings of the Upper Nile Valley stood firm in their own local domains. The Egypt of the Hyksos was not as well organized as under the Old Kingdom and Middle Kingdom. But its literature and culture far surpassed anything in Palestine at that time, which was also in political and economic chaos.

Some scholars believe the Exodus took place during the time of the Hyksos; but others contradict this. Unfortunately, Scripture and archaeological evidence do not obviously enforce one another at this point. The most probable date of the Exodus (1446 B.C.) is discussed in the chapter "Bible Chronology." A Hyksos ruler was probably the "pharaoh who did not know Joseph" (Exod. 1:8). The Semitic Hyksos probably felt a

The Valley of the Kings

For a thousand years, the pharaohs of Egypt were buried in the desolate area known as the Valley of the Kings. Located along the Nile near the city of Thebes, it became the resting place of thirty or more kings, among them the greatest Egypt ever knew.

The Egyptian culture took great care in preparing the dead, to insure their security in the afterlife. It was believed that one must place in his tomb everything needed to make the afterlife happy. So the kings filled their tombs with great wealth and then marked the site of the tomb with a huge stone monument *(pyramid)*.

Many workers were used to build the elaborate tombs, and they knew that within them lay treasures of all descriptions. In order to protect these treasures, the king of the reigning dynasty hired guards to patrol the valley. In spite of these precautions, grave robbers began to plunder the tombs, stripping them clean. Thus, many of the kings were moved to secret burial sites to protect and preserve their bodies and coffins.

King Thutmose, greatly disturbed by this looting, decided to keep secret the location of his tomb. He hired a trusted friend, Ineni, to oversee its construction. It is believed that Ineni hired prisoners to do the actual work and then slaughtered them when it was completed, in order to guard the royal secret. Even this plan failed, for thieves continued to plunder the riches that lay within the tombs. When King Thutmose's tomb was discovered in 1899, little remained in it but the massive stone sarcophagus.

No area has ever been surrounded with such mystery as the Valley of the Kings. The riches that lay there evoked wickedness in the hearts of men who sought to strip it bare. As late as the 1800s, men continued to seek its wealth. However, the valley was eventually saved by the efforts of archaeologists who unearthed the greatest find to date, the tomb of King Tutankhamen.

rivalry with the Hebrews and wanted to suppress them as much as possible. Even after the Hyksos were overthrown, the rulers of Egypt oppressed the Hebrews.

After about a century, King Kamose of Thebes broke the power of the Hyksos in Egypt and united the nation under the city of Thebes once again. Kamose, his younger brother Ahmose, and their successors reformed the religion of Egypt once again. These alterations in religion were a political tactic. The priests who controlled the various shrines and towns fought to gain political power over the pharaoh. They revived the worship of Amun, combined it with the religion of Re, and named the new national god Amun-Re. This prepared the way for a new epoch in Egyptian politics, called the New Kingdom (1575–1085 B.C.). Ahmose married his sister, Princess Ahmose-Nofretari, and claimed that she was the wife of Amun. This gave both of them spiritual prestige.

E. The New Kingdom. The New Kingdom formally began when Ahmose's son, Amenhotep I, succeeded him in 1546

B.C. Notice that Amenhotep named himself after his father's god, Amun-Re; he also called himself the "Son of Re."

Gradually the Egyptians came to think of their pharoahs as gods in the flesh, and they worshiped them as such. For example, the official Egyptian history showed that when Thutmose II died (*ca.* 1504 B.C.), he "went forth to heaven and mingled with the gods."[5]

Other pharaohs of the New Kingdom followed the custom of naming themselves after Amun-Re (e.g., Amenophis, Tutankhamen). When Hatshepsut assumed the power of the pharaoh after the death of Thutmose II (she was the only woman to ever do so), she called herself "Daughter of Re." She described herself as "altogether divine," and said that all the gods of Egypt promised to protect her.

Her son, Thutmose III, also held this idea of divine protection for the pharaoh. When his general, Djehuti, won a great victory at Joppa, he sent a dispatch to Thutmose III that said: "Rejoice! Your god Amun has delivered to you the enemy of Joppa, all his people, and all his city. Send people to lead them off as captives, in order that you may fill the house of your father Amun-Re, king of the gods, with male and female slaves. . . ."[6]

The Sphinx. This massive figure with the body of a lion and the head of King Khaf-Re represents the god Horus guarding the city of the dead at Giza. Built during the Old Kingdom period of Egypt (2800–2250 B.C.), the Sphinx has come to symbolize the mystery of the past.

The Nile–Red Sea Canal

The idea of a canal linking the Mediterranean and Red seas is about 4,000 years old. The first canal was probably built by Pharaoh Sesostris I (reign 1980–1935 B.C.). Egypt's foreign commerce at that time was a royal monopoly. Middle Kingdom pharaohs believed in courting the favor of their neighbors. Sesostris I or another pharaoh of that era built a canal to increase commerce with his southern neighbors in Punt (possibly modern Somaliland).

During the time of the pharaohs, the Nile River divided into three great branches that passed through the delta and emptied into the Mediterranean Sea. The easternmost branch (which has silted up since the time of Christ) was the branch from which the Nile–Red Sea canal was built. The canal seems to have run from the Nile at Bubastis (modern Zagazig) through the land of Goshen to join Lake Timsah. There it turned south, passing through the Bitter Lake and another canal connecting it with the Red Sea. The earliest written record of the canal is the inscription of one of Hatshepsut's trading expeditions to the Punt. Remains of the canal's masonry work show that it was about 45 m. (150 ft.) wide and 5 m. (16 ft.) deep. The canal was gradually filled by sandstorms and fell into disuse.

About 600 B.C., Pharaoh Necho tried to reopen the Nile–Red Sea canal. Herodotus recorded the undertaking: "The length of this canal is equal to a four days' voyage, and is wide enough to admit two *triremes* (war galleys) abreast. . . . In the prosecution of this work under Necho, no less than 10,000 Egyptians perished. He at length desisted from his undertaking, being admonished by an oracle that all his labor would turn to the advantage of a barbarian."

Strabo (*ca.* 63 B.C.–A.D. 21) stated that Darius of Persia carried on the work, then stopped on the false opinion that the Red Sea was higher than the Nile and would flood Egypt. The Ptolemies made the canal navigable by means of locks.

During the Roman occupation of Egypt, Roman Emperor Trajan (reign A.D. 98–117) added a branch to the canal. This later fell into disuse, as the earlier canal had. A Muslim caliph ordered his men to fill in part of the canal as an act of war in A.D. 767, and it was never reopened.

The Suez Canal, opened in 1869, directly linked the Red Sea with the Mediterranean, without using the Nile.

The succeeding pharaohs of the New Kingdom, especially Amenhotep III (1412–1375 B.C.), constructed great tombs for themselves that extolled the powers of Amun-Re. He was their claim to immortality.

Amenhotep IV shunned the worship of Amun-Re in favor of the sun god, Aton. He renamed himself Akhnaton and founded a new capital city at Amarna, where he tried to establish Aton as the new universal god of Egypt. But when he died in 1366 B.C., his successor Tutankhamen moved the capital back to Thebes and restored Amen-Re as the leading god of the empire. Tutankhemen's tomb contained many symbols of Osiris, the god of the dead, and other evidence indicates that the worship of Osiris was becoming more prominent at this time.

The elderly king Rameses I began the nineteenth dynasty

The Merneptah stele. Merneptah ruled Egypt in the latter half of the thirteenth century B.C. He fought to defend the Egyptian Empire against the invasion of Mediterranean peoples into the Delta. The Merneptah stele commemorates the king's Palestinian campaign, in which he claims to have destroyed Israel. This is the first historical monument on which the name of Israel is inscribed.

with his short one-half year reign (1319–1318 B.C.). This dynasty revived the glory of ancient Egypt for a brief time, following the political disorder that Akhnaton had caused. Rameses' son, Sethi I, began new wars of conquest that pushed into Palestine, driving out the Hittites.

The pharaohs of this new dynasty established their capital at Karnak in the Nile Delta. Though they still gave homage to Amun-Re, they raised the worship of Osiris to a new level of royal favor. They dedicated the city of Abydos in honor of Osiris, and glorified the god of the dead in their majestic tombs at Abu Sinbel and the temples of Medinet Habu. The Rameses pharaohs also elevated the worship of Re-Harakhti, in whom they combined the qualities of Horus (the sky god) and Re (the sun god). But they still considered Amun-Re to be the chief god of their religious system.

Rameses II chose his son, Merneptah, to succeed him in 1232 B.C. Merneptah and the remaining kings of the nineteenth dynasty gradually lost the power that the Rameses kings had acquired; but Merneptah launched ruthless raids against Palestine. Archaeologists have translated an inscription from a stone column called the Israel Stele, on which Merneptah describes his victories in that area: "Carried off is Ashkelon; seized upon is Gezer; Yanoam is made as that which does not exist; Israel is laid waste, his seed is not. . . ."[7]

This would have been during the time of the judges; so Merneptah's description confirms the disorganized situation in Israel, where "there arose another generation . . . which knew not the Lord nor yet the works which he had done for Israel" (Judg. 2:10). However, Merneptah's troubles at home did not allow him to stay in Palestine, and so he left the scattered tribes of Israel at the mercy of the Philistines.

Pharaoh Sethnakht reunited the Egyptians city-states in about 1200 B.C. His son, Rameses III (1198–1167 B.C.), fought off invasions by the "People of the Sea"—Philistines who landed on the Mediterranean shores of Egypt. His artists chiseled great relief carvings in the Temple of Medinet Habu that describe these victories. But Rameses III died at the hand of an assassin, and his successors slowly lost their grip on the government. Ironically, the priests of Amun gained more prestige during the same periods.

F. Third Intermediate Period. Around 1100 B.C., a Nubian general named Panehsi appointed one of his lieutenants named Hrihor as the high priest of Amun at Karnak. Hrihor soon became commander-in-chief of the army itself, and took the throne from Rameses XI (1085 B.C.). This began a new pattern in Egyptian government: Each pharaoh appointed one of his sons to become the high priest of Amun as the boy's first step to the throne. The royal family claimed to be the high religious family from this point on, using the influence of Amun to assert their authority.

At this time, David and Solomon were building Israel to the

Madame Pharaoh

Ancient governments seldom allowed women to attain positions of leadership. The few women who succeeded in claiming the throne did so by violence or by gradually assuming the powers of a weak male monarch. The first method was used by Athaliah, the only woman to rule Judah, who seized power by murdering her grandsons (2 Kings 11:1-3). The second method was used by Hatshepsut, who slowly assumed the role of pharaoh from her half-brothers.

Hatshepsut (reign 1486–1468 B.C.) was the only surviving child of Pharaoh Thutmose and Ahmose. Ahmose (her mother) was the only descendant of the old Theban princes who had fought and expelled their foreign rulers, the Hyksos. Many Egyptians believed that only the descendants of this line were entitled to rule. In fact, Thutmose had ruled by virtue of his marriage to Ahmose, since the country refused to submit to the rule of a woman.

To provide a pharaoh for the throne when her father died, Hatshepsut married Thutmose II, her half-brother by one of Thutmose's lesser wives. (The Egyptians saw nothing wrong in brother-sister marriages. They felt this made the blood line purer.) But at the time of his coronation, Thutmose II was sickly. He was dominated by his wife,

Hatshepsut, and her mother Ahmose. His reign lasted no more than three years.

Thutmose III, another half-brother of Hatshepsut, was then proclaimed pharaoh; but Hatshepsut acted as regent for the young pharaoh. An inscription tells us: "His sister, the Divine Consort, Hatshepsut, ad-

---

height of its power. When David's commander-in-chief, Joab, drove young Prince Hadad of Edom out of his native land, Hadad's servants took him to Egypt (1 Kings 11:14-19). One of the pharaohs took him in, and Hadad married the pharaoh's sister-in-law. Hadad then returned to harass King Solomon (1 Kings 11:21-25). So Egypt figured in the political affairs of Israel throughout this period (cf. 1 Kings 3:1; 9:16).

But the Egyptian empire gradually disintegrated, and princes of Nubia carved out the southern territory with their capital at Napata. These Nubian kings also claimed to have the special favor of Amun. "The state was to be considered as a model theocracy and its king the true guardian of unadulterated Egyptian character and culture."[8] Egypt's troubles were justed the affairs of the Two Lands [i.e., Upper and Lower Egypt] by reason of her designs; Egypt was made to labor with bowed head for her, the excellent seed of the god, who came forth from him."

Instead of surrendering her regency when Thutmose came of age, Hatshepsut assumed the titles of the pharaoh. At her temple in Deir el-Bahri, she expended great efforts to make her reign legitimate. Her architect, Senmut, sculptured on the walls a series of reliefs showing the birth of the queen. The god Amon is shown appearing to Ahmose, and he tells her as he leaves: "Hatshepsut shall be the name of this my daughter. . . . She shall exercise the excellent kingship in this whole land." The artist followed court traditions so closely that he pictured Hatshepsut as a boy. The relief shows Hatshepsut's coronation by the gods, and her parents' acknowledgment of her as queen. They represent Thutmose I as saying: "Ye shall proclaim her word, ye shall be united at her command. He who shall do her homage shall live, he who shall speak evil in blasphemy of her majesty shall die."

Hatshepsut's reign brought the greatest prosperity following the collapse of the Middle Kingdom. Extensive building and rebuilding of the temples was carried out under the direction of Senmut. Hatshepsut ordered huge obelisks from the Aswan quarries, had them inscribed to proclaim the queen, and topped them with gold which reflected the sun so that they could be seen from both sides of the Nile.

Hatshepsut's relations with other nations were peaceful. She was most proud of an expedition to the land of Punt (perhaps modern Somaliland). Five vessels laden with jewelry, tools, and weapons, as well as a great statue of the queen, sailed down the Nile and through a canal connecting the Nile with the Red Sea. When the ships returned, they were loaded "very heavily with the marvels of the country of Punt; all goodly fragrant woods of god's land, heaps of myrrh-resin, of fresh myrrh-trees, with ebony and pure ivory, with the green gold of Emu, with incense, with baboons, monkeys, and dogs. . . . Never was the like of this brought for any king who has been since the beginning."

After Hatshepsut had been pharaoh for seventeen years, young Thutmose III brought her reign to an abrupt end. Perhaps because he had waited so long in the background, Thutmose attempted to completely purge the records of her reign. Inscriptions in her temples were chiseled off. Obelisks were sheathed with masonry, covering Hatshepsut's name and the record of their erection. Her statues were hurled into the quarry. But Thutmose III did not succeed in obliterating Hatshepsut's fame.

---

much like Israel's during this time; both had a divided kingdom.

Kings of Libya (to the west) toppled the weak pharaohs of Thebes in the tenth century B.C. They hired soldiers from the region of the Nile Delta to keep the peace in Lower Egypt.

One of these Libyan kings, Sheshonk I, sacked the temple of Jerusalem in the fifth year of King Rehoboam (1 Kings 14:25-26; note that the Bible calls him "Shishak"). Sheshonk and the other Libyan kings adopted the traditional worship of Amun-Re. But even with this symbol of national power, they failed to realize their dream of reviving the Egyptian empire.

The Nubian (Ethiopian) princes moved down the Nile and defeated the Libyan kings around 700 B.C. For the next 50 years, they attempted to reunite Egypt. One of these new kings (the Bible calls him "Zerah") attacked Judah with an enormous army. Undoubtedly, he was trying to secure his eastern border, as so many pharaohs had done before him. But Asa soundly defeated him: ". . . Ethiopians were overthrown, that they could not recover themselves" (2 Chron. 14:13).

The Assyrians attacked Judah soon afterwards. King Hoshea of Judah appealed to a new Ethiopian king for help, but the Ethiopians could do nothing. ". . . Therefore the king of Assyria shut him [Hoshea] up, and bound him in prison" (2 Kings 17:4). The Assyrians captured Judah, then marched into Egypt and overthrew the Ethiopian monarchy in 670 B.C.

G. The Late Period. But the Assyrians could not maintain their hold on Egypt, and 7 years later Prince Psamtik of Sais drove them back to the Sinai Peninsula. Psamtik reunited Upper and Lower Egypt and established the twenty-sixth dynasty, reviving Egyptian culture until 663 B.C. (when the Persians conquered Egypt). Psamtik reestablished the worship of Amun-Re as the national god of Egypt. But his priests were not able to exert the controlling and unifying influence that royal priests once had over the Egyptian people.

Egyptian religion now degenerated into a variety of animal cults. The kings of the twenty-sixth dynasty built temples in honor of certain sacred animals, such as the crocodile and the cat. "So extreme was the zeal of this epoch that it became the custom to embalm each one of the sacred animals at death and bury it ceremoniously in special cemeteries dedicated to the purpose."[9]

Nekau ("Necho") succeeded his father Psamtik I as pharaoh in 610 B.C. He recognized the growing menace of Babylon, and marched through Canaan in order to help the Assyrians fight this common enemy. King Josiah tried to stop him at Megiddo, but Nekau defeated him and continued on his march (2 Kings 23:29-30). Nebuchadnezzar destroyed the Egyptian army at Carchemish on the Euphrates River in 605 B.C. But Nekau escaped, captured the new king of Judah, and made Judah a buffer state between Babylon and Egypt

Periods of Egyptian History

Period	Dates	Bible Events
I. Early Dynastic Period (Dynasties 1–2)	3100–2800 B.C.	
II. The Old Kingdom (Dynasties 3–6)	2800–2250 B.C.	
III. First Intermediate Period (Dynasties 7–9)	2250–2000 B.C.	Abraham comes to Egypt
IV. The Middle Kingdom (Dynasties 9–12)	2000–1786 B.C.	Joseph and Jacob come to Egypt
V. Second Intermediate Period (Dynasties 13–17)	1786–1575 B.C.	
VI. The New Kingdom (Dynasties 18–20)	1575–1085 B.C.	The Exodus (1446 B.C.)
VII. Third Intermediate Period (Dynasties 21–25)	1085–663 B.C.	Sheshonk I ("Shishak") sacks the temple (927 B.C.)
VIII. The Late Period (Dynasties 26–31)	663–332 B.C.	The Exile (586 B.C.); refugees flee to Egypt
IX. The Ptolemaic Period	332–30 B.C.	
X. The Roman Era	30 B.C.–A.D. 395	Mary and Joseph escape to Egypt (4 B.C.)

Figure 15

(2 Chron. 36:4). When Nebuchadnezzar attacked Judah in 601 B.C., Egypt was able to stop him temporarily. Pharaoh Apries encouraged King Jehoiakin to resist the Babylonian intruders. But Nebuchadnezzar succeeded in capturing Jerusalem in 586 B.C. and carried its people into exile. Nebuchadnezzar installed Gedaliah as governor of the new Judean province; but Gedaliah's subjects murdered him within a few months (2 Kings 25:25). Afraid that the Babylonians would slaughter them in revenge, the remaining Jews of Jerusalem fled to Egypt. Among them was the prophet Jeremiah (Jer. 43:5-7).

King Cyrus of Persia conquered the Babylonian Empire in 539 B.C.; his successor, Cambyses, took Egypt in 525 B.C. The Persians placed puppet kings on the throne of Egypt for the next century, and each of them gave lip service to the god Amun-Re. But the real power behind the throne was the army of Persia, not the traditional mystique of the Egyptian gods.

H. The Ptolemaic Period. Alexander the Great conquered Egypt in 332 B.C. He died nine years later and the Ptolemy family took charge of Egypt and Palestine. The Ptolemies placed members of their own family on the throne at Thebes, and they tried to recapture the grandeur of Egypt's golden age. For example, Ptolemy Euergetes II made Amenhotep I a god in 140 B.C.; by revering this pharaoh who established Egypt's New Kingdom, Euergetes hoped to pass himself off as a true Egyptian. But the native people of Egypt only gave him token loyalty. He had to depend on the Roman armies to protect him from the attacks of the Seleucid Empire north of Palestine.

The Roman emperor, Pompey, captured Jerusalem in 63 B.C. and broke the back of the Seleucid threat; but Egypt was tottering on the brink of collapse. At last Cleopatra emerged from the Ptolemy family to try to save the nation by political chicanery and bribes. She courted the favor of both Augustus Caesar and Mark Anthony; but when Caesar's fleet defeated hers at Actium in 30 B.C., Cleopatra committed suicide in despair. From that time, Egypt came under the shield of imperial Rome.

During their brief time on the throne, the Hellenistic rulers planted Greek cities on the coast of Egypt and brought Greek settlers into the country. Thus they added foreign elements to the Egyptian way of life, especially to Egyptian religion.

The Egyptians were more receptive to the process of Hellenization than the Jews were. Priests gave Egyptian gods the names of their Greek counterparts: Horus became Apollo; Thoth became Hermes; Amun became Zeus; Ptah became Hephaistos; Hathor became Aphrodite; and so on. Egyptians worshiped the Ptolemaic rulers and their wives, much like they had worshiped the pharaohs.

Hebrew vs. Egyptian Wisdom

The Hebrew sages who wrote the Old Testament books of Proverbs, Ecclesiastes, Job, and some of the Psalms may have been influenced by Egyptian sages who wrote similar literature. But Hebrew "wisdom literature" has a basic difference from the wisdom of other cultures.

Hebrew wisdom centered around Almighty God; it said that "the fear of the LORD is the beginning of wisdom" (Prov. 1:7). This wisdom would guide an individual in day-to-day living. The wisdom of God, as reflected through Old Testament wisdom literature provided the Jewish people with a basic commonsense morality that dictated individual conduct in many circumstances.

Egyptian wisdom also attempted to establish the rules of proper conduct for daily life. Wisdom for the Egyptian, however, centered on the individual. It was based on studying and recording wisdom of the sages, and on disciplining oneself to accept life with its many paradoxes. Being well-versed in the wisdom writings was an important part of Egyptian education; it opened doors to careers and privileges that were otherwise unobtainable.

The Egyptian scholars produced a sophisticated form of wisdom verse. One popular form is seen in the "Instructions" or accumulations of practical sayings. Many Bible scholars acknowledge that the "Instruction of Amen-em-opet" shows a strong similarity to the Book of Proverbs. Amen-em-opet divides his "Instruction" into thirty parts, a structure which is similar to the thirty wise sayings of Proverbs 22:17 to 24:22. Both books show concern for the protection of the defenseless; they call for the fair treatment of widows and orphans, and emphasize the value of knowledge. Amen-em-opet advises: "Do not lean on the scales nor falsify the weights. . . ." Proverbs 20:23 says, "The LORD hates people who use dishonest scales and weights." The Egyptian's philosophy on a life well lived was: "Better is poverty in the hand of the god than riches in a storehouse; better is bread, when the heart is happy, than riches with sorrow." It is similar to Proverbs 15:16-17: "Better to be poor and fear the LORD than to be rich and in trouble. Better to eat vegetables with people you love than to eat the finest meat where there is hate."

The injustices of life are reflected in "The Admonition of an Egyptian Sage," which observes: "In truth, the poor now possess riches and he who was not even able to make sandals for himself possesses treasures. . . . He who had not any servants is now become master of (many) slaves and he who was a nobleman has now to manage his own affairs." Ecclesiastes 9:11 and 10:7 declare a similar thought: "Wise men do not always earn a living, intelligent men do not always get rich, and capable men do not always rise to high positions. . . ," And "I have seen slaves on horseback while noblemen go on foot like slaves."

Study of these ancient documents has added to our understanding of the Old Testament, but there is still considerable debate over what relationship existed between Hebrew and Egyptian wisdom. Perhaps Hebrew wisdom influenced the development of the surrounding cultures, and what we see in Egypt is really a reflection of Hebrew work.

Jews who settled in Egypt during the Babylonian exile developed thriving Jewish communities there. Aramaic papyri show that there was a prominent Jewish colony at Aswan, on the island of Elephantine. This group did not live in close conformity with the Law of Moses, and they finally abolished animal sacrifice. The community was destroyed soon after 404 B.C.

Other Jewish communities fared better, and under the Ptolemies they received legal status. The Letter of Aristeas claims that Ptolemy I carried off over 100,000 Jews from Palestine and used them as mercenaries in the Egyptian armed forces. These Jews continued to worship God, but they were able to adjust to the Graeco-Roman way of life.

Ancient tax receipts show that there were Jewish tax collectors in Egypt. Jews also served in other government offices. In a letter that Claudius wrote to the Alexandrines, he asked that Jewish candidates not be allowed to run for the office of *gymisiarch*, who was in charge of the athletic games that were offensive to strict Jews (cf. 1 Macc. 1:14-15).

The ancient historian Philo says that 1,000,000 Jews lived in Egypt. They knew little Hebrew or Aramaic. For this reason, the Hebrew Bible was translated into Greek, the *Septuagint* version. The Jews of Alexandria were the first to use the Septuagint; later it was read in synagogues throughout the Roman Empire.

Philo of Alexandria was a Jewish philosopher who adopted the Greek ideas of Stoicism and Platonism. He dressed Jewish beliefs in the categories of Greek philosophic thought.

From Alexandria came the allegorical interpretation of Scripture. This Egyptian city became an important center of Jewish scholarship in the intertestamental period.

When Mary and Joseph hid the infant Jesus there in about 4 B.C. (Matt. 2:13-15), several Jewish communities remained in the Nile Delta area where they had settled in Jeremiah's time. We assume that Mary and Joseph found refuge in one of these villages.

7

THE BABYLONIANS AND ASSYRIANS

The Babylonians and Assyrians lived in the region known as *Mesopotamia* (Greek, "between the two rivers"). The ancient historian Herodotus gives this name to the broad plains between the Tigris and Euphrates Rivers, bounded on the north by the Zagros Mountains and on the south by the Persian Gulf. The Bible mentions several cities of Mesopotamia and some of the significant leaders of the Babylonians and Assyrians. Indeed, these two cultures brought the eventual downfall of Israel and Judah. Yet the people of Mesopotamia were affecting the lives of the Israelites many centuries before that final encounter.

THE SUMERIANS

The earliest known inhabitants of Mesopotamia lived in the southern part of what is now Iraq. These people are simply called "proto-Euphrateans," for lack of a better term. The first identifiable people of this group were known as *Sumerians*. The old West Semite form of the name appears to have been *Shinar*, so the Old Testament refers to them as the people of the "plain of Shinar." The Sumerians were not Semites, nor were they Indo-Europeans. They spoke a language unlike any other, either ancient or modern.

The Sumerians began building small towns along the banks of the Tigris and Euphrates sometime after 7000 B.C. The relics of these early communities show that the people were primitive farmers.

The Sumerians developed a township system of government, in which the temple of the local deity was the center of economic, cultural, and religious life. So integrated were the religious and civil functions that these ancient societies are called the "archaic religious states." This term describes the antiquity and the religious character of their organization.

The town was ruled by a council led by a mayor or *ensi*. The *ensi* also acted as the high priest of the town, ministering at a temple that stood at the center of the community. The temple was the town's center for worship, education, and government. At the temples of E-Anna in Uruk archaeologists have found the earliest evidence of writing dating from about 3000 B.C.

Each Sumerian city developed its own style of pottery. Archaeologists have found beautiful examples of their pottery art at Hassuna, Samarra, Halaf, Ubaid, and Uruk (Warka). The Sumerians also developed great skill as jewelry makers.

A. "Ur of the Chaldees." One of the foremost cities of Sumer was Ur. This city-state came to the chief position among the towns of Sumer several times in its history. The Bible refers to it as "Ur of the Chaldees" (Gen. 11:28). This city was the home of Terah and Abram (Abraham), ancestors of the Hebrew nation (Gen. 11:28-31).

Located on the banks of the Euphrates River, Ur was an important trading post dedicated to the god Sin and the goddess Nin-gal. Clay tablets from Ur explain that it was located in the district of the Kaldu people, which is why the biblical writers called it "Ur of the Chaldees."

B. Larsa. Northeast of Ur stood the city of Larsa. The Bible probably refers to this site when it mentions the "king of Ellasar" who attacked Sodom and Gomorrah and the other "cities of the plain" (Gen. 14:1-2). The people of Larsa worshiped the sun god Shamash.

C. Erech. Just over 24 km. (15 mi.) west of Larsa stood the town of Erech. Many scholars believe this was the home of the "Archevites" who later petitioned King Artaxerxes to stop the restoration of Jerusalem (Ezra 4:9).

Erech was the center for the worship of the goddesses Ishtar and Nana, two of the best-known pagan deities. Unlike the other Sumerian towns, Erech was the home of Semitic people. In its ruins archaeologists have found bricks bearing the names of Semitic kings.

THE AKKADIANS

In the northern region of Mesopotamia lived the Akka-dians, who had a more advanced civilization than their neighbors to the south. The Akkadians developed one of the first systems of writing. They were ingenious builders and military strategists. Like the Sumerians, the Akkadians built each of their cities around a temple that honored a local deity.

A. Agade (Akkad). The northern region took its name from the town of Agade, which many English-speaking schol-ars called Akkad. Some believe that the Bible calls this city Sepharvaim (cf. 2 Kings 17:24).

B. Nippur. Another important city of the Akkadians was Nippur, located 56 km. (35 mi.) southeast of Babylon. Nippur was the chief religious center of the region, devoted to the god En-lil. But the Bible makes no reference to this city.

THE EARLY BABYLONIANS

The Akkadian cities were eventually dominated by Elam, a strong city-state to the southeast. In about 2300 B.C., King Sargon of Agade rebelled against the Elamites and united the Akkadians under his rule. He called himself "King of the Four Zones," referring to the major cities of the region—Kish, Cutha, Agade-Sippar, and Babylon-Borsippa.

Sargon established an efficient system of roads and postal service to unite his domain. He began an imperial library that eventually collected thousands of clay tablets.

The Table of Nations says that "Cush begat Nimrod: he began to be a mighty one in the earth" (Gen. 10:8). It is doubtful that the Hebrew term here should be translated as *Cush* (an ancient name for Ethiopia); rather it should be *Kish,* the city where the Sumerians believed the gods established a new line of kings after the great flood. Moreover, the state-ment that Nimrod "began to be a mighty one in the earth" should better be read, "He was the first dictator in the earth." Thus many scholars believe that Nimrod was another name for Sargon of Agade. He was indeed a "mighty hunter (of men) before the Lord" (Gen. 10:9).

Sargon's dynasty lasted for only three generations. Akkad then came under the influence of Ur, the great commercial center of Sumerians. A few Akkadian cities, such as Lagash (ruled by a priest named Gudea) resisted this trend. But the Sumerian city-states of Ur and Larsa dominated Mesopotamia for over 200 years. The region gradually drifted back to the control of Elam.

A. Hammurabi (ca. 2000 B.C.). Semitic invaders from Canaan and the Arabian Desert wrested Mesopotamia from Elamite control in about 2000 B.C. The ruler of Babylon, a man named Hammurabi, emerged as the new ruler of the land "between the two rivers."

Hammurabi united the cities of Mesopotamia much as Sargon had done before him. He set up a royal postal system, a new network of roads, and an effective chain of command for his government officials. Hammurabi organized the laws of Mesopotamia into a simplified written form. These laws were carved upon a massive stone column found at Susa. Modern scholars have acclaimed Hammurabi's Code of Law as "a monument of wisdom and equity."[1]

About this time, Abraham and his family left Ur and moved to Canaan, where God promised to make them a great nation.

Gudea. This is one of a series of statues representing Gudea, the governor or king of Lagash, one of the major Sumerian cities. The serenity and dignity of this portrait sculpture make it a remarkable work of art.

The Babylonian Empire fades from the picture of Bible history for several generations.

B. Babylonian Literature. The cuneiform tablets and stone monuments of Babylon provide considerable information about life in the Babylonian Empire during the time of Abraham. This literary evidence runs the gamut from very personal letters to huge public inscriptions boasting of the king's power and prestige.

The best-known document from this period is Hammurabi's Code of Law. Hammurabi used this great declaration to assert that the gods sanctioned his rule. He wrote: "I, Hammurabi, the perfect king among perfect kings, was neither careless nor inactive in regard to the citizens of Sumer and Akkad, whom En-lil bestowed upon me and whose shepherding Marduk committed unto me. Safe places I continually sought out for them, I overcame serious difficulties, I caused light to shine for them. With the awesome weapons that Zababa and Ishtar entrusted to me, with the wisdom Ea allotted to me, with the ability Marduk gave me, I uprooted enemies above and below, I extinguished holocausts, I made sweet the expanse of the fatherland with irrigation. . . . I am the preeminent king of kings, my words are precious, my ability has no equal. According to the command of the sun god, the great judge of heaven and earth, may my law be displayed in the fatherland."

This passage illustrates the governmental ideals of one of the great conquerors of history. On this great stone stele, Hammurabi lists 282 laws to regulate everyday life in the empire.

Archaeologists have found many clay tablets that describe the worship of various Babylonian gods. Statues and carvings of these gods are not very impressive. In fact, it seems that the Babylonians paid more homage to the king than to the god he represented. The gods were patriotic symbols of the various Babylonian cities. Thus Babylonian travelers were careful to honor the gods of cities that they visited, lest they offend the native citizens.

Religion colored every aspect of Babylonian life. The ruins of Babylonian cities contained inscriptions of prayers for every conceivable occasion. Some of these prayers are addressed to no god in particular, and run something like this: "May the god who is unknown be favorable to me."

Other religious texts from Babylon confess the sins of the worshiper and call upon the gods for forgiveness. Scholars call one of these tablets "The Lament of the Righteous Sufferer."

Unfortunately, few of the documents from ancient Babylon describe the political events of that day. We must reconstruct the history from casual clues on royal monuments and letters. So Babylonian literature is of little help in establishing the dates of biblical events; for this we must depend on the records of the second great culture of Mesopotamia—the Assyrians.

THE EARLY ASSYRIANS

In the northwestern reaches of Mesopotamia lived the Assyrians, a war-like people who used the Zagros Mountains as their stronghold. These Semitic tribes settled in the area before Sargon of Agade united the lower Mesopotamian region. They were proud and independent.

Because they were proud of their heritage, the Assyrians kept careful records of their royal lineage. These Assyrian king lists help us to establish the dates of many Old Testament events.

The king lists show that the Assyrians began flexing their muscles in the Near East shortly after Hammurabi's dynasty ended. An eastern nation known as the Kasshites sized control of Babylon around 1750 B.C. and began a series of wars with Assyria that lasted until 1211 B.C. These wars covered the time of Israel's bondage in Egypt, the Exodus, the conquest of Canaan, and the early years of the judges. At the same time Egypt was vying for control of the Near East. All three nations—Assyria, Babylon and Egypt—marched their armies across Palestine in their pursuit of world supremacy.

A. Shalmaneser I (ca. 1300 B.C.). The first great Assyrian conqueror was Shalmaneser I, who built the capital city of Calah. Shalmaneser expanded the Assyrian territory beyond

Nineveh

The powerful city of Nineveh (built by Nimrod, the great-grandson of Noah) presents us with mystery piled on mystery. Even so, as scholars assemble the puzzle, the accuracy of the Bible becomes more apparent.

Nineveh was undoubtedly one of the oldest large cities in the world. The record of its beginnings go back to Genesis 10:11-12: "From that land he went into Assyria, and built Nineveh, Rehoboth-Ir, Calah, and Resen between Nineveh and Calath; that is the great city" (RSV).

The Khoser River flowed eastward from the Tigris through Nineveh. These two rivers, plus a canal that was constructed to carry water from the Tigris to the edge of the city's western wall, provided water for moats, fountains, irrigation, and drinking.

From 1100 B.C., Nineveh was a royal residence. During the reign of Sargon II (722–705 B.C.), it served as the capital of Assyria. Sennacherib (705–681 B.C.) especially loved Nineveh and made it the chief city of his empire: "So Sennacherib king of Assyria departed, and went and returned, and dwelt at Nineveh" (2 Kings 19:36).

Sennacherib made many improvements at Nineveh. He had massive walls constructed and built the oldest aqueduct in history there. It was part of a canal that brought water from the mountains 56 km. (35 mi.) away.

All of these improvements cost money; but the conqueror Sennacherib had no problem raising money, a great deal of which came from tribute.

No one knows the precise age of Nineveh, but the city is mentioned in Babylonian records that extend back to the twenty-first century B.C. Nineveh was also mentioned in the records of Hammurabi, who lived between 1792 and 1750 B.C. We do, however, fix a more precise date for the city's destruction.

The prophet Nahum wrote lyrically about Nineveh's destruction: "Woe is the bloody city! It is full of lies and robbery. . . . The noise of a whip, and the noise of the rattling of the wheels, and the prancing horses, and of the jumping chariots" (3:1-2).

Nineveh was destroyed in August 612 B.C. It fell after a two-month siege carried out by an alliance among Medes, Babylonians, and Scythians. The attackers destroyed Nineveh by releasing the Khoser River into the city, where it dissolved the buildings' sun-dried brick. This was a remarkable fulfillment of Nahum's prophecy: "The gates of the river shall be opened, and the palace shall be dissolved" (Nahum 2:6). Nineveh was lost for well over 2000 years.

Two centuries after Nineveh's destruction, the Greek soldier and historian Xenophon passed near it on his famous trip to the Black Sea. Although he mentioned seeing the remains of the quay as he marched along on the dry riverbed, he assumed it was a wall belonging to ancient Larsa.

Writing about the city of Mosul in the twelfth century A.D., Benjamin of Tudela wrote: "This city, situated on the Tigris, is connected with ancient Nineveh by a bridge. . . . Nineveh lies now in utter ruins, but numerous villages and small towns occupy its former space." Others also wrote about the place that was Nineveh, but Henry Layard was the first archaeologist to identify the site; he made the discovery on December 22, 1853.

The most famous biblical person connected with the drama of ancient Nineveh was Jonah. Controversy has swirled about this man during the last two centuries, as some scholars have questioned the three days that he spent in the "great fish." But the story of Jonah and Nineveh was in wide circulation during the ministry of Jesus, and Jesus referred to Jonah several times (e.g., Matt. 12:39–41; 16:4).

the Euphrates River and his son, Tiglath-Ninib, captured the enemy city of Babylon. With the aid of the Hittites, Tiglath-Ninib's son incited a civil war that divided the Assyrian nation.

Subsequent Assyrian leaders were able to unite their nation in the face of rather formidable foes. By the time Assyria entered the Old Testament record, it had earned a reputation for military prowess.

B. Assyrian Literature. Most of the Assyrian literature that modern archaeologists have found comes from its later history. It records Assyria's incessant wars with Babylon and other rival nations. Most of the Assyrian king lists were written after 1200 B.C., using older records that have not survived.

THE GOLDEN AGE (1211–539 B.C.)

The last Kasshite king of Babylon drove the Assyrians out of his territory by 1211 B.C. This established an uneasy balance of power between the Babylonians and Assyrians, allowing both nations to rise to their zenith.

A. Nebuchadnezzar I (ca. 1135 B.C.). The people of Babylon ousted the Kasshite kings in 1207 B.C. and placed a new family of native kings on the throne. The sixth king in this line was Nebuchadnezzar I, who began his reign around 1135 B.C. Nebuchadnezzar suffered several defeats at the hands of the Assyrians, but he was able to expand the realm of Babylon. He was also successful in pushing back the Elamites on his eastern border. His son and grandson made successful raids upon Assyrian territory.

Babylon. This painting by Maurice Bardin shows the city of Babylon in its glory during the reign of Nebuchadnezzar (605–562 B.C.). The city proper was surrounded by double-walled fortifications and connected to the newer area across the Euphrates River by a pontoon bridge. To the left behind the wall is a ziggurat; to the right, the temple of Marduk.

B. Tiglath-Pileser I (ca. 1100 B.C.). The Assyrian king Tiglath-Pileser I conquered many surrounding nations during his reign. He plunged deep into the heart of Babylonian territory and captured the city of Babylon for a short time. Tiglath-Pileser's court scribes erected an eight-sided stone monument to record his victories, and he rebuilt the old capital city of Asshur. Saul took the throne of Israel at about this time.

For the next two centuries, Babylon and Assyria fell on hard times. Civil war, conspiracy, and seige combined to weaken them and thwart their desire for conquest. As these two giants struggled with their problems, the nation of Israel enjoyed its own "golden age" under the reigns of David and Solomon.

Tiglath-Pileser II (*ca.* 950 B.C.) began a new line of kings in Assyria. These kings renewed Assyria's efforts to build an empire that would blanket the known world.

C. Ashurbanipal III (885–860 B.C.). The next king of Assyria, Ashurbanipal III, led his armies against the Arameans of the north and then marched west to the Mediterranean coast. Ashurbanipal forced conquered cities to pay heavy tribute to his royal treasury and he often sent captured kings to the prisons of his capital city (Nineveh) to guarantee that his subjects would remain loyal. He conducted these military campaigns during the reigns of Ahaziah and Athaliah of Judah. He also rebuilt the old Assyrian capital of Calah.

D. Shalmaneser II (860–824 B.C.). The next Assyrian king, Shalmaneser II, continued the conquests of his father. He turned his eyes south to the divided kingdoms of Israel and Judah. King Ahab of Israel and Ben-hadad of Damascus joined forces to resist these invaders (1 Kings 20:13-34). Ahab's successor, King Jehu, submitted to the Assyrians. A black obelisk-shaped monument of Shalmaneser shows Jehu bowing down to the Assyrian king. Shalmaneser boasted that he was "trampling down the country like a wild bull."[2]

The Assyrian Empire suffered serious setbacks under Shalmaneser's descendants. His son Shamshi-Ramman IV (824–812 B.C.) defeated an alliance of Babylonians, Elamites, and other eastern peoples. The next king tried to unite

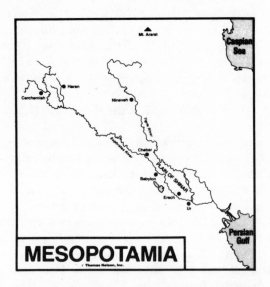

MESOPOTAMIA

Babylon and Assyria by bringing Babylonian religious symbols into Nineveh. But the strategy failed. His Babylonian
subjects rebelled and a series of famines and military defeats
pointed to Assyria's gradual decline.

E. Tiglath-Pileser III (745–727 B.C.). Tiglath-Pileser III
revived Assyria's hope of becoming a world empire. He
regained the Babylonian territory, recaptured the Aramean
cities, and returned Assyria's army to the battlefield of Palestine. Tiglath-Pileser's royal documents say that foreign cities
were "desolated like an overwhelming flood" by his sudden
advance.[3] Tiglath-Pileser captured Israel and Damascus in
732 B.C., setting Hoshea on the throne of Israel as a puppet
ruler (2 Kings 15–16).

F. The Destruction of Israel. King Hoshea foolishly decided to rebel against Tiglath-Pileser's successor, Shalmaneser
IV. He made an alliance with the pharaoh of Egypt and
stopped paying tribute to the Assyrian capital. Shalmaneser
attacked and captured Hoshea, then laid seige to the city of
Samaria. Shalmaneser died just before the city surrendered in
721 B.C. (2 Kings 17).

This was Israel's final gasp. The new Assyrian king, Sargon (722–705 B.C.), deported the people of Israel to the hinterlands of the expanding Assyrian Empire. These tribes would never return to the Promised Land.

G. The Destruction of Judah. Shalmaneser and his successors, Sargon (722–705 B.C.) and Sennacherib (705–681 B.C.), had to quell several revolts in the defeated nation of Israel (2 Kings 17:24–18:12). Sennacherib captured the fortified cities of Judah and demanded the surrender of Jerusalem (2 Kings 18), but he had to withdraw his forces to fight Merodach-baladan, the rebel king of Babylon.

Having lived under Assyrian rule since 1100 B.C., the Babylonians took this opportunity to declare their independence from the expanding Assyrian Empire. Sennacherib defeated Merodach-baladan, but a more powerful king named Nabopolassar came to the throne of Babylon. He was able to unite the city-states of the old Babylonian Empire and restore much of the former glory of Babylon. Nabopolassar and his son Nebuchadnezzar II led their armies against the Egyptian pharaoh Necho, who was trying to gain control of the weakening Assyrian Empire. Their armies met at Carchemish, where the Babylonians defeated the Egyptians in one of the great battles of the ancient world (604 B.C.).

The Egyptian pharaohs provoked rebellion among the kings of Ju᾿ ᾿h to distract their Babylonian foes. When Jehoiakim of Judah refused to pay tribute to Nebuchadnezzar II, the Babylonian king captured Jerusalem and deported part of its population in 597 B.C. (2 Kings 24:8-17). Jehoiakim's successor Zedekiah also followed the bad advice of the Egyptians, and Nebuchadnezzar attacked Jerusalem again. This time he destroyed the city's defenses and took most of the population into captivity (2 Kings 25). Thus the divided kingdom of Israel and Judah met its final end in 586 B.C.

H. The Glory of Nebuchadnezzar II. Nebuchadnezzar invaded Egypt and the coastal cities of Palestine to secure the borders of his new empire. For more than twenty years after the fall of Jerusalem, Nebuchadnezzar reigned over the mighty Babylonian Empire. His architects raised the capital city of Babylon to the height of its splendor, adorning it with the famed hanging gardens.

"There was a conscious effort on the part of the leaders to return to the old forms and customs. It has been said that this period might properly be called the Renaissance of Old Babylonia."[4]

YEARS OF DECLINE

The Assyrians and Babylonians began to lose their grasp of Mesopotamia as the Persian Empire grew stronger. Nineveh, capital of Assyria, fell to a group of Scythian tribes known as the Umman-Manda in 606 B.C. These tribes used the resources of Nineveh to build an empire of their own.

In Babylonia, Nebuchadnezzar's successors made corrup-

Winged bull. This winged, man-headed bull guarded the palace of the king of Assyria during the ninth century B.C. A fine example of Assyrian art, the figure with its long plaited beard and hair tells us something of the appearance of the people of that day.

tion and assassination a way of life. They broke off diplomatic relations with the Medes—the tribal chieftains of Nineveh—thinking that these renegades had no use in their political schemes.

Belshazzar took the throne of Babylon in 553 B.C. and attempted to revive popular interest in the ancient religions of the empire, neglecting the status of his armed forces. He did not anticipate the sudden rise of Cyrus the Great, who absorbed the Medes and pushed north to subdue other tribes of Asia Minor. Finally Cyrus sent his armies against Babylon. The stodgy government of Belshazzar proved to be an easy prey. Babylon fell to the Persians, giving Cyrus control of all Mesopotamia.

ART AND ARCHITECTURE

We have learned much about the life of the Babylonians and Assyrians from relief carvings found in the ruins of Nimrud and Nineveh (magnificent capitals in the prime of Assyria). For example, one carving depicts a savage lion "hunt" in which lions are released into an arena and slaughtered by a king in his chariot, shooting arrows while protected by his spearmen!

From an early period, Babylonian and Assyrian altars showed scenes of war. Their wall paintings and cylinder seals portrayed scenes of animal and plant life. Only a few sculptures have survived from the Assyrian culture, the best-known being the statue of Ashurnasirpal II now in the British Museum.

Assyrian architecture emphasized the ziggurat, and is probably represented best by the palace built by Sargon II in what is now known as Khorsabad.

The palace had a triple entrance leading into a large court measuring 90 m. (300 ft.) on each side. The walls were carved with reliefs of the king and his courtiers, and were plastered in sections with vari-colored designs. To one side of the court

Lyre. This reconstructed Lyre from Ur (twenty-fifth century B.C.) consists of a sound box attached to two uprights, which are decorated with mosaic inlay and the gold head of a bull. Attached to the uprights is a crossbar, half of which consists of silver tubing. A Mesopotamian craftsman probably fixed the strings at the bottom of the sound box and then attached them to the cross bar at the top.

were offices and service quarters, and to the other were six temples and a ziggurat. Behind the court were the living quarters of the king. Beyond these were rooms of state including a brightly painted throne room.

Much Assyrian art focuses on battle scenes showing dead and dying soldiers, or on hunting scenes depicting wounded and dying animals. Babylonian art reflects the Sumerian influence. They used brick panels (some enameled and in relief) on walls and gates. They also built ziggurats, a Sumerian contribution. Babylon itself was the site of the ziggurat known in the Bible as the "Tower of Babel" (Gen. 11:1-9). All that remains are the ground plan and traces of three large stairways leading to its summit. A geometrical description found on a cuneiform tablet (dated about 229 B.C.) describes the tower as having two stories plus a tower of five stages, crowned by a sacred shrine at the top. However, the Greek historian Herodotus said the Tower of Babylon was built in eight stages surrounded by a ramp and having a sanctuary.

The Babylonian palaces often were decorated with paintings. During the dynasty of Hammurabi, the painted themes were mainly mythological motifs, war scenes, and religious rites.

Babylonian sculpture is represented by cult statues of deities and rulers. One of the most important discoveries is a head in black granite, which might be that of King Hammurabi. The rendering is almost impressionistic.

RELIGION

Assyrian religious practices were almost identical with those of Babylonia, except that their national god was called Ashur while Babylonia's national god was called Marduk.

The Babylonians modified the Sumerian religion. Besides Marduk, their important gods were Ea (god of wisdom, spells, and incantations), Sin (moon god), Shamash (sun god and god of justice), Ishtar (goddess of love and war), Adad (god of wind, storm, and flood), and Marduk's son, Nabu (scribe and herald of the gods).

Babylonian temple services were held in open courts where there were sacrifices, burning of incense, and festivals.

LITERATURE OF THE GOLDEN AGE

The inscribed clay tablets unearthed by archaeologists have contributed greatly to our knowledge of Assyria, Babylonia, and the ancient Middle East.

Most of the inscriptions are administrative, economic, and legal documents. Many are dated in relation to significant historical events. They bear the distinctive *cuneiform* (wedge-shaped) writing.

Archaeologists have found more than 5,000 tablets inscribed with myths, epic tales, hymns, lamentations, and proverbs. Except for the proverbs and some essays, all the Babylonian and Assyrian literary works are written in poetic form.

The literary influence of Babylonia and Assyria upon the Old Testament is seen in the fact that hundreds of words and phrases used in the Hebrew Bible are directly paralleled in the cuneiform tablets. Three primary texts found in cuneiform

The Behistun Inscription

Kings of the Ancient Near East often prepared monuments to commemorate their victories. From these monuments, scholars have learned a great deal about the ancient world. Biblical events and persons are frequently mentioned. One of these commemorative monuments, the Behistun inscription, enabled scholars to decipher ancient Akkadian (i.e., the eastern division of the Semitic languages).

The town of Bisitun or Behistun lay on the main caravan route between Baghdad and Tehran. King Darius I of Persia (521–485 B.C.) had a record of his exploits carved on the mountainside nearby, 108 m. (345 ft.) above a spring where travelers stopped and 31 m. (100 ft.) above the highest point to which a man could climb. To insure that his work would not be defaced, Darius instructed his workers to destroy the way to get to the inscription after their work was completed.

In 1835, a British officer named Sir Henry Rawlinson began the hazardous task of copying the inscription. To copy the top lines, he had to stand on the topmost step of a ladder, steadying his body with his left arm and holding his notebook with his left hand, while writing with his right hand.

To the top of the inscription is a winged disk (representing the god Ahura-Mazda) and twelve figures. The inscription shows Darius treading on his rival Gaumata. To

Darius' left are two attendants and before the king are nine rebels, roped together.

The inscription itself is in three languages: Old Persian, Elamite, and Babylonian (a form of Akkadian). After they deciphered the old Persian inscription, scholars worked on the hypothesis that the other two texts contained the same narrative. Edward Hincks, rector of a parish church in Ireland, and Henry Rawlinson published their interpretation of the cuneiform characters. This provided the key to the decipherment of other Akkadian inscriptions.

A copy of the Behistun inscription was also found at Babylon, and an Aramaic version was discovered among the Jews of Elephantine Island. Darius made sure his fame was spread from one end of his extensive empire to the other.

In part, the Behistun inscription reads: "I am Darius. . . . By the grace of Ahura-Mazda I am ruler of twenty-three lands including Babylonia, Sparda (Sardis?), Arabia and Egypt. I put down the rebellions of Gaumata and eight others . . ."

Due to the great height of the inscription from the road, one wonders how Darius expected travelers to read of his glory. However, his trilingual proclamation has benefited scholars in a marvelous way—a way the king never dreamed.

are very similar to Old Testament themes. These are the creation, the flood, and the lament of the righteous sufferer (cf. the Book of Job). For a further description of the cuneiform stories of the creation and flood, see Chapter 5, "Pagan Religions and Cultures."

OTHER ARCHAEOLOGICAL EVIDENCE

Sifting through other archaeological clues, we find that Assyrian culture closely resembled Babylonian culture—except that the Assyrians tended to be more barbaric. For example, the Assyrians buried their dead with the knees drawn up to their chins. They buried them under houses instead of in cemeteries.

The favorite pursuits of Assyrian kings were war and hunting, which is reflected in their art and writings. Archaeological finds indicate that the Assyrians were generally a merciless and savage people.

In 1616, Italian traveler Pietro della Valle (1586–1652) recognized the ruins of Babylon. And between 1784 and 1818, several "digs" took place at this site. But the most important was done here after 1899, by the Deutsche Orient Gesellschaft under the direction of German archaeologist Robert Koldewey (1855–1925). He traced the outermost wall of Babylon over about 31 sq. km. (12 sq. mi.) and excavated the Processional Street, the Ishtar Gate, and the foundations of two palaces of King Nebuchadnezzar II.

What do the archaeological discoveries tell us about Babylonia? First, that the people were essentially urban, although their economy was based on agriculture. Babylonia consisted of 12 or more cities surrounded by villages and hamlets. The people served under an absolute monarch.

Second, these finds tell us there were three social levels of citizens: *awelin,* the free man of upper class; *wardu* or slave; and *mushkenu,* free man of lower class. Parents could sell their children into slavery if they desired. However, it seems that most slaves were acquired as prisoners of war and were treated humanely (considering the era).

The family was the basic unit of society, with marriages arranged by parents. Women had a few legal rights but were subordinate to men. Children had no rights.

Third, we find that the population of Babylon was somewhere between 10,000 and 50,000. Babylonian streets were winding, unpaved, and meandering. The average house was a one-story mud brick structure with several rooms grouped around an open court.

The well-to-do Babylonian usually had a two-story house that was plastered and whitewashed. The ground floor had a reception room, kitchen, lavatory, servants quarters and sometimes a private chapel. Furniture consisted of low tables, high-backed chairs, and beds with wooden frames. Utensils were made of clay, stone, copper and bronze. Reeds were utilized for baskets and mats. Like the Assyrians, the Babylonians buried their dead (in many cases) underneath the house. Pots, tools, weapons, and other items were buried with them.

Babylonians had considerable engineering "know-how" that they used in maintaining canals and reservoirs. They prepared maps, mastered early mathematics, and developed timetables for planting and harvesting.

8

UGARIT AND THE CANAANITES

The Canaanites lived in the land of Palestine before the Hebrews arrived. Until 1928, our knowledge of the Canaanites was limited to three sources.

One source was the archaeological work at cities in Palestine such as Jericho, Megiddo, and Bethel. These cities yielded pre-Israelite building remains, pottery, house utensils, weapons, and similar items—but no inscriptions. Scholars certainly value these other items, but written evidence is usually the most important tool in reconstructing the past. In the long run the historical value of inscriptions outweighs physical evidence. Here we have in mind such things as myths, legends, royal chronicles, legal texts, and business records.

The second source of our information on Canaan was the literature of contemporary people who lived outside Canaan. A good example of this are the Tell el-Amarna Letters, sent by Canaanite princes in Palestine to the pharaoh in Egypt. These letters were written mainly to Amenhotep III and his son Akhnaton in the 1400s or early 1300s B.C. As we shall see Canaan was an extension of Egyptian power for much of the Canaanites' history.

A late Egyptian story (eleventh century B.C.) gives us another view of Canaan. This story concerns the journey of Wenamon, an official of the Temple of Amun at Karnak, to Byblos in Phoenicia to get lumber for the sacred boat of his god. The story suggests that Egypt's control over Canaan had slipped severely from the time of the Tell el-Amarna Letters, for the Canaanites treated Wenamon disrespectfully and were slow to meet his request.

Various Akkadian texts from the east and Hittite texts from the north also give us interesting facts about Canaanite customs. For example, Hittite laws are very specific and seem to deal with every possible civil offense. Akkadian texts describe elaborate temple rituals and sacrifices. These documents suggest that the cultures of that area were quite sophisticated.

Our third source of facts on Canaan and its people was the Old Testament. Scripture tells us the Hebrews pushed the Canaanites out of their land and in some cases eliminated entire cities (Josh. 11:10–12:24). Even a quick reading of Scripture shows us that the Canaanites never ranked highly with Old Testament writers. The Old Testament writers spare no effort in painting the Canaanites as evil and immoral people, and their religion as strange and obnoxious (Judg. 2:2; 10:6-7). The account of such an unsparing attack con-

Ugarit. This aerial view shows part of the excavation at Ugarit (Ras Shamra), located in present-day Syria near the Mediterranean coast. The Canaanites worshiped the god Baal, and the Old Testament prophets frequently condemned them for their religious practices. Written records at Ugarit have enabled scholars to understand the beliefs and rituals so abhorred by the prophets. Clay tablets found at the site have also provided keys to the meanings of Old Testament Hebrew words not previously understood.

vinces some modern scholars that the Old Testament is unduly biased against the Canaanites. But Scripture is amazingly accurate and objective, and does not exaggerate the truth when it tells us of the Canaanites. An archaeological discovery in northern Syria in 1928 confirms the Bible's portrayal of the Canaanites. This discovery provided a vast new store of information about Canaanite civilization.

In the spring of 1928, a Syrian peasant farmer working in his fields heard a blade of his tilling machine strike what he assumed was a hidden rock. Looking closer, he saw that his blade had sliced off the top of an unusually large hole in the ground; it looked like an ancient tomb. This accidental discovery began an exciting excavation of a Canaanite city, which yielded fascinating historical objects and the remains of several significant monuments.

As French archaeologists dug deeper into the city, they found vast amounts of ancient texts on clay tablets. Could it be that they had stumbled upon Canaanite literature, written by Canaanites in their native language? The answer was yes.

THE CITY OF UGARIT

The ancient name of this site was Ugarit. Although the name of Ugarit was mentioned in documents such as the Tell el-Amarna Letters, biblical scholars did not know Ugarit's exact location. The discovery of 1928 solved the problem. The modern Arabic name for this territory in Syria is Ras Shamra, meaning "fennel head." (*Fennel* is a fragrant flower whose seeds are used for making aromatic ointments; much of it is grown in this area.)

A. Description of the Area. What survives of Ugarit today is a large round mound of earth about 20 m. (65 ft.) high, over 900 m. (1,000 yds.) at its widest point, and almost 640 m. (700 yds.) at its greatest length. It is located about 0.8 km. (0.5 mi.) from the Mediterranean coast, in line with the easternmost tip of the island of Cyprus. Scientists began excavating the area in 1929 and have continued to the present, except for the years during World War II.

Weapons and tools. Archaeologists examine a hoard of 74 copper and bronze artifacts hidden under the house of Ugarit's high priest. The weapons and tools, never used, may have been an offering made by a bronze smith to the high priest.

B. Ugaritic Texts. Scholars soon deciphered the Canaanite texts from Ugarit and translated them into several modern languages. This was due largely to the efforts of Hans Bauer, a German, and the Frenchmen Charles Virolleaud and Edouard Dhorme.

We might say the Ugaritic texts were "cosmopolitan," since the writings were found in seven different languages: Egyptian, Cypro-Minoan Linear B, Hittite, Hurrian, Sumerian, Akkadian, and Ugaritic. So the Ugaritic tablets contained *hieroglyphic* (Egyptian), *cuneiform* (Hittite), and *linear* (the remaining five) forms of writing.

Researchers found that most of the texts were in the Akkadian syllabic script, which they knew from the cities of Mesopotamia. Akkadian was used for most of the business, law, administrative, and international documents at Ugarit. But archaeologists found that a unique Ugaritic alphabetic script was used for recording the great myths, epics, and legends of the city.

The traditional cuneiform script uses hundreds of different symbols; but on many tablets of Ugarit only 30 separate symbols appeared, suggesting that they used a system like an alphabet. The words were often separated by a divider symbol, something archaeologists had not seen on other cuneiform tablets. Most of the words were built from three basic consonants, the same pattern followed by Semitic languages such as Hebrew, Aramaic, and Phoenician. In addition, a few of the Ugaritic texts were written from right to left, while cuneiform is nearly always written from left to right.

These peculiarities convinced the researchers that Ugarit's tablets introduced them to an alphabet that had been unknown hitherto.

Here is the Canaanite alphabet:

a	y	p
b	k	s
g	s	q
h	l	r
d	m	t
h	d	g
w	n	t
z	z	i
h	s	u
t	c	s

The following sequence of letters of our English alphabet survived from this old alphabet: ab–d–h–klmn–pqr–t.

C. Other Archaeological Data. Archaeologists noticed five separate levels in the mound of Ugarit, and they found signs of human occupation at each level. Level Five (at ground level) contained evidence of a small fortified town at Ugarit as far back as a major flood. No pottery was discovered at this level. Level Four and part of Three date back to the Chalcolithic Period. Diggers did find pottery here. Level Three dates to the Early Bronze Age, about 1,000 years before Abraham. Here the excavators found signs of skillful work with metals. The top layers, Levels One and Two, bring us into the golden age of Ugarit, 1550–1200 B.C. This takes us from the Old Testament patriarchal period into the time of the judges. Ugarit was destroyed at the end of this period, apparently the victim of earthquake and invaders that the scribes of Ugarit called "Sea Peoples." There are only traces of occasional settlement at Ugarit after 1200 B.C.

Diggers unearthed two temples at Ugarit dedicated to the god Baal and his father Dagon. These temples are similar in structure to the one Solomon built. Both of the Ugaritic temples have rooms that might have been used somewhat like the holy place and the holy of holies in Solomon's temple.

Archaeologists unearthed several other buildings at Ugarit; some of these contained the libraries that give us most of our Ugaritic literature. The diggers found what must have been a plush royal palace, with 67 rooms and halls. It measured 119 m. by 82 m. (130 yd. by 90 yd.). The researchers discovered that many people of Ugarit placed burial vaults directly beneath their homes. Channels carried water from ground level into the tombs. Some archaeologists believe these channels were used to make pagan offerings to the dead.

Scientists also found storage jars over one meter (39 in.) high, and several beautiful golden bowls that were surely the work of professional goldsmiths. One bowl featured the engraved picture of a hunter on a chariot aiming his arrows at gazelles and bulls.

Archaeological researchers found 74 weapons and tools under the floor of a single Ugaritic house. Inscriptions on five of these items show that the collection belonged to a high priest (*rb khn*, as the letters would be written in their English counterparts). Apparently, ancient worshipers gave the priest these tools and weapons as offerings or gifts for their blessings and rituals.

Archaeologists also discovered several religious statues and cult objects at Ugarit. Among them were a few small golden amulets in the shape of nude women, surely relating to Ugarit's fertility cult. On the lid of an ivory box, the excavators found a carved picture of a bare-breasted goddess, holding several ears of grain in each hand. A goat on each side stood on hind legs, trying to nibble on the grain. Another ivory slab has a picture of a goddess nursing two children. This is a familiar feature in Near Eastern religious literature and art. Mortals and minor gods were supposed to receive power and prestige by suckling at the breasts of a goddess.

The researchers found a few small bronze statues of the god Baal, showing his left hand lowered and right hand raised, as if he were ready to strike a blow or lead a war cry. A larger slab of stone featured a picture of Baal wearing helmet and skirt and waving a club or mace in his right hand. He holds a spear in his left hand.

CANAANITE GOVERNMENT

Unlike Egypt, Mesopotamia, or Asia Minor, early Canaan had no single ruler whose power extended over the entire country. The Canaanites never produced a famous pharaoh or king. The cities were each governed by a petty ruler. The association of rulers held power over all Canaan.

A. City-State Concept. Canaan was composed of several city-states, self-ruling and to some degree, self-sufficient. A king, more properly called a lord, ruled in each city-state. In the Middle Bronze Age (2000–1500 B.C.) and the Late Bronze Age (1500–1100 B.C.), each of these territories was usually under the actual control of the Egyptians or the neo-Hittites. Note that Joshua 12 lists 31 kings with whom the Israelites battled in the conquest of Canaan.

B. Ugarit's Kings. It is hard for historians to establish exactly when, and by whom, the dynasty of petty kings started in Ugarit's history. Kings of the Late Bronze Age employed a seal that bears the inscription, "Yaqarum son of Niqmad King of Ugarit." This seal probably dates back to the nineteenth century B.C.

Biblical scholars don't know who provided community leadership in Ugarit over the next few centuries. But we are able to trace the rulers of Ugarit from the fourteenth century B.C. to the destruction of Ugarit in the eleventh century B.C. These late Ugaritic rulers, in order of succession, are:

1. Ammishtamru I
2. Niqmad II
3. Ar Khalba
4. Niqmepa
5. Ammishtamru II
6. Ibiranu
7. Niqmad III
8. Hammurapi'

At least the first two in this list were faithful vassals of Egypt and wrote regularly to that country. We find evidence of this in the Amarna letters.

Niqmad II (or Niqmaddu, as it may be spelled) lived at the same time as a famous Egyptian pharaoh, Akhnaton, also known as Amenhotep IV (*ca.* 1360 B.C.). The names of Akhnaton and his equally famous wife, Nefertiti, appear on alabaster vases found at Ugarit. Coaxed by the promise of more land, Ugarit's Niqmad II shifted his loyalty from the Egyptian pharaoh to a Hittite king, Shuppiluliuma. Niqmepa enjoyed one of the longest reigns of all the Ugaritic rulers, (*ca.* 1336–1265 B.C.). He sided with the Hittites against the Egyptians and the Pharaoh Rameses II at the famous battle of Kadesh in 1285 B.C. The fight ended in a stalemate and the rival nations formed a peace treaty. Ugarit benefited from this pact.

The fifth king on our list, Ammistamru II, was Niqmepa's son. Ammistamru should be remembered for a written record of his marriage and divorce from his wife, who was an adulteress. The Hittites forced Ammistamru II and his son, Ibiranu, to provide money and troops to defend them against a new menace on the horizon, the Assyrians. These easterners were led by Shalmaneser I and Tukulti-Ninurta I.

The reigns of the final Ugaritic kings, Niqmad III and Hammurapi', were brief and without significance. During their time a western enemy, the "Sea People," appeared to have become a more dangerous threat than the Assyrians while some natural disasters such as earthquakes may have weakened the city-states. The "Sea People" attacked, burned, decimated, and buried the city of Ugarit in about 1200 B.C. So it remained until it was rediscovered in A.D. 1928 by the Syrian farmer.

THE LAND OF CANAAN

Though Ugarit is never mentioned in the Bible, it is part of the land of Canaan. Let us look at the wider area of Canaan as it is described in the Old Testament.

A. The Meaning of *Canaan*. Scholars still debate the meaning of *canaan*, as they do the boundaries of the territory

Golden bowl. This artifact from Ras Shamra shows wild goats in the inner circle. In the outer circle a hunter stands in a two-wheeled chariot with drawn bow, pursuing a gazelle that leaps gracefully away. Running ahead are three wild bulls and one of the hunter's dogs. Hunting from the chariot was popular sport for the wealthy Canaanites. The hunter tied the reins to the chariot pole and then wrapped the ends around his waist to give greater stability and to leave his hands free for shooting.

indicated by this term. In the nineteenth century, scholars thought *canaan* was linked with the Semitic verb *knc*, which in Arabic means "to bow, be low," and in Hebrew, "to be subdued, humble oneself." So they interpreted *Canaan* to mean something like "lowland." Language experts have now abandoned this approach, but we should not overlook the words of Genesis 9:25, "Cursed be Canaan, a servant of servants shall he be unto his brethren." It is hard to miss the idea of inferiority here. Here *Canaan* may indeed be tied with the Hebrew root *knc*, "to be low."

Most scholars today feel *canaan* is related to the cuneiform word *kinahhu*, which comes to us from the Hurrians of Mesopotamia. This word means "reddish purple," and it refers to the murex snail found on the shores of the Mediterranean, which secretes a purple dye. The dye was one of the chief products of Canaan; hence it was called "the land of the purple dye." Phoenicians used the dye in the clothing industry. In fact, the Canaanite word for *Phoenician—phoinike—*is very close to the word *phoinix,* meaning "reddish purple."

B. Canaanite Boundaries. It is one problem to define *canaan.* It is just as difficult to determine the country's boundaries.

1. Biblical Evidence. We find the first clear biblical statement on this matter in Genesis 10:19: ". . . And the border of the Canaanites was from Sidon, as thou comest to Gerar, unto Gaza; as thou goest, unto Sodom and Gomorrah, and Admah, and Zeboim, even unto Lasha (in the Dead Sea area?)." On the basis of this verse, we may define Canaan as a long, thin area parallel to the southeast shore of the Mediterranean, covering areas populated by southern Phoenicians (Sidonians) and Philistines. No eastern boundary is designated, but we think it was the Jordan River.

2. Akkadian References. God's promise of land to Abraham takes on more significance when compared to an Akkadian text found at Ugarit. The text is a letter from the Hittite king Hattusilis III (thirteenth century B.C.) to his vassal, Niqmepa, king of Ugarit. Niqmepa had complained to the Hittite king that traveling merchants from Ur were making life difficult for residents of Ugarit. Some scholars believe Abraham was a traveling merchant with far-flung commercial interests. His 318 troops (Gen. 14:14) may have been bodyguards for the traveling merchants.

To relieve the situation at Ugarit, the Hittite king placed several restrictions on the merchants. One was that they could visit Ugarit only at harvest. The merchants were also prohibited from buying land or personal real estate in Ugarit with profits from their business. If Abraham was a merchant forbidden to buy real estate, then the promise offering him "all this land" takes on a new meaning. Man says: You can't have this land. God says: I am giving it to you.

C. God's Word and Canaan. Beginning with Abraham, and through following generations, God promised Canaan to individuals (a patriarch), then groups (the Israelites under Moses and Joshua). But the land of Canaan had to be conquered; it was not delivered on a silver platter to the Israelites.

God's word to His people was: "And the city [Jericho] shall be accursed, even it, and all that are therein, to the Lord: and they utterly destroyed all that was in the city, both man and woman, young and old, and ox, and sheep, and ass, with the edge of the sword" (Josh. 6:17a, 21).

CONQUEST OF CANAAN

It is easy to say, as some scholars do, that Canaan was not conquered as the Bible describes, but was instead penetrated slowly by the Israelites. Some people feel the description of these "holy wars" or "wars of extermination" springs from the imagination of later writers who distorted the historical events. It is equally convenient to view the events as historical, but chalk them up as an early stage in the development of the conscience of the old Israelites. But perhaps the conquest of Canaan can be better understood in light of these facts:

A. Mercy Grant. The land of Canaan was given to the Israelites on the basis of God's mercy, not their merit. We find no suggestion that the Israelites considered themselves a superior people. Their God was superior—the *only* God.

B. God's Orders. Canaan was attacked by the Israelites because God gave the order. Israel did not take the first step

El. Many scholars believe the seated deity shown on this stone relief was El, the leader of the Ugaritic gods. His left hand is upraised in a gesture of benediction as he accepts an offering from a worshiper.

on its own. This was not a fulfillment of any long-held dream of expansion on Israel's part. In fact, Scripture makes no reference to Israel's having a standing army until David's time.

C. War as a Way of Life. The wars against Canaan never became models for later action by the Israelites. God's will for His people in the world was spelled out first in Genesis 12:3: "And in thee shall all families of the earth be blessed."

D. Booty. Taking booty from the defeated enemy was a common practice in that day and has remained so throughout history. But God's Word prohibited the Israelites from taking personal booty from the conquered people. Everything was to be devoted to the Lord. Silver, gold, and vessels of bronze and iron were to be placed in the Lord's treasury, not private coffers (Josh. 6:18-19).

E. No Dual Standard. The Israelites are not exempt from God's Word. There was no dual standard here. An Israelite named Achan gave in to the temptation to sneak a bit of Canaanite spoil for himself. As a result, he and his family were devoted to destruction (Josh. 7, especially vv. 24-26). When the Israelites sinned as a nation, they were punished—i.e., defeated by their enemies—just as other nations were.

F. Enslavement. When the Israelites entered Canaan, they could have followed three courses of action regarding the Canaanite people. They could kill them, expel them, or make them slaves. Except in actual battle situations, the Israelites appear to have chosen the last option most often, for the Canaanites continued to live in Palestine long after Joshua's death. This is seen in the story that Solomon's father-in-law, the Egyptian pharaoh, marched against the city of Gezer in Canaan, wrested it from the Canaanites, and gave it to his daughter as a wedding present (1 Kings 9:16). Judges 3 states that Canaan was a nation left by God to test the Israelites (Judg. 3:1-3).

G. Immorality. The Bible firmly states that the Canaanites' religion and lifestyle were immoral. The Canaanites destroyed themselves by their sinful living. This is what God means when He tells Abraham, "but in the fourth generation they [Abraham's descendants] shall come hither again: for the iniquity of the Amorites [Canaanites] is not yet full" (Gen.

15:16). God will not give the land to His people too soon, He will wait until evil has run its full course.

The Lord said to His people through Moses, "Thou shalt not bow down to their gods, nor serve them, nor do after their words. . . . Thou shalt make no covenant with them, nor with their gods. They shall not dwell in thy land, lest they make thee sin against Me: for if thou serve their gods, it will surely be a snare unto thee" (Exod. 23:24a, 32-33).

UGARIT LITERATURE

Does the literature found at Ugarit confirm what the Old Testament says about the Canaanites?

Let us look at the texts from Ugarit written in the unique alphabetic cuneiform script discussed above. These texts may be divided into two groups. The first is *legends* or *epics,* in which the main characters are human. The second category is *myths,* in which the action of the gods is the main feature. Let us first look at the myths.

A. Myths. Most of the Ugaritic myths revolve around Baal and the other gods associated with him. Baal was the god of sky and rain. His two major opponents were Yamm (god of the sea) and Mot (god of death).

1. The Baal Cycle. We call the longest of the Canaanite myths the Baal Cycle. Scholars do not agree on the sequence of this story's episodes, which are found on about one dozen clay tablets. But we can accept this general version:

Baal and Yamm are engaged in a fierce war. It is not merely a wrestling match in the sky to be observed by amused spectators. The outcome is deadly serious for believers in Baal. If Baal triumphs, the land will be fertile that year, and farmers and residents can breathe a bit easier. But if Mot wins, disaster will follow—death and sterility will rule. It may mean the year of the locust plague, or one of drought.

We learn from one of the first tablets in this series that Yamm sends two messengers to El, head of the gods, to ask that he give Baal to the messengers: "Give up, O gods, him whom you harbor. . . . Give up Baal . . . Dagon's son, so that I may inherit his gold." El yields and hands over Baal. Angered, Baal lashes out in revenge, but is restrained by the goddesses Anath and Ashtoreth. For the moment, Yamm is victor over Baal.

But we see that another text puts the shoe on the other foot. In this episode, Baal defeats Yamm. Baal's weapons are two magic clubs furnished by Kothar-wa-Khasis, god of craftsmanship and inventor of tools, weapons, and musical instruments.

A long text of the Baal Cycle introduces us to the goddess Anath, Baal's consort. Baal had three daughters as well: Talliya, goddess of dew; Padriya, goddess of the clouds; and Arsiya, goddess of the earth.

Corbelled Vault. A passage or stairway probably led to this stone vault under the main floor of a Canaanite house. The people of Ugarit believed the dead could not rest if they were deprived of water, and so they devised elaborate systems to provide it. Often water was poured into a pipe above ground and flowed into a gutter, which led into a pit next to the burial chamber. A window cut into the wall supposedly allowed the dead access to the water. Archaeologists call this type of chamber a *corbelled vault,* because the tighty fitted stone masonry forms a stone gable or *corbel.*

Anath is both goddess of war (She fights for her husband's causes.) and goddess of love and sensuality, a common combination of attributes in ancient goddesses. Her slaughterhouse tactics against Baal's opponents are described in detail: "Anath swells her liver with laughter/Her heart is filled with joy/For in Anath's hand is victory/For knee-deep she plunges in the blood of soldiers/Neck-high in the gore of troops/Until she is sated." This slaughter results in fertility for the land: "She draws water and washes/With dew of heaven/Fat of earth." Similar blessings are contained in Isaac's words to Jacob (or Esau, as Isaac thought), in Genesis 27:28: "God give thee of the dew of heaven, and the fatness of the earth." This blessing is found again in Isaac's word to Esau (Genesis 27:39).

The next story tells us how Baal attempts to lure Anath into convincing El to give him a palace. No favor or request from Baal seems too much for Anath to honor. She tells Baal that all he need do is ask, and she will deliver. She reminds him of her past achievements: "Have I not crushed Yamm, El's darling?/ Nor annihilated the great god River?/Have I not muzzled the dragon/Nor crushed the crooked serpent/Mighty monster of seven heads?/I have crushed Mot, darling of the earth god's. . . ." As the narrative ends, Anath appears before El and demands that he honor Baal's request for a palace. She threatens El with violence if he does not fulfill the request. El is so frightened by his daughter that he hides from her in his own house!

Another text describes a different meeting between Baal and Yamm, with Yamm the victor. But in this version Baal has carnal relations with a young cow before going to the underworld in order to provide an heir. Apparently the Canaanites saw nothing wrong in allowing their gods to practice bestiality.

These texts allow us to understand the cosmic battles in Ugaritic myths between the god-forces of barrenness and productivity, sterility and fertility—Yamm and Baal, Mot and Baal. The Old Testament has many passages that read much like these showdowns in the sky. One example is: "Awake, awake, put on strength, O arm of the Lord . . . Art thou not it that hath cut Rahab, and wounded the dragon? Art thou not it which hath dried the sea, the waters of the great deep . . . ?"

(Isa. 51:9-10). Or Psalm 74:13-14: "Thou didst divide the sea by Thy strength: thou brakest the heads of the dragons in the waters. Thou brakest the heads of leviathan in pieces, and gavest him to be meat to the people inhabiting the wilderness." We even find similar declarations in the New Testament, especially in connection with the great red dragon with seven heads and ten horns, defeated by Michael and his angels (Rev. 12:3-17).

How shall we interpret verses such as these? Did the poets of Israel borrow the myth of the cosmic battle from her Canaanite neighbors? Probably not. Literary material such as this was common currency throughout the ancient Near East.

Biblical writers deliberately made references to familiar myths. It seems impossible to avoid this conclusion. What would allusions to a dragon or leviathan mean to Isaiah's audience, unless the people were already familiar with stories about the creatures? But the Israelite authors did not simply copy Canaanite thoughts in their writing. If they had, we would expect to find Canaanite creation myths in the Pentateuch and the opening chapters of Genesis, and we do not. Instead, the mythical beasts crop up in Scripture at a relatively late date, when Israel was firm in its belief in God who is One,

City gate. Past this entrance lay Ugarit, one of the oldest cities in the world and one of the largest city-states of the Phoenicians. At the king's palace of Ugarit, excavators discovered the foreign office archives, which contained letters to the Egyptians and the Hittites and bills of shipping to Tyre, Sidon, Ashdod, Crete, and other ancient sites. The people of Ugarit built a massive trading empire.

without rival. Isaiah and the Psalmist are not affirming Canaanite myths as truths, but borrowing their contents to use as poetic imagery for celebrating God's sovereignty.

2. Fertility Myths. Two more myths from Ugarit will round out our discussion of this branch of literature. One myth concerns the marriage of Yarih, the moon god, to Nikkal, moon goddess from Mesopotamia. Nikkal bears a child to Yarih. Yarih's words to Nikkal show that fertility of the womb and fertility of the land are linked: "I shall make her fields into vineyards/The field of her love into orchards."

The second myth is often called "The Birth of the Good and Gracious God." It opens with a banquet at which wine flows freely. The text is divided into sections, the tenth being the last and most crucial. El is about to create two women who will become either his wives or daughters, depending on his ability to impregnate them. He creates these females and seduces them, and they both become pregnant. One bears a child called Dawn (Shahar), and the other bears a child called Dusk (Shalim). Later, El makes love to these same women and they produce seven sons between them. These sons are "the good and gracious gods." They are destined to be gods of fertility, and are first suckled at the breasts of "the Lady" (Asherah, wife of El?). El sends them to the wilderness for seven years, until things take a turn for the better. It has been suggested this text was connected with a ritual intended to end a string of bad years and start a productive cycle for Ugarit.

Fertility religions such as Ugarit's place great emphasis on reproduction in the land, in crops, and in the womb. This emphasis helps explain their stress on sexual unions.

The Bible and the Canaanite texts at Ugarit use the words *qadesh* and *qedesha*, which mean "holy one"—the first masculine, the second feminine. At Ugarit these "holy ones" were homosexual priests and priestesses who acted as prostitutes.

We find strong Hebrew reaction against this "cultic prostitution" in passages such as Leviticus 19:29, "Do not prostitute thy daughter, to cause her to be a whore," and Deuteronomy 23:17, "There shall be no whore (*qedesha*) of the daughters of Israel, nor a sodomite (*qadesh*) of the sons of Israel." One of

The Legend of Keret. This epic, written on four tablets in cuneiform alphabetic script, tells of the prosperous King Keret of Ugarit. The story says that Keret was distressed by the death of his wife and her failure to bear any heirs to the throne. The god El told him to demand the hand of the beautiful daughter of the king of Udum. Keret made the appropriate vows, besieged the capital of Udum, and won the king's daughter. In time, he had sons and daughters of his own. Keret fell ill, but El intervened to restore his health.

Josiah's reforms was "to break down the houses of the sodomites" (2 Kings 23:7).

B. Legends. We should examine two important Canaanite legends about ancient kings. One story is the Legend of Keret, named for its major character, the son of El. Keret is king of Hubur. His wife is taken from him and his family killed. Much of this story contains the advice from El to Keret on where to find a new wife. Keret is told to go to Udum (Edom?), where King Paebel has a beautiful daughter, Hurriya. Keret's quest is successful. The couple is happily united and starts a new family, which grows to seven boys and a girl. Later Keret becomes fatally ill.

Here El, leader of the gods, steps in again. He uses magic to restore Keret's health: "I myself will perform the magic/I shall indeed stay the hand of the disease/Exorcising the demon. . . ." We find it interesting that in using magic, the god appeals to an outside power.

One of Keret's sons, Yassib, soon rebels against his father for his bland leadership. Keret says, "May Horon (god of the plague and the nether world) break, O my son/May Horon break your head/Ashtoreth, name of Baal, your pate. . . ." So we see this story begin and end with a troubled father.

The second legend deals with a king called Aqhat, son of Danel (*not* the Daniel of Scripture) and his wife Donatiya.

Kothar-wa-Khasis (the god of crafts) makes a beautiful bow for Aqhat, which draws the attention of Anath, goddess of war. Anath desires the bow for her arsenal, but Aqhat rejects her offers for it.

Amath has Aqhat killed by one of her cohorts, Yatpan, who assumes the form of an eagle.

Father Danel retrieves Aqhat's remains from the stomach of the eagle and buries his son. Aqhat's sister, Pigat, goes to Yatpan to revenge her brother's death. Meanwhile, Danel enters a seven-year period of mourning for Aqhat. The text ends here, but many scholars feel there is probably more to the legend.

Why was this legend written? Nobody is certain. The story probably hints at the sacred office of the king as holder of fertility, because the text says that after Aqhat's death "Baal failed for seven years . . . without dew, without showers." Danel is called several times *mt rp'e,* "the healer," or "dispenser of fertility."

Aqhat's father, Danel, is especially interesting to us in this legend. The prophet Ezekiel dampened his people's false hopes of deliverance (Ezek. 14:12-23) by saying that an individual will be saved only if he is righteous. To stress the point, Ezekiel says: "Though these three men, Noah, Daniel, and Job, were in [the land], they should deliver but their own souls by their righteousness" (vv. 14, 16, 18, 20). Three verses insert, "they shall deliver neither sons nor daughters."

Scholars have no problems identifying Noah and Job in the Bible. But who is Daniel? Is it the same Daniel of whom Ezekiel speaks in 28:3: "Thou [the prince of Tyre] art wiser than Daniel; there is no secret that they can hide from thee"? Many writers have suggested that the Daniel whom Ezekiel mentions is not his contemporary, the prophet Daniel, but the Daniel of Canaanite legend. In the Book of Daniel, Daniel is spelled in Hebrew *dny'l.* But in all of Ezekiel's passages, Daniel is spelled *dn'l,* exactly as the name Danel is spelled in the Aqhat story.

If the Hebrews knew of the Canaanite leviathan and mentioned it in their religious literature, could they not have done the same with Danel?

CONCLUSION

We know that the Hebrews lived next to the Canaanites and were familiar with their lifestyle, world view, religion, and literature. Many times the Hebrews adopted the Canaanite religion. Think of the bull image built by Jeroboam at Bethel and Dan (1 Kings 12:28-29); in Ugaritic texts, El is often called "the Bull." Or recall the frequent references to such Canaanite objects as the Asherah or Asherim (Exod. 34:12; Deut. 7:5; 12:3; 16:21; Judg. 6:25; 1 Kings 14:15; and others).

Much of the prophets' stern warning was a reaction against the Canaanites. At times the Hebrews freely borrowed from the Canaanites.

From which areas of Canaanite life did they borrow? Certainly from their architecture and their literary techniques. Our knowledge of the workings of Hebrew poetry (especially Psalms and Proverbs) is due in great part to valuable poetic texts found at Ugarit. The Hebrews even referred to their language as "the language of Canaan" (Isa. 19:18).

But these borrowings were rarely religious. To be faithful to its God, Israel had to stand apart from its pagan neighbors. It dared not tamper with what God called loathsome and unacceptable to Him. Yahweh and His spokesmen challenged Israel to live above the surrounding cultures, to be separate from them, and be a witness and a challenge to them.

9

THE PERSIANS

Persians ruled Palestine during the last century of Old Testament history. The Bible speaks of that period in the narratives of Esther, Daniel, Ezra, Nehemiah, and two verses at the end of 2 Chronicles. For the Jews this was a period of restoration and reconstruction. For the Persians it was a period of imperial expansion.

The Jews had been exiled to Babylonia for nearly 60 years when the Persians conquered that land in 539 B.C. Two years later Cyrus II, the Persian king, granted the exiles permission to return to their homeland. He then pressed on toward the conquest of Egypt, a feat accomplished by his son in 525 B.C.

Palestine was swept into the great empires of Babylon, Persia, Greece, and Rome over a period of 650 years. However, only the Persians are remembered for their contributions to the Jewish people. The other empires are regarded in the Bible as evil and hostile to the Jews.

EARLY HISTORY

The Persians knew what it meant to be exiled. They had been forced to migrate for over a thousand years. Their ancestors had originally lived near the steppes of southern Russia. They were pressured by other migrating peoples about 2000–1800 B.C. to move into the plains of Central Asia. They took with them their Aryan names, traditions, and language. This Indo-Iranian language has some closeness to Greek and Latin. When these Aryans reached their new homeland in the vast region between India and Mesopotamia, it appears they introduced the horse and chariot. Pottery from that period has been discovered showing pictures of horses. Iron and copper reins have also been uncovered.

Of the tribes which settled in northern Iran only the Medes and Persians are of significance to this study, since they had the most influence on Bible people and times. Their emergence as people of importance took nearly a thousand years.

By about 700 B.C. Media and Persia were established, although they were subject to Assyria. Assyria had by that time conquered the northern kingdom of Israel. The Persians freed themselves from Assyrian dominance in 681 B.C., when Achaemenes was their king. However, the Assyrian cuneiform became the basis for the Persian system of writing. His two sons quarreled among themselves when they inherited the throne, and they divided the kingdom into two parts. Very soon, however, one of those kingdoms, called Parsa, was absorbed by Media. The other kingdom, centered in a region called Anshan, provided the basis for the eventual Persian Empire and the first dynasty, the Achaemenid dynasty, that lasted until 330 B.C.

At the beginning of the seventh century B.C., when Judah was subject to Nebuchadnezzar of Babylon, the Medes were still a semi-nomadic people. Their ruler was Phraortes (675–653 B.C.), who resided at Ecbatana (near modern Hamadan), a city that later became one of the capitals of the Persian Empire. In a battle against Assyria in 653 B.C. Phraortes was killed.

Cyaxares, his son, reorganized the army and introduced better weapons for his warriors. He extended his control over the Persian kingdom, which paid tribute to him. When he was about to defeat the Assyrians, however, the Medes were forced to withdraw to protect their eastern regions from Scythian invaders. Twenty-eight years later Cyaxares attacked Assyria again and took the city of Asshur in 614 B.C. He joined forces with Nabopolassar of Babylon, who had defeated Assyria in battle on an earlier occasion (626 B.C.), to capture Assyria's capital, Nineveh, in 612 B.C.

Babylonia continued westward conquests. She defeated the alliance of the Assyrians and Egyptians at Carchemish in 605 B.C. and took over the Assyrian Empire. The Babylonians would control affairs in the Near East for the next sixty years.

Babylonia and Media marched on parallel routes westward in order to subdue the nations under them. Cyaxares took his forces on campaigns into northern Mesopotamia, capturing Armenia and Cappadocia as far as the kingdom of Lydia to the west and Parthia to the east. The Babylonians campaigned in Syria, Phoenicia, and Palestine. However, while these two kingdoms rivaled each other for power, Persia began its rise toward dominance of the Near East.

THE RISE OF CYRUS THE GREAT (550–529 B.C.)

Cyaxares' granddaughter was married to Cambyses I, Persian king of Anshan. The son born out of this marriage was Cyrus II, known as Cyrus the Great. Under Cyrus II the Persian power had to be reckoned with. When he was crowned king of Anshan in 559 B.C., the Persians still paid tribute to Media. By about 550 B.C. Cyrus had defeated his grandfather, Astyages, king of the Medes, and taken his capital, Ecbatana. Cyrus then gave himself the title of "king of the Medes" and made Ecbatana his headquarters. By permitting the Median officials to remain in office, he won their allegiance to him.

All of the Median Empire fell to Cyrus. He marched westward and claimed Armenia, Cappadocia, Cilicia, Lydia, Greek city-states in Asia Minor, and Greek islands. Eastward, his conquests included all of Iran. There were still two powerful rivals, however: Babylon and Egypt. Before a march against Egypt could be made, Babylon had to come under Persian rule.

In conquering Babylonia, Cyrus entered the arena of biblical history. To understand the impact Cyrus had upon the ancient world, we should review the last days of Babylonia, his arch rival.

A. The Reign of Nabonidus. Nabonidus, the last ruler of

the Babylonian Empire (555–539 B.C.), believed that an alliance with Cyrus II of Anshan might destroy his rival, Media. He relied on the alliance for protection and made no efforts to strengthen his own country. Instead of building his military forces, Nabonidus spent his time with literature, religion, and a study of Babylon's past. The work of Nabonidus has proved invaluable in establishing dates. He brought in the cult of the moon-god, Sin, the patron deity of Haran, from which his family originally came. Before long he was driven from Babylon by priests who did not like his religious reforms. He lived in exile in Teima in northern Arabia for ten years, beginning in 552 B.C. Nabonidus left his son Belshazzar as regent in Babylon during this time. When Nabonidus returned to Babylon in 543 B.C., the kingdom was weakened and divided. The priests were still dissatisfied, for they felt themselves robbed of their former glory since Sin had replaced Marduk as the god of Babylon.

B. Daniel and the Writing on the Wall. The Old Testament records that Daniel served under Belshazzar, who ruled Babylon in the absence of his father, Nabonidus. The book bearing Daniel's name tells that Belshazzar provided a banquet for a thousand nobles. Among the excesses at the party were drunkenness and the defiling of vessels captured from the Jerusalem temple. When the handwriting on the wall appeared, neither the king nor his sages could read the strange inscription. Finally, Daniel was called. He first rebuked the king for his pride. The same pride which brought Nebuchadnezzar down for a short time, would bring Belshazzar down, according to the meaning Daniel gave to the inscription: "MENE, MENE, TEKEL, UPHARSIN" (Dan. 5:25). Daniel interpreted these Aramaic words (literally, "number, number, weight, divisions") to mean that "God hath numbered thy kingdom, and finished it. . . . Thou art weighed in the balances and art found wanting. . . . Thy kingdom is divided and given to the Medes and Persians" (Dan. 5:26-28).

Even after hearing this dire message, Belshazzar did not repent. Instead, he made Daniel the third in rank in the kingdom, as if to overrule God's decision by including this

The Book of Esther:
A Glimpse of Persia

The Book of Esther records events that occurred during the reign of Ahasuerus (Xerxes) in the fifth century B.C., at Shushan (Susa), a capital city of the Persian Empire. Since Esther's story centers around intrigues at the royal court, it gives much detail about the customs and life at this time.

Persian feasts were famous for their magnicence. Esther 1 gives a glimpse of the opulence of these feasts. It describes the common Persian manner of eating by reclining on couches or beds (v. 6), and it states that all drinking utensils were made of gold, no two being alike (v. 7). The Greek historian Xenophon said the Persians prided themselves on their number of drinking vessels. When the Greeks destroyed the Persian Empire, a part of their spoil consisted of golden drinking horns and cups.

Esther shows the inner workings of the royal Persian court, as well as special laws relating to the king. Esther 1:14 mentions the seven princes of Persia and Media who "saw the king's face." These were chief nobles who were intimate advisors of the king (cf. Ezra 7:14).

Only a person summoned by the king could visit him without penalty. This gave dignity to the monarch and protected him from assassination. Esther feared going to Ahasuerus without being called because the punishment for such a visit was death (Esther 4:11). Also, no one was allowed to visit the king in mourning clothes, such as sackcloth (Esther 4:2). Yet Esther did so.

Bowing in reverence to nobles was a common custom (Esther 3:2). Everyone bowed in the presence of the king; to refuse to bow was an insult.

Herodotus mentions that the king kept records of royal benefactors. These records are probably referred to in Esther 2:23 and 6:1-3. One of the greatest favors the king could bestow upon a loyal subject was to dress him in clothing the king himself had worn (Esther 6:8).

The Book of Esther tells of other interesting Persian customs outside the royal court. The Persian Empire boasted a highly organized postal system. Letters sent by couriers were forwarded with amazing speed (Esther 3:13). Swift horses or other animals were used to make the dispatch travel even faster (Esther 8:10). As in other areas of the ancient Near East, letters were "signed" by the imprint of one's seal of a signet ring on the document.

By faithfully reflecting the manners and customs of Persia during the days of the empire, the Book of Esther serves as a reliable historical record of the period.

man of God in his government. The Bible solemnly observes: "In that night was Belshazzar the king of the Chaldeans slain. And Darius the Median took the kingdom being about threescore and two years old" (Dan. 5:30-31).

C. The Identity of "Darius." Critics have been quick to argue that the Bible is mistaken in the reference to Darius in Daniel 5:31. Secular records bear out that Cyrus II took Babylon in 539 B.C., and they do not know of a Darius who conquered and ruled Babylon. Some critics feel the book was not written by Daniel or even during his lifetime but by a second-century B.C. writer who wanted to encourage the Jews to be faithful to God in resisting Antiochus IV, who had attempted to Hellenize Palestine. Such a writer might be more interested in telling an inspiring story than in carefully recording the facts. Other scholars suggest identifications of Darius.

Some have speculated that Darius was really Gobryas (or Gubaru), one of Nebuchadnezzar's generals. He had become Babylonian governor of the province of Elam, a province at the edge of Persia. When he saw the rise of Persian power, he deserted to Cyrus and joined him in undermining the power of Babylon. Gobryas and Cyrus easily took Babylon since the priesthood of the god Marduk was waiting to aid the Persians. Belshazzar, left by Nabonidus to defend the city, was unable to defend his capital because of his drunkenness. Cyrus followed Gobryas into Babylon without a battle. There he received a hero's welcome and was immediately crowned "king of Babylon."

Documents of that period reveal why Cyrus was so popular as the conqueror of Babylon. He restored Marduk as the deity of the state, along with the priestly order. He also maintained strict discipline among his occupation forces so that plundering and rape were avoided.

D. Cyrus' Decree. Cyrus committed himself to a policy of restoration. Unlike the Assyrians and Babylonians, who uprooted and exiled conquered people from their countries, Cyrus believed that it was in his best interest to permit the people to return to their native countries and to rebuild their temples. His was a policy of religious polytheism.

The new policy was welcomed by the Jewish communities. Jews had been in exile from Israel since 723 B.C. and from Judah since 586 B.C. They viewed the growing power of Persia as a God-sent sign of the end of their captivity. They comforted themselves with prophetic messages of Babylon's downfall such as Jeremiah 25; 50; 51. Isaiah assured them that Cyrus was anointed by God for a special mission even though he did not know God (Isa. 45:1, 4).

Ezra 1 records the decree of Cyrus to restore captured people to their homelands as the Jews received and understood it. In addition to releasing them, the decree granted the Jews permission to rebuild the temple and to set up organized worship of the God of Israel. Ezra has the decree instructing the neighbors of the Jews to send them off with a personal travel gift as well as a free-will offering for the reconstruction of the temple. Cyrus even returned those valuable articles which had been taken out of Solomon's temple by Nebuchadnezzar in 586 B.C. The items included 30 gold platters, 1000 silver platters, 29 vessels of various kinds, 30 golden bowls, 410 bowls of silver, and 1000 "other vessels" (Ezra 1:9-10). Cyrus also contributed to the reconstruction from the royal treasury. This contribution was later verified during the reign of Darius when a memorandum in Aramaic was found in the fortress in Ecbatana. That memorandum is recorded in Ezra 6:3-4.

E. The Jewish Response. The Jews responded with enthusiasm to Cyrus' offer. The year the order was issued (538 B.C.), many Jews prepared to return home. We should remember their decision to return was not an easy one. Those who had followed Jeremiah's advice (Jer. 29:5 ff.) had become rooted in Babylonia. They had bought homes, planted orchards, and established businesses in exile. Babylonian business tablets reveal to us Jewish names, indicating the Jews' good standing in Babylonia at that time. These ancient "Zionists" had to give up all they had built in exile to return to a poor homeland. Those starting the long and dangerous journey from Babylon to Palestine needed trust in God, a pioneering spirit, and a strong will to rebuild their land.

Sheshbazzar, "the prince of Judah," was the first governor of Judah. Sheshbazzar, whose name in Babylonian *(Shamash-apalusur)* means "Shamash has guarded the sonship," was responsible for temple treasures during the trek to Jerusalem (Ezra 1:11; 5:14). He was possibly the son of Jehoiachin, Shenazzar (1 Chron. 3:18).

Historians do not agree on Sheshbazzar's identity. Some argue that the Sheshbazzar named in Ezra 1:11 is identical with Zerubbabel of the family of David, who led the first return (Ezra 2:2). Zerubbabel was a leader next to Jeshua. But we are not told that Sheshbazzar was an active leader, while Ezra lays special emphasis on Zerubbabel's role as Davidic leader in the reconstruction period. In the Jewish response to Darius, Sheshbazzar is mentioned as the governor who saw the foundations of the temple laid. Sheshbazzar may have died soon after his return to Jerusalem and perhaps his middle-aged relative, Zerubbabel, took over the governorship. The prophet Haggai refers to Zerubbabel as "governor" (Hag. 1:1, 14).

Soon after the Jews' arrival in Jerusalem, Sheshbazzar instructed his people to follow Cyrus' order to rebuild the temple. Zerubbabel of David's family and Jeshua the high priest led the people in thanksgiving and laid the foundation of the temple. The priests and Levites led the people in praise. "Because he is good, for his mercy endureth for ever toward Israel" (Ezra 3:11). Only those who had seen the glory of Solomon's temple could compare it with the humble structure being built before their eyes. Those who remembered cried, while younger Jews shouted for joy at witnessing this new beginning. They knew this fulfilled God's promises to the prophets based on His covenant with Abraham (Ezra 3:12-13).

The Jews in Palestine sought to obey Mosaic Law. They sacrificed burnt offerings morning and evening (Ezra 3:2; cf. Deut. 12:5-6); celebrated the Feast of Booths (Num. 29:12);

Shushan (Susa). This ancient city in southwestern Persia became a capital city of the Persian Empire. Here Darius I built his palace, which was restored by Artaxerxes I and Artaxerxes II. Many of the events in the Book of Esther occurred in this palace.

and observed the fixed festivals (Num. 29:39). They willingly gave what they could afford for building the temple—a total of 61,000 gold drams, 5,000 pounds of silver, and 100 priestly garments (Ezra 2:69).

F. Daniel under the Persians. Daniel's life in exile had covered the rise and fall of Babylonia. He had witnessed the beginning of the Exile (*ca.* 606 B.C.), the fall of Babylon (539 B.C.), and the first waves of Jewish people returning to Palestine (*ca.* 538 B.C.). God had used Daniel to proclaim Babylon's fall into Persian hands (Dan. 5). Daniel then served the Persians for a few years after the fall of Babylon.

It seems most likely that the "Darius" of Daniel 6 should be identified with the Persian ruler named Gubaru. Gubaru became governor of the largest Persian province, "Babylonia and across the River." His domain included Babylonia, Assyria, Syria, Phoenicia, and Palestine. He appointed 120 governors and 3 commissioners (Dan. 6:1) to protect his province. Gubaru made Daniel a commissioner. Daniel's two colleagues and the governors wanted Daniel dismissed, even though his work and judgment were beyond criticism. They attacked his personal life. A pious Jew, Daniel regularly prayed to God, facing Jerusalem (Dan. 6:10). His enemies convinced Gubaru to order that no one should pray to any god or person, save the king (Dan. 6:12). As the governors expected, Daniel defied this order. He was tried and found guilty, and cast into a lions' den, from which God rescued him by a miracle (Dan. 6:22).

During Gubaru's first year of rule, Daniel meditated on Jeremiah's prophecy of the 70 years of exile (Dan. 25:11, 12; 29:10). Daniel confessed the sins for which the Jews were exiled, and prayed that the Lord might again deal graciously with His people and restore them to Jerusalem. Suddenly the archangel Gabriel revealed to Daniel that after 70 weeks (an unknown period of time) the people and Jerusalem would be restored, and atonement for their sins would be made. Gabriel said everlasting righteousness would be accomplished on their behalf (Dan. 9:24).

Daniel's last prophetic vision appeared in the third year of Cyrus, king of Persia (Dan. 10:1). By this time Daniel was too old to join the Jews returning to Palestine. God revealed His glory to Daniel as Daniel sat on the bank of the river Tigris (Dan. 10:4ff.). God's messenger told Daniel of the future of the Persian Empire. Daniel's vision foretold that three kings after Cyrus would rule Persia (Cambyses, Pseudo-Smerdis, and Darius), before a fourth (Xerxes) would spend his life fighting the Greeks (Dan. 11:2). One hundred years later the Persian Empire was taken by Alexander the Great (*ca.* 323 B.C.). For the next century and a half, two divisions of Alexander's empire would fight on the soil of Palestine—the Ptolemaic kingdom of Egypt ("king of the south") and the Seleucid kingdom of Syria ("king of the north"). Indeed, Palestine would be captured by the Seleucids around 200 B.C. (Dan. 11:17ff.), and ruled by them until the coming of Antiochus Epiphanes. Antiochus was to battle the Ptolemies of Egypt until the Romans' "ships of Kittim" demanded his withdrawal (Dan. 11:30). Enraged, Antiochus would go to Jerusalem and "set up the abomination of desolation" (Dan. 11:31).

The kingdom of God triumphed over the enemy forces in Daniel's vision. God's guidance of history assured Daniel and the Jews that God would accomplish everything according to His purpose. The Jews' future was not bright; they were destined to be ruled by Persians, Greeks, and Romans, and would endure great suffering (Dan. 11:40-45; 12:1). But ultimately the Jews would be raised and "shine brightly like the brightness of the expanse of heaven" (Dan. 12:3). God made a special promise to Daniel: "You will enter your rest and rise again for your allotted portion at the end of the age" (Dan. 12:13).

G. Cyrus' Death. Cyrus reached his goal of building an empire even greater than Babylon. He organized his empire into 20 satrapies (provinces). A satrap (governor) ruled each province, and was responsible to the king. Each satrap was checked by officers who also answered directly to the great king. The officers were the king's "eyes" in each province. Any attempt to go against the king's interests was reported to Cyrus at his great palace at Pasargadae, near the eastern shore

Darius and Xerxes. This relief from Persepolis shows King Darius I on the throne and crown prince Xerxes behind him. A very powerful Persian king, Darius compiled a code of laws, quelled revolutions within the empire, and established Susa as its new capital. The Jews prospered under the reign of Darius I. The Book of Esther refers to his son, Xerxes, by the name "Ahasuerus."

of the Persian Gulf. Cyrus created a large park there with his palace, shrines, and other structures.

Cyrus continued to fight in the East until he died in 530 B.C. He was buried at Pasargadae in a tomb 10.7 m. (35 ft.) high. (The tomb chamber is only 3.2 x 2.2 m. [10.5 x 7.5 ft.].) Guards stood near the tomb to protect the body of the dead king Cyrus. The corpse was placed inside the tomb in a limestone sarcophagus, which was placed on a funeral couch. The beloved Cyrus was buried with swords, earrings, fine clothing, and tapestries.

CAMBYSES II (529–522 B.C.)

Cyrus' son, Cambyses, took over the kingdom after his father's death. Like his father, he was a capable man and a good general. Cambyses had represented Cyrus at the new year's festival (called "the Akita Festival") in Babylon ever since Cyrus became king of Babylon. Cambyses had also stood in the capital as the king's official successor when Cyrus was on a military trip, in case harm came to the king. After his coronation, Cambyses looked westward to expand his empire.

Egypt had escaped foreign rule until this time. Pharaoh Amasis, who was disliked by his people, ruled Egypt with the aid of hired Greek soldiers. Cambyses took Memphis in 525

B.C., when neither Amasis nor his son, Psamtik II, could resist the Persian troops. This marked the start of Persian rule over Egypt.

Egyptians hated foreign rule. The false rumor that Cambyses had killed the sacred Apis bull was an outrage easily believed by simple people. The priests of certain temples were angry because they no longer received free supplies from the state. They were required instead to work the soil and raise fowl for sacrifice. These changes were all the Egyptians needed to reject the Persian rule. Archaeological evidence suggests that Cambyses respected Egypt's religion. But the Egyptian revolt forced him to pull the reins tighter. On his return from Egypt, Cambyses was told that Smerdis had seized rule of Persia. Cambyses knew it could not have been Smerdis, his half-brother (also known as Barfiya), because his aides had already killed Smerdis to prevent an uprising of this sort. Gaumate, a Median who claimed to be Smerdis (Pseudo-Smerdis), had really led the revolt. Cambyses did not live to deal with Gaumate. He died near Mount Carmel in 522 B.C., possibly by suicide.

DARIUS I (522–486 B.C.)

Darius was a distant relative of Cambyses. He bore Cambyses' spear in his battle with Egypt, and kept up with new political developments. Darius plotted against Gaumate, who backed the religious interests of the Medians and Magian priests. Darius and his forces killed Gaumate in a fortress in Media.

A. Strengthening the Empire. Darius first acted to unite the empire. It was crumbling on all sides because of separate patriotisms in the satrapies. Leaders of the provinces tried to grab power in Media, Elam, Babylon, Egypt, and even in Persia. Darius stemmed each revolt by sending loyal generals to subdue rebel forces. In two years Darius was recognized as a great king over most of the empire. He established Susa as the new capital of the kingdom, and built a palace there (521 B.C.). Next he created a code of law to be obeyed throughout his empire (*ca.* 520 B.C.). This law code resembles the Code of Hammurabi (*ca.* 1775 B.C.). Darius also appointed Persians to sit with native leaders as judges, and imposed taxes to be enforced by new officers.

B. Darius and Palestine. In the first difficult years of his reign, Darius had to deal with the temple in Jerusalem. Builders had laid the foundation of the temple, but no further work had been done (Ezra 4:5). The Jews concentrated on building homes and reestablishing their lives in the desolate land. Knowing the rumors of Cambyses' opposition to Egypt's religious practices, the Jews in Palestine may not have felt eager to request Cambyses' aid in rebuilding the temple.

But Darius wanted to win the Jews' loyalty to his throne, and he was more tolerant of the Jews than earlier Persian rulers had been. God sent two prophets to stir the hearts of Jews in Palestine: Haggai and Zechariah. Both of these men stressed the importance of finishing the temple. Haggai shamed the people by pointing out the poor progress they had made on the temple since their arrival in Jerusalem. The Jews had been in Palestine for over 15 years, but only the foundations of the temple were in place. The Jews were continually frustrated by drought (Hag. 1:10-11), blasting winds, hail, and mildew (Hag. 2:17). Still, they found time to build fine houses for themselves. Haggai twice challenged them with these words: "Consider your ways!" He warned that God would withhold His blessing until the temple was rebuilt (Hag. 2:18-19).

Zechariah prophesied between 520 and 518 B.C., a longer time than Haggai. Zechariah's gloomy picture of the disillusioned Jews agrees with that of Haggai (Zech. 1:17; 8:10). God reassured the people through Zechariah of the future glory of Jerusalem.

The Jews and their leaders were stunned by the prophetic words. Their new eagerness to obey God led them back to work. Zerubbabel and Jeshua (Joshua) began rebuilding three weeks after the first prophetic oracle (late 520 B.C.). Their loyalty to the Lord was noted by Haggai: "Then Zerubbabel, the son of Shealtiel, and Joshua the son of Jehozadak, the high priest, with all the remnant of the people, obeyed the voice of the Lord their God and the words of Haggai the prophet, as the Lord had sent him. And the people showed reverence for the Lord" (Hag. 1:12, NASV). God sent Haggai with words of further encouragement: "I am with you" (Hag. 1:13), and "take courage, Zerubbabel, take courage also, Joshua . . . , and all you people of the land take courage . . . and work; for I am with you" (Hag. 2:4, NASV).

But opposition soon came. Tatnai, the newly appointed Persian governor, tried to halt the renewed efforts to rebuild the temple. The Jews claimed they were carrying out Cyrus' orders. They asked Tatnai to check royal records for Cyrus' memorandum telling the Jews to go to Jerusalem and restore their temple (Ezra 5:10-16). The order was found at Ecbatana, Cyrus' home in his first years of rule. The order was written in Aramaic, and its instructions are recorded in Ezra 6:3-5.

Now it was clear to the Jews that God was with them! Darius told Tatnai not to interfere with the work on the temple (Ezra 6:6-7). Further, Darius ordered that the royal provincial treasury pay for the building expenses, as well as for the necessary sacrifices—young bulls, rams, and lambs for a burnt offering to the God of heaven, and wheat, salt, wine, and anointing oil; "according to the appointment of the priests, which are at Jerusalem, let it be given to them day by day without fail" (Ezra 6:9). It seems that Darius continued Cyrus' custom of allowing nations in the empire to worship their native gods, that "they may . . . pray for the life of the king, and of his sons" (Ezra 6:10). Anyone who disobeyed this order was warned of severe penalties: destruction of his house and execution (Ezra 6:1).

Darius established good relations with his Jewish subjects. As his forces marched through Palestine on their way to fight in Egypt, the Jews assured Darius that they would not trouble his men. During the winter of 519-518 B.C., Darius managed to regain control of Egypt, by the same quiet manner he had used with the Jews. He respected the religious traditions of Egypt and encouraged the digging of a canal from a branch of the Nile to the Gulf of Suez. (The project had been started by the Pharaoh "Necho" 70 years earlier and abandoned.)

Before Darius left their land, Egyptians accepted him as their ruler and gave him the title of Egyptian king.

C. Darius and the Greeks. Darius reestablished the Persian Empire from Egypt to India, as far east as the Indus River. He did not bring the Scythians in southern Russia under his rule, though he gained a foothold across the Bosporus by taking Thrace (513 B.C.).

At his death in 486 B.C., Darius I controlled a larger and stronger empire than he had inherited. Darius improved the government of the empire, placed strict military control on the semi-independent governors, introduced coinage, standardized weights and measures, and took an interest in the welfare of his subjects. But his new taxes were to cause the empire's downfall.

Darius was buried in a royal tomb at Persepolis. After his burial, his son Xerxes was made king.

XERXES I (486–465 B.C.)

Some scholars think Xerxes I is the famous "Ahasuerus" of the Book of Esther. He faced the same problems as his father, Darius. His empire was crumbling, largely because of new taxes. But Xerxes did not have Darius' interest in holding the loyalty of his subjects. He made grave errors of judgment in his military actions. He angered the priests of Egypt by taking their temple treasures. He burned Athens, and lost any support he might have claimed in Greek cities. He destroyed Babylon's temples and ordered that Marduk's golden statue be melted down. The Jews had prospered under the peaceful reign of Darius and had completed their temple. But when the Jews wanted to rebuild the walls of Jerusalem, their enemies falsely accused them of rebellion. The Jews were not permitted to complete the walls.

In his third year of rule, Xerxes organized a royal party for all of the princes, governors, and high army personnel in the empire's 127 satrapies from India to Nubia (Esther 1:1-3). All of the events of the Book of Esther occurred under Xerxes' reign.

ARTAXERXES I (465–424 B.C.)

Xerxes was murdered in his bedroom in 465 B.C. His younger son, Artaxerxes (Longimanus) took over a weakened Persian Empire. Artaxerxes tried to keep the empire together with many battles in Bactria, Egypt, and Greece. He accepted the peace formula known as the treaty of Callias (449 B.C.), which postponed a full-fledged war with Greece.

We can appreciate the activities of Ezra and Nehemiah against this background of international rebellion and plotting. The Jews again attempted to rebuild the walls of Jerusalem. The nobles of Samaria this time saw the building as a sign of rebellion. They told Artaxerxes that a strong Jerusalem would be a danger to the security of the empire. They told the king he should check the records to see for himself that Jerusalem was a "rebellious and evil city" (Ezra 4:12, RSV), and that the king's treasury was in danger: "If this city be builded, and the walls set up again, then will they not pay toll, tribute, and custom, and so thou shalt endamage the revenue of the king" (Ezra 4:13). They also advised that in that case the king "will have no possession in the province beyond the River" (Ezra 4:16, NASB). The search of records in the royal library confirmed the nobles' point. ". . . It is found that this city [Jerusalem] of old time hath made insurrection against kings, and that rebellion and sedition have been made therein" (Ezra 4:19). Artaxerxes ordered work on the walls stopped until a later order changed the situation (Ezra 4:21).

Despite his feelings against a walled Jerusalem, Artaxerxes viewed the Jews favorably. He gladly provided funds for Ezra's mission (*ca.* 458 B.C.). The loyalty of Jews in Judea strengthened his position in Syria, and in Egypt. He reinforced Cyrus' order in a special order of his own that permitted Jews in the Persian Empire to return to Palestine. We know from Scripture that Artaxerxes gave gold, silver, and lavish utensils to the temple (cf. Ezra 8:26-27), and promised to pay for all the temple needs from the royal treasury (Ezra 7:16-20). The king impressed the Jewish leaders with his gifts, promises, and encouragement to do "whatever is commanded by the God of heaven . . . for why should there be wrath against the realm of the king and his sons?" (Ezra 7:23). Artaxerxes also exempted priests, Levites, and temple workers from paying taxes (Ezra 7:24).

Artaxerxes supported Ezra's wish to teach the people of Judea the Law of God. Ezra was well qualified by his own study and careful observance of the Law. "Ezra had prepared his heart to seek the law of the Lord, and to do it, and to teach in Israel statutes and judgments" (Ezra 7:10). Artaxerxes ordered Ezra to teach the people of the law, and to make them accountable for their actions before courts and judges (Ezra 7:25). The sword of the Persian government backed up the God-centered Jewish system of law: ". . . Whosoever will not do the law of thy God, and the law of the king, let judgment be executed speedily upon him, whether it be unto death, or to banishment, or to confiscation of goods or to imprisonment" (Ezra 7:26).

Fifteen hundred Jews, including Levites who were responsible for the temple treasures (Ezra 8:24ff.), joined Ezra in his mission early in 458 B.C. This group experienced God's presence during their long and dangerous journey. Ezra records: "He delivered us from the hand of the enemy, and of such as lay in wait by the way" (Ezra 8:31). They arrived late the same year.

By this time over 50,000 exiles had returned to Judea. According to Nehemiah 7, most lived in towns located in and around Jerusalem. The region from Jericho to Bethel was the northern limit, from Bethel to Zanoah the western, from Zanoah to En-gedi the southern, and from Beth-Zur to Jericho the eastern. The big problem Ezra faced on arriving in Palestine was intermarriage. He knew the history of his people well enough to recall that in the past intermarriage had caused idolatry and corruption. Ezra pleaded with his people to stay pure as the people of God living by the Law of Moses, lest they return to exile. In prayer (Ezra 9:6-15), Ezra shows us his deep hope that the present generation would not repeat the mistakes of the past. Ezra was aware God might leave no remnant in another act of judgment.

Those who had intermarried confessed their sins and were willing to divorce their "foreign" wives (Ezra 10:3, 11, NASV). The Jews set up a divorce court, and by the winter of 458 B.C. they had settled the matter of intermarriage. A list of the divorces was added to the end of the Book of Ezra (chap. 10).

We know little about Ezra's whereabouts after this episode until we find him some years after in Jerusalem with Nehemiah (Neh. 8). Perhaps Ezra fulfilled his mission of teaching the Law throughout Judah, or had been away reporting the success of his mission to the Jews of Babylonia or to the court of Artaxerxes.

Persian troops moved through Palestine four years later (454 B.C.) on their way to Egypt. The mood was tense in the satrapy of "beyond the River," to which Judea belonged. The satrap of this province revolted against Artaxerxes. Fortunately for Judea, Artaxerxes quickly stemmed this rebellion.

In 445 B.C., Nehemiah's mission accomplished what the Jews had hoped for. Nehemiah, a Jew, was a cup-bearer to King Artaxerxes at Susa. Nehemiah had heard that his fellow Jews were not allowed to rebuild the walls of their city. He realized how dangerous the situation was for the Jews. The changeable times, the dislike of the Samaritan leaders for the Jews of Judea, and the nearly successful extinction of the Jewish people by Haman were good reasons for Nehemiah's distress. After prayer (Neh. 1:5-11), and with deep concern for his brothers in Judea, Nehemiah spoke with Artaxerxes. The king gave Nehemiah permission to rebuild the walls of Jerusalem (Neh. 2:5, 7-8). Escorted by the royal cavalry, Nehemiah arrived in Jerusalem in 445 B.C.

Nehemiah was soon opposed by Sanballat, Tobiah, and Geshem (Neh. 2:10, 19; 4:1-2). But Nehemiah checked the work to be done on the walls and made sure that construction was started immediately, before the Jews' opponents could gather forces. During these tense days workers used one hand to build and the other to hold a weapon for defense (Neh. 4:17). The wall was finished after only 52 days of work. The

Israelites had worked very hard during the day and guarded the walls at night. When the walls were done, Levites and singers came from all around Jerusalem to dedicate the structure with song. Nehemiah arranged two choirs to walk in opposite directions around the walls, singing praises to God as they drew nearer each other. Amid the singing and sacrifice at the temple, the people were so happy that their enemies could hear the joyous sounds from a great distance (Neh. 12:43).

Nehemiah remained governor of Judea for 12 years. He wanted to restore Jerusalem to its former glory. Until now few people had risked living in Jerusalem, exposed to invaders and surprise attacks (Neh. 7:4). With their wall rebuilt, the Jews agreed that at least 10 percent of their people would move from their homes and villages to live in Jerusalem (Neh. 11:1). In this way Jerusalem quickly became a thriving city in which all the citizens of the province had an interest—many had friends or relatives there now. Nehemiah was also successful in gaining social reforms in his province: He abolished lending money at unfairly high rates (Neh. 5:7), and restored lost property (Neh. 5:11).

Sometime during Nehemiah's governorship, Ezra returned to Jerusalem. Ezra read the Law to the assembly of people (Neh. 8:2) and helped the Jews understand how they should live according to the Law. This instruction continued during the Feast of Booths (Neh. 8:18). A solemn assembly at Jerusalem (Neh. 9:38; 10:29) made its own agreement to uphold the Law. This group also faced specific problems of its community: intermarriage (Neh. 10:30); Sabbath observance (Neh. 10:31); contribution of one-third of a shekel for the temple service (Neh. 10:32-33); and support of priests and Levites with first fruits and tithes (Neh. 10:34-39).

Nehemiah returned to Artaxerxes in 433 B.C. He was privileged to return to Jerusalem later (Neh. 13:6), when he used his royal authority to expel Tobiah (Neh. 13:7). Nehemiah also required the citizens of Jerusalem to support the Levites and singers (Neh. 13:10ff.), to enforce the Sabbath observance (Neh. 13:15ff.), and to forbid intermarriage (Neh. 13:23ff.).

PERSIA'S DECLINE

Like other great powers of the ancient world, Persia eventually passed its peak of influence and began a long period of decay. Military defeat, political intrigue, and economic blunders contributed to the empire's failure.

A. Political Maneuvers. The death of Artaxerxes in 424 B.C. opened a new era of secret plotting in the royal courts of Persia. Xerxes II was killed while intoxicated. His assassin, a son of Artaxerxes' concubine, was killed by Ochus, son of another concubine. Ochus, who already had support from the Babylonian army, found Susa's army unsympathetic to its new ruler, Darius II. Darius was forced to deal with Ochus and other pretenders to the throne by having them cruelly executed. He maintained Persian interests in Greece with Sparta's help. When tension arose between the Jews in the Elephantine region of Egypt and the local Egyptians, Darius and the Persians did not intervene.

B. Growing Jewish Power. The Jews enjoyed good relations with the Persians during the years of Persia's decline. They served as hired soldiers in Persian forces. Jews stationed at Syene (modern Aswan) at the southern border enjoyed relative independence. On the island of Elephantine opposite Syene in the Nile River, one Persian fortress was manned entirely by Jews. They even built a temple on the island, where they sacrificed animals to God. The sacrifice of rams offended the native Egyptians, especially the priests of Khnum, who regarded the sacrificial ram as a sacred animal. The priests destroyed the Jews' temple when the Jewish governor left to report to Susa in 410 B.C. Jews of the Nile asked Jerusalem for advice on rebuilding their temple. They said the temple had stood since before Cambyses' conquest of Egypt. After repeated requests for aid, Jewish leaders in Jerusalem told the colony in Egypt to rebuild their temple and to continue offering meal and incense. But because the local Egyptians strongly disliked them, the Jews never rebuilt their temple at Elephantine.

C. Final Phase. The last 70 years of the Persian Empire were filled with plotting and murders. The last Persian king, Darius III, was a capable ruler who faced the impossible task of uniting a splintering empire while trying to withstand the onslaught of the great general of Macedonia, Alexander the Great. Alexander reached Persepolis in 330 B.C. after defeating Darius at Gaugamela. In 330 B.C., Alexander looted and burned Darius' palace.

The Persians' rule had brought relative peace and prosperity to Jews in Palestine. The Jews' temple and Torah had flourished, and much of the Oriental culture of Persia had been adopted by the Jews. Jewish life in Palestine under the Greeks would change for the worse.

PERSIAN CULTURE

The Persians left an indelible mark upon the life of the Jews. Various aspects of Persian culture changed the life of Jewish people in New Testament times and beyond.

A. Art and Architecture. Persian art reflected the life of the court. Persian rulers cut fine royal reliefs into rocks to celebrate their victories over enemies. In the Behistun relief, Darius is shown defeating the rebels (521 B.C.). These victory reliefs show foreign subjects offering tribute to Darius.

Persian rulers also prided themselves on their beautiful palaces. Cyrus followed the style of the Median palace of Ecbatana in building his capital, Pasargadae.

King Darius chose Persepolis as the setting for his palace in 520 B.C. Building and magnifying Persepolis began with Darius' successor, and lasted to the fall of Persepolis under Darius III in 330 B.C.

Even after eight years of warfare, Xerxes found time to develop the buildings of Persepolis. Archaemenid art reached its peak during the last 13 years of Xerxes' reign.

The royal tombs also show us the Persians' desire for lavishness. The tomb of Cyrus II was simple compared to the rock-hewn tombs of Darius I, Artaxerxes I, and Darius II near Persepolis.

The whole Persian Empire contributed materials and artisans to imperial projects. Natural, three-dimensional figures; a fondness for animal themes; and the refined art of miniatures are contributions of the Persians. We find many of these characteristics in synagogues and other Jewish buildings of the post-exilic period in Palestine, such as the synagogue at Capernaum.

B. Language. Persian is a branch of the Indo-Iranian language group. It has similarities to Latin and Greek. (The Persian word for god is *daiva*, related to Latin *deus* and English *divine*.) The ancient Persians knew and used the Elamite, Babylonian, and Old Persian languages. The Behistun Rock records the Achaemenid dynasty up to Darius I in these three languages.

Old Persian was written in *cuneiform*, or wedge-shaped figures. People used the language only for official court documents and inscriptions. Official correspondence was aided by the use of Aramaic, a language that was used from Persia to Egypt. The Aramaic script became the model for a new Hebrew script that was used to record the Old Testament. The Jews borrowed many Aramaic words. In Hebrew, for example, the word *dat* ("decree") comes from the Persian *data*.

Aramaic words found their way into other languages as well. Our English word *paradise* comes from the Persian word for garden palace, *pairi-daeza*.

C. Religion. The chief god of the Persian system of religion was Ahura-Mazda, "the wise Lord." The official priests were called the Magians. The king believed Ahura-Mazda granted him the right to rule; he was the "image" of the god, in a very real sense.

The Persians believed in nature gods such as Air, Water, Heaven, Earth, Sun, and Moon. They did not worship these gods in temples. Instead, they sacrificed animals in open fields, to the accompaniment of chanting from a Magian priest. The Persians also burned sacrifices to their gods.

In the middle of the sixth century B.C., Zarathustra began to reshape Persian religious thought into what later became known as Zoroastrianism.

The conflict of good and evil was basic to Zarathustra's teachings. Zoroastrianism recognized Ahura-Mazda as its only god, but Ahura-Mazda was in eternal conflict with the evil spirit Angra Mainyu. Zarathustra opposed sacrifices and offerings of drink. He started the worship of Ahura by perpetual fire. The Persians built fire temples for this purpose.

This popular religion challenged the Jews to state their faith in clear terms. Jewish rabbis founded academies to preserve the truth of God's Word and to combat the intriguing doctrines of the Zoroastrians.

In the New Testament we read how "the magi" came to worship the baby Jesus in Bethlehem (Matt. 2:2). They may have been representatives of the priestly caste of the Zoroastrian religion.

Persia profoundly altered the course of Israelite history. The apocalyptic ideals of Persian philosophy are strongly represented in the apocryphal books of the intertestamental period. So persuasive was the influence of Persia that it is difficult to isolate Israelite art and architecture from the Persian influences. The Aramaic language (a late Persian dialect of Assyrian) became the standard language of Jewish politics and religion after the intertestamental period.

FOOTNOTES

Chapter Two: *"Bible History"*
[1]William Hendriksen, *Survey of the Bible* (Grand Rapids; Baker Book House, 1977), p. 79.
[2]Gleason L. Archer, *A Survey of Old Testament Introduction* (Chicago: Moody Press, 1964), p. 199ff.
[3]Leon Wood, *A Survey of Israel's History* (Grand Rapids: Zondervan, 1970), p. 88ff. Cf. Archer, p. 212ff. *See also* "Chronology."

Chapter Three: *"Bible Chronology"*
[1]Edwin R. Thiele, *The Mysterious Numbers of the Hebrew Kings* (Grand Rapids: William B. Eerdmans Publishing Company, 1965), p. 30.
[2]*See* Gleason L. Archer, *A Survey of Old Testament Introduction* (Chicago: Moody Press, 1964).
[3]*See* Robert Anderson, *The Coming Prince* (Grand Rapids, Mich.: Kregel Publications, 1975) and Alva J. McClain, *Daniel's Prophecy of the Seventy Weeks* (Grand Rapids, Mich.: Zondervan, 1940).

Chapter Four: *"Archaeology"*
[1]But the Egyptians never allowed a genuine alphabet to develop; this step was taken in about 1500 B.C., by political prisoners at the turquoise mines at Serabit el-Khadem in central Sinai. From their proto-Sinaitic inscriptions, the idea of an alphabet spread northward to Canaan, where we find evidence of experiments with alphabets shortly afterwards. One of the most famous of these is the writing of Ugarit (Ras Shamra). The scribes of Ugarit used cuneiform symbols alphabetically to express their own Semitic dialect, which closely resembled Hebrew. Other experiments undoubtedly led into the Hebrew alphabet, although we cannot trace its beginnings.
[2]Colin McEvedy, *The Penguin Atlas of Ancient History* (Middlesex: Penguin Books, 1967), p. 28.
[3]Howard M. Jamieson, "Jericho," *The Zondervan Pictorial Encyclopedia of the Bible* (Grand Rapids: Zondervan, 1975), pp. 451-452.
[4]George Steindorff and Keith C. Seele, *When Egypt Ruled the East*, rev. ed. by Keith C. Seele (Chicago: University of Chicago Press, 1957), p. 221.
[5]W. H. Morton, "Gibeah," *Interpreter's Dictionary of the Bible*, Vol. 2 (Nashville: Abingdon Press, 1962), p. 391.
[6]Now the Gezer calendar has been upstaged by an inscription found at Izbet Sarta (probably the biblical Ebenezer) near Aphek. This newly found inscription is at least a century older.

Chapter Five: *"Pagan Religions and Cultures"*
[1]O. G. Gurney, *The Hittites* (Baltimore: Penguin Books, 1952), pp. 149–150.
[2]George Steindorff and Keith C. Seele, *When Egypt Ruled the East*, rev. ed. by Keith C. Seele (Chicago: University of Chicago Press, 1957), p. 77.
[3]W. W. Hallo and W. K. Simpson, *The Ancient Near East: A History* (New York: Harcourt Brace Jovanovich, 1971).
[4]J. B. Pritchard, ed., *Ancient Near Eastern Texts Relating to the Old Testament* (Princeton, N.J.: Princeton University Press, 1969).
[5]C. H. Gordon, "Ancient Near Eastern Religions," *Encyclopedia Britannica*, 15th ed., Vol. 12 (Chicago: Encyclopedia Britannica Educational Corporation, 1974).
[6]Yehezkel Kaufmann, *The Religion of Israel* (Chicago: University of Chicago Press, 1960), p. 21.
[7]A. Leo Oppenheim, *Ancient Mesopotamia: Portrait of a Dead Civilization*, 2nd ed. (Chicago: University of Chicago Press, 1976).
[8]*The Tree of Life* (New York: Viking Press, 1942), p. 263.

Chapter Six: *"The Egyptians"*
[1]J. A. Wilson, "Egypt," *Interpreter's Dictionary of the Bible*, Vol. 2 (Nashville: Abingdon Press, 1962), p. 42.
[2]The Egyptians also used a simplified form of hieroglyphics called the *hieratic* script (from the Greek *hieratikos,* "pertaining to the priest's office").
[3]J. A. Wilson, "Egypt," p. 42.
[4]George Adam Smith, *The Historical Geography of the Holy Land* (New York: A. C. Armstrong and Son, 1906), p. 157.
[5]George Steindorff and Keith C. Seele, *When Egypt Ruled the East* (Chicago: University of Chicago Press, 1957), p. 40.
[6]Steindorff and Seele, *When Egypt Ruled the East,* p. 57–58.
[7]J. B. Pritchard, *Ancient Near Eastern Texts Relating to the Old Testament* (Princeton, N.J.: Princeton University Press, 1969), p. 231.
[8]Steindorff and Seele, *When Egypt Ruled the East,* pp. 270–271.
[9]Steindorff and Seele, *When Egypt Ruled the East,* pp. 139–140.

Chapter Seven: *"The Babylonians and Assyrians"*
[1]Lewis Spence, *Myths and Legends of Babylonia and Assyria* (London: George G. Harrap and Company, 1916), p. 21.
[2]George W. Gilmore, "Assyria," *The New Schaff-Herzog Encyclopedia of Religious Knowledge*, Vol. 1, ed. by Lefferts A. Loetscher (Grand Rapids, Mich.: Baker Book House, 1977), p. 330.
[3]Dorothy Ruth Miller, *A Handbook of Ancient History in Bible Light* (New York: Fleming H. Revell Company, 1937), p. 102.
[4]Miller, *A Handbook of Ancient History in Bible Light,* p. 117.

ACKNOWLEDGMENTS

The Publisher gratefully acknowledges the cooperation of these sources, whose illustrations appear in the present work.

Aleppo Museum, 6; Ashmolean Museum, 55; Bildarchiv Preussicher Kulturbesitz, 46, 129; British Museum, 111, 117, 154; G. G. Cameron, 158; Dover Publications, 114; Egyptian National Museum, 118, 134; Lee Ellenberger, 76; Giraudon (Paris), 146; L. H. Grollenberg, 71; Iraq Museum, 156; Israel Department of Antiquities and Museums, 121; Israel Government Press Office, 27; Israel Government Office of Tourism, 4; Gustav Jeeninga, 79, 91, 176; The Louvre, 158; Metropolitan Museum of Art, 136; Ministry of Culture and Information, 12; Naples Museum, 106; Thomas Nelson, Inc., 17; Oriental Institute, 2, 49, 87, 150, 188, 191; Pontificum Institutum Biblicum (Jerusalem), 100; Religious News Service, 22; Claude Schaeffer-Forrer, 162, 164, 169, 171, 174, 178; S. J. Schweig, 34; Trans World Airlines, 132; John C. Trever, 11; William White, 74, 124.

The Publishers have attempted to observe the legal requirements with respect to the rights of the suppliers of photographic materials. Nevertheless, persons who have claims are invited to apply to the Publishers.

INDEX

This index is designed as a guide to proper names and other significant topics found in *The World of the Old Testament*. Page numbers in italics indicate pages where a related illustration or sidebar appears. Headings in italics indicate the title of a book or some other important work of literature. Use the index to find related information in various articles.

A

Aaron, *22*
Aaron's calf, 105
Abdon, *48*
Abel, 17, 54
Abib, 33, 35, *38*
Abijam, *25*, *40*, 42
Abimelech, *48*
Abner, *42*
Abraham ("Abram"), *6*, 16–17, 50–51, *52*, 124, 129, *139*, 144, 165, 170
    Abrahamic covenant, 188
Abu Simbel, 134
Abydos, 134
Abyssinia, 125
accession dating system. *See* dating, accession year.
Achaemenes, 182
Achaemenid dynasty, 202
Achan, 172
Actium, 140
Adad, 157
Adam, 16, 54, *56*
Admah, 170
Admonition of an Egyptian Sage, 141
Adonijah, *121*
Aegean Sea, 6
aerial photography, infrared, 78
Africa, 8, 125
Agade, *12*, 145
    See also Akkad; Sargon of Agade.
Agade-Sippar, 145
Ahab, *25*, 29, 30, 35, *40*, 41, 97–98, 151

Ahasuerus, 66, *185*, *191*
    See also Xerxes II.
Ahaz, *25*, *58*, 61–63
Ahaziah, *25*, 38–41, 59, 151
Ahmose, 131, *136*
Ahmose-Nofretari, 131
Ahura-Mazda, *159*, 202–203
Ai, 24, 87–88
Akhnaton, 7, 94, *118*, 134, *161*, 168
    See also Amenhotep IV.
akitu, 120
Akkad, 10, *12*, 89, 145–146
    See also Agade.
Akkadian language, 14, 71, 115, 162, 164, 170
Akkadians, 6, 14, 94, 107, 145–146, *159*
alabaster, *2*
Albright, W. F., 72, 90, 109
Alexander the Great, 9, 32, 98, 128, 140, 190, 201
Alexandria, 142
allegorical interpretation of Scripture, 142
altar, *121*
Amalek, battle of, 24
Amarna, *46*, 133
    Amarna Age, 6–7, 93
    Amarna tablets, 94, 161, 167
Amasis, 191

Amaziah, *25*, 28, *58*, 60
Amenemhet I, 129–130
Amenhotep I, 131–132, 140
Amenhotep II, *47*
Amenhotep III, 44, *46*, 133, 161
Amenhotep, IV, 94, 109, 134, 168
    See also Akhnaton.
Amenophis, 132
Ammishtamru I, 167
Ammishtamru II, 167
Ammonites, 47, 62
Amon, *25*, *60*, 64, 108, *136*
Amorites, 86, 92
    invasion, 86
Amos, 31
Amun, 130, 135, 140
Amun-Re, 114, 131–135
Anath, 113, 174, 179
Anathoth (Anata), 74
Angra Mainyu, 203
aniconic worship, 105
animals, 185
    animal cults, 138
ankh, *114*
Anshan, 183
Antiochus III, 32
Antiochus IV (Epiphanes), 185, 190
Anu, 114
Anubis, 106
Aphrodite, 140
Apiru, 45
Apis, 192
Apollo, 140
apostasy, *48*

Apries, 139
Apsu, 110–112
Aqhat, Legend of,
    178–179
aqueduct, *149*
Ar Khalba, 167
Arabia, 10, 124, *159,*
    184
Arad, 87
Aramaic language, 84,
    141–142, *159,* 164,
    184, 202
Arameans, 151
archaeology, *4,* 13–14,
    67–102, *87, 174*
  dating techniques,
    77–78
  recording methods,
    78–80
  underwater, 74
Archevites. *See* Erech.
architecture, 101
Aristeas, Letter of, 142
Aristotle, 9, 13
ark, Noah's. *See* Noah.
ark of the covenant, 26,
    27, 97
Armenia, 183
Arphaxad, 52–53
Arsiya, 174
Artaxerxes I, 66, 144,
    188, 195–200
Artaxerxes II, *188*
Aruru, 114
Aryans, 181
Asa, *25, 28, 29, 40,* 41,
    138
Ashdod, 96
Asherah, 177
Ashkelon, 135
Ashtoreth, 178
Ashur, 71, 157
Ashurbanipal III, 151
Ashurnasirpal II, 155
Asia, 8, 181
Asia Minor 70, 95, 124,
    167, 183
assassination, *185*
Asshur, 151, 182
Assyria, 8, 29, 72, 97–
    98, *149,* 182–183
Assyrians, 11, *29,* 35,
    62, 107, 138, 143,
    148, *154,* 168,
    182–183
  kings, 34–36, *57,*
    148, 151
  language, 17

literature, *17,* 150
  religion, 104, 157
astrology, 11, *35,* 118
  Assyrian, 11, *29*
  Babylonian, 11
Astyages, 183
Aswan, 125, *136,* 141,
    200
Athaliah, *25,* 38, 59,
    136, 151
Athena, 104
Athens, 8, 195
Aton, 108, 133
Atum, 108
Augustus Caesar, 128,
    140
Avaris, 92
Azariah, *25,* 28, *58,*
    60–61
  See also Uzziah.

B

Baal (god), 30, 105,
    108, *162,* 165,
    173–175, 179
Baal Cycle, 173–177
Baal-hermon, 108
Baal-peor, 108
Baal-zephon, 108
Baasha, *25, 40,* 42, 98
Bab edh-Dhra, 88
Babel, 10, 18, 156
baboons, *136*
Babylon, 8, *29,* 64, 69,
    71–72, 98, 112,
    120, 138, 145–160,
    182, 195
  fall, 189
Babylon-Borsippa, 145
Babylonia, 29, *159,*
    181, 186
Babylonian Empire,
    12, 145–160
Babylonian captivity,
    64, 186–187
Babylonians, 1, 11, 64,
    119, 139, 143,
    145–160
  kings, 183
  language, *159*
  literature, *117,*
    147–148
  religion, 104, 112,
    145, 157
Bactria, 196
Baghdad, 159
Balkan Sea, 95
bamah, 88

Bardin, Maurice, *150*
basalt, *100*
Bauer, Hans, 164
bed, *185*
Beer-sheba, 74, 83
Behdet, 129
Behistun inscription,
    71, *159,* 201
Bel and the Dragon, 120
Belshazzar, 69, 155,
    184
Ben-hadad, 151
Benjamin, 21
Benjamin of Tudela,
    149
Bethel, 91, 161, 180
Bethlehem, 1
Beth-shemesh, 5
Beth-Yerah, 88
Beth-Zur, 197
Bezaleel, 118
Bible, 1, 10, *34,* 67–69,
    117, 149
  chronology, 33–66
  history, 15–32
Bir es-Safadi, 83
*Birth of the Good and
    Gracious God, The,*
    177
Bisitun. *See* Behistun.
Bitter Lake, *133*
Black Sea, 8, 95, *149*
blasphemy, *136*
Book of the Dead, 124
Bosporus, 195
Bouchard, 124
brickmaking, *20*
British Museum, 155
bronze, *164*
Bronze Age, 80, 84
Bubastis, *133*
bull, *157, 169*
"Bull of Heaven", 114
burial, multiple, 92
burial ground, 90
burial objects, *74, 131*
burning bush, 22
burnt offering, 17
Bur-Sagale, 35
Byblos, 161
Byzantine Empire, 76

C

Caesarea Maritima, 74,
    79, 91, 102
Cain, 16–17, 54
Cainan, *52,* 53, *56*
Calah, *34,* 71, *149*

Caleb, 24, 47
calendar, 34, *35*
  Egyptian, 12
  Jewish, 33, 65
  lunar, 33
  Persian, 65
  See also Gezer Calendar.
Callias, Treaty of, 196
Cambyses I, 140, 183, 189, 200
Canaan, *6, 7, 22,* 44, *46,* 86, 93, 113, 138, 146, 168
  conquest of, 148, 171–173
  See also Palestine; Israel.
Canaanites, 86–87, 90, 94, 103, 161–180
  alphabet, 165
  city planning, 86
  gods and goddesses, 108, *162*
  government, 167–168
  legends, 113
canal, *133, 136*
Capernaum, 27
  synagogue, *27,* 102, 202
Cappadocia, 183
caravan, 159
carbon isotope dating, 77
Carchemish, *29,* 138, 153, 183
Carmel, Mount, 30
cataract, 126
Chalcolithic Period, 82–83, 85, *100,* 165
  See also Copper-Stone Age.
Champollion, Jean Francois, 71, 124
chariot, *169*
Cherith, brook, 29
child sacrifice, 90
China, 7
Christ. *See* Jesus Christ.
Christianity, 15
church, 10
Church of the Holy Sepulchre, 99
Cilicia, 183
Claudius Caesar, 142
clay tablet, 11, *35, 46,*
52, *57,* 71, *117, 162, 178*
Cleopatra VII, 128, 140
clothing, *2, 185*
coffin, *131*
coin, 76
Constantine, 99, 102
copper, *164*
Copper-Stone Age, 82
  See also Chalcolithic Period.
corbelled vault, *174*
cosmogony, 110
couch, 185
covenant, *22,* 188
Creation, 1, 15, 50, *52,* 54, 57, *117*
  date, 15–16
  Egypt myths, 110–111
cremation, 83
Crete, 130
cults, religious, 4
cuneiform writing, 10–11, *35,* 71, 84, 94, *117,* 157, 164, *178,* 202
Cutha, 145
Cyaxares, 182–183
Cypro-Minoan Linear B, 164
Cyprus, 164
Cyrus II ("the Great"), 31, 65, 140, 155, 181, 183, 186–191, 194, 196, 201
  Cyrus' decree, 186–187

D

Dagon, 165
Daian-Assur, 35
Damascus, *29,* 151
Damietta Branch, 125
Dan, 180
Danel, 178
Daniel, *29,* 31, 64, 178, 181, 185, 189–191
Darius I ("the Great; the Mede"), 65, 71, *106, 133, 159,* 185, *188, 191*
Darius II, 200
Darius III, 201
Darius the Mede. *See* Darius I.

date (chronological). *See* dating.
dating, 33–66, 77
  accession year, 36, 41
  nonaccession, 36, 39, 59
  radiocarbon, 77
  sequence, 72
David, 8, 26, 42–43, 80, 85, 97, 118, 135–136, 151, 172
Dawn (Shahar), 177
Dead Sea, 13, 83, 88, 98
Dead Sea Scrolls, 13
  See also Qumran.
death, *22,* 120.
  See also burial objects; funeral customs; mummy.
death penalty, 18
Debir, 72, 96
Deborah, 26, 48
Decalogue. *See* Ten Commandments.
Deir el-Bahri, 12, *136*
demotic (Egyptian) script, 124
Deutsche Orient Gesellschaft, 159
deVaux, Roland, 101
Dhorme, Edouard, 164
Diaspora, 9
Divided Kingdom, 28–30, 39
divination, 116–118
Djehuti, 132
dog, *136, 169*
dolmen, 84
Donatiya, 178
Dusk (Shalim), 177

E

Ea, 111, 115, 147, 157
E-Anna, 144
Early Bronze Period, *73,* 83–90, 165
eating, *185*
Eber, 52–53, 89
Ebla (Ibla), 6, 14, 52, 89
  tablets, 14, 89
ebony, *136*
Ecbatana, 183, 187, 194, 201
Ecclesiastes, Book of, 141
eclipse, 35, 64

Eden, 16
Edict of Constantine, 10
Edom, 136
Egypt, 2–5, 8, 13, *20, 22, 29,* 32, 71, 84–87, 90, 92, 105, 113, 119, 126–142, 148, 153, 161, 167, 183, 190, 198, 200
  Lower Egypt, 13, 129, 138
  pyramids, *131*
  Upper Egypt, 129, 138
Egyptian captivity, 20, 148
Egyptians, 1, 64, 103, 123–142, 153, 167–168, 183
  history, 54, 128–142
  language, *22,* 123–125
  paintings, 106, *129*
  religion, 103–122, *124,* 128
Ehud, *48*
El, 105, 107, *171, 175*
Elah, *25, 40,* 42
Elam, 4–5, 146, 186, 192
Elamites, 145, 150
  language, 71, *159*
Elephantine Island, 141, *159,* 200
Eli, 26
Eliezer, *22*
Elijah, *29,* 30–31, 119
Elisha, *29,* 30–31
Ellasar, 144
Elon, *48*
empires, origin of, 5
Emu, 136
En-gedi, 83, 197
Enkidu, 114–115
Enki/Ea, 104, 107
Enlil, 107–108, 115, 145, 147
Enoch, 54–55, *56*
Enos, 54–55, *56*
Enuma Elish, 110–112, *117,* 120
Ephraim, tribe of, *76*
Epic, Babylonian, *117*
epochal genealogy, 54
Erech, 10, 144
Esarhaddon, *29*
Esau, 20, 175

Essenes, 99
Esther, 66, 185
Esther, Book of, 181, *185, 188, 191*
Ethanim. *See* Tishri.
Ethiopia, 138
  See also Nubia.
Ethiopians, 126
  rulers of Egypt, 29
Euergetes II, 140
Euphrates River, *6,* 93, 138, 143–144, *150*
Europe, 83
Eve, 16, 54
excavation, archae-ological, *87, 91*
  See also archaeology.
Exile, *29,* 31, 33, *60,* 65, *139,* 141, 186, 189
Exodus, the, 7, *20, 47,* 130, *139,* 148
Ezekiel, 31, 65, 179
Ezra, 31, 66, 181, 186, 196–198

F
falcon, *114*
feast days, *185*
Feast of Booths. *See* Feast of Taberna-cles.
Feast of Ingathering. *See* Feast of Taber-nacles.
Feast of Tabernacles, 33, 188, 199
Feast of Weeks, 33
Fertile Crescent, 82
fertility cults, *6*
Fisher, Clarence S., 72
Flood, the, 18, 50, *52,* 113
Flood myths, 113
Franciscan monks, 99
funeral customs, *174*
  See also death; tomb.

G
Gabriel (archangel), 189
Galilee, Sea of, 88
Garden Tomb, 99
Garstang, John, 87
gate, *176*
Gaumata, *158*

Gaza, 170
gazelle, *169*
Geb, 110–111
Gedaliah, *60,* 65, 139
genealogy, 54
Genesis, Book of, 15, *55*
Gerar, 170
Gerizim, Mount, 102
Gershom, *22*
Geshem, 98, 198
Gezer, 97, 135, 172
Gezer calendar, 97
Ghassul, 82, *100*
Ghassulian Period, 82
giant, 17
Gibeah, 97
Gibeon, 96
Gideon, 26, *48*
Gihon, 97
Gilgamesh Epic, 114, 120
Giza, 132
glacis wall, 93
Glueck, Nelson, 74, 91
goat, *169*
God, *141*
gods, pagan, *6,* 103–122
  See also proper names of various gods, such as Baal, and proper names of various pagan peoples, such as Canaanites.
gold, *136, 157, 169,* 196
Golgotha, 102
Goliath, 26
Gomorrah, 89, 144, 170
Gordon, C. H., 116
Gordon's Calvary, 99
Goshen, *133*
grave, *71*
Greece, 9, 95, *106,* 181, 196
Greeks, 8, 73, 103–104, 107
  cities, 8
  language, 9, 71, 181, 202
  philosophy, 14
  religion, 104, *106*
Gubaru, 189
Gudea, *146*
Guzana, 35

H

Habiru, 45, *46*, 94
Hadad, 136
Hagar, 19
Haggai, 31, 65, 188, 193
Halaf, 144
Halo, W. W., 109
Ham, 18
Haman, 198
Hamitic languages, 124
Hamito-Semitic language, 124
Hammurabi, 146–147, 156
Hammurabi, Code of, 147, 192–193
Hammurapi, 168
Haran, *6,* 51, 184
Hasmoneans, 32
Hassuna, 144
Hathor, 106, 140
Hatshepsut, 46, *47, 132, 133, 136*
Hatti, 5
Hattushash, 19
Hattusilis III, 170
Hazor, 5, 93, 97
Hebrews, 20
  language, 11, 53, 142, 164, 180
  script, 98, 202
Hebron, 43, 72, 90–91
Helena, 99
Heliopolis, 110, 130
Hellenism, 9, 140
  Hellenistic Age, 9, 13, *73,* 99
  Hellenistic kingdoms, 9, 13
hemerology, 117
hepatoscopy, 116–117
Hephaistos, 140
Herculaneum, 14
Hermes, 140
Hermopolis, 108, 110
Herodians, 32
Herodium, the, 101
Herodotus, *133,* 143, 156, *185*
Hezekiah, *25,* 28, *57, 58,* 63, 97
hieroglyphics, 71, 85, 125, 164
high priest, *164*
Hincks, Edward, *159*
history, 2, 80

Old Testament, 2, 15–32
Hittites, 6, *49,* 95, 103, 109, 134, 149, 162
  texts, 164
holy days. *See* feast; festival; *proper names of various holy days, such as* Feast of Tabernacles.
holy of holies, Jewish, 27
Homer (poet), 8, 13
horns (of altar), *121*
Horon, 178
horse, *141,* 185
Horus, 107, 121, 132, 135, 140
Hosea, 31
Hoshea, *25, 58,* 61–62, 138, 152
house, *4,* 159–160
Hrihor, 135
Hubur, 178
Hulda Gates, 101
Humbaba, 114
hunting, *169*
Hurrians, 6, 92
  invasion of Palestine, 86
  language, 164, 169
Hurriya, 178
Hyksos pharaohs, 45, 49, 92–93, 130, *136*
Hyrcanus, John I, 32

I

Ia-a-u, 35
Ibiranu, 167
Ibzan, *48*
iconography, 105
idolatry, 5, *29,* 105
Iliad, the, 8
immortality, 122
Inanna, 104
incest, *136*
India, 9, 84, 181, 195
Indo-Aryan tribe, 92
  See also Hurrians.
Indo-Europeans, 84, 143
Indo-Iranian language, 181, 202
Indus River, 195
Ineni, *131*

infanticide, 23
Intertestamental Period, 9, 32
Iran, 183
Iraq, 4, 143
Ireland, *159*
Iron Age, *73,* 80, 96–97
Isaac, 19, 49, *50,* 175
Isaiah, 29, 31
Isaiah, Book of, 11
Ish-bosheth, 42–43
Ishmael, 19
Ishtar, 104, 114, 144, 147, 157
Ishtar Gate, 159
Isis, 121
Islam, 15
Israel (nation), 7, 27, 29, 33, *34,* 37, *38,* 42, 46, 60, 98, 109, 134–135, 143, 148, 182
  First Commonwealth, 8
  Second Commonwealth, 8
  Divided Kingdom, 28
  kings (table), *25*
  United Kingdom, 26–27
Israel (person). *See* Jacob.
Israel (place), 30–31, 136–137, 181–182
  See also Palestine; Canaan.
Israel Stele, 135
Israelite Period (archaeological), 86
Israelites, 11, *22,* 47, 90, 94, 105, 123, 127, 172, 199
Italy, 9
ivory, *136*

J

Jacob, 19–20, 44, 49, *50,* 130, *139,* 175
Jacob's Well, 102
Jair, 48
Jambres, *22*
Jannes, *22*
Japheth, 18
Jared, 55, *56*

Jehoahaz, *25, 58,* 60, 64
Jehoash (Joash), *25,* 28, *58,* 59–60
Jehoiachin, *25, 60,* 64
Jehoiakim, *25, 60, 64*
Jehoiakin, 139, 153
Jehoram, *25,* 38–41, 54, 59
See also Joram.
Jehoshaphat, *25,* 28, 38–41
Jehovah, 23
Jehu, *25, 29, 34, 40, 58,* 59, 151
Jephthah, 26, 44, 47, *48*
Jeremiah, *29,* 31, 74, 139
Jericho, *4,* 5, 24, 45, 81, 86–87, 92, 101, 161, 170, 197
Jeroboam I, 8, *25, 40,* 42–43, 180
Jeroboam II, *25, 58,* 60, 98
Jeroboam's calf, 105, 180
Jerusalem, 8, 26, *27, 29,* 64, 89, 97–98, 137, 139, 144, 188–189
  restoration temple, 31
  sieges, *29,* 32, *57*
Jeshua, 188, 193
Jesus Christ, 1, 14, *149*
  birth, 1, 9, 32, 102, 142, 203
Jethro, 21, 46
jewelry, *136*
Jews, 8, 9, 181, 186–202
  customs, *22*
  religion, 15, *141*
Jezebel, *29,* 30, 59, 119
Jezreel, 30
Joash, king of Israel. See Jehoash.
Joash, king of Judah, *25, 58*
Job, 179
Jonah, *149*
Jonah, Book of, 149
Joppa, 132
Joram, 39–41, 59

Jordan River, 13, 24, 30, 82, 84, 170
Jordan Valley, 74
Joseph, husband of Mary, *142*
Joseph the patriarch, 20–21, 49, *50,* 130, *139*
Joseph's tomb, 99
Josephus, Flavius, 101
Joshua, 7, 24, 47, 85, 88, 95, 170
Josiah, *25,* 28, *29,* 35–36, *60,* 64, 138, 178
Jotham, *25,* 28, *58,* 61–62, 64
Judah, 8, 28, *38,* 63, 98, *136,* 138, 143, 151, 153, 181–187
  fall, *29*
  kings, *25,* 35, *60* (table), *25*
  return from Exile, 31
Judaism. See Jews.
Judea, 196–198
judges, 7, 26, *42,* 44
Jupiter, 104
Justin Martyr, 102

K

Kadesh, 23, 168
Kaldu people, 144
Kamose, 131
Karnak, 135, 161
Kasshite, 150
Kaufmann, Yehezkel, 116
Kenyon, Kathleen, 72, 85, 88, 92
Keret, Legend of, *178*
Khaf-Re, *132*
Khir-bet-el-Kerak. See Beth Yerah.
Khirbet Qumran. See Qumran.
Khnum, 200
Khonsu, 105
Khorsabad, *149,* 155
Khoser River, *149*
Kings, Valley of the, 12, 131
Kingu, 111, 113
Kish, 10, 145

Koldewey, Robert, 159
Kothar-wa-Khasis, 174, 179

L

Laban, 20
Lachish, 72, 96, 98
Lagash, 146
Lamech, 17, 56
Lament of the Righteous Sufferer, the, 148
lamp, *73*
languages, 5, 18
Larsa, 108, 144
Lasha, 170
Late Bronze Age, *73,* 88, 93–96, 167
Latin (language), 181, 202
law, *185*
  Persian, 192–193
Law of Moses, *22,* 141, 188, 197
Layard, Sir Austen Henry, 71, *149*
Leah, 20
leap-year days, 34
Lebanon, 7, 70
lecanomancy, 117
legends, 178–179
leprosy, *29*
Levites, 199
libanomancy, 117
Libya, 137
Libyans, *49*
linear writing, 164
lion, *132*
Longimanus, 196
  See also Artaxerxes I.
Lord, *141*
Lot, 19
Lugal-banda, 114
Lydia (place), 183
lyre, *157*

M

Maat, 108
Maccabeans, 32, 98
Maccabees, First and Second Books of, 32
Macedonia, 9
Magi, 203
  See also Jesus Christ, birth.
Mahalaleel, *56*

Malachi, 32
Manasseh, king of Judah, *25*, *29*, *58*, *60*, 64
Manetho, 128
Marduk, 111–113, 157, 186, 195
Marduk, Temple of, Babylon, 108, *150*
Mari, *6*, 91
Mark Antony, 140
Mary, mother of Jesus, 142
Masada, 101
mask, *12*
Masoretic Text, 51, 53–54
Mattathias, 32
McEvedy, Colin, 92
Medes, *149*, 155, 182
Media, 182–183, *185*, 192
Medinet Habu, 95, 134
Mediterranean Sea, 5, 86, 90, 95, 102, 123, *133*, 170
Mediterranean area, 6–8, 151, 162
Megalithic culture, 83
Megiddo, 87, 97, *121*, 138, 161
Megiddo Pass, Battle of, 93
Memphis, 108
Menahem, *25*, *58*, 61
Menander, 13
Menes, 129
menology, 117
Meribah, 22
Merneptah, 95, *134*, 135
Mesolithic Period, 81
Mesopotamia, 2–6, 54, 70, 75, 82, 86, 91, 108–109, 113, 143, *152*, 154, 164, 167, 177, 181
Mesopotamian literature, 14
Messiah, 16
Methuselah, 56
Micah, 31
Middle Bronze Age I, 86, 88–91, 167
Middle Bronze Age II, *73*, 92–93

Middle East, 6
Middle Kingdom, 129–130
Middle Stone Age. *See* Mesolithic Period.
Midian, *22*, *48*
Minerva, 104
Minoans, 6
miracle, 30
Miriam, *22*
Mishor, 109
Mitanni Empire, 92
Moab, 23, *48*
Moabites, 29, 105
monism, 105
monkeys, *136*
monotheism, 109, *117*
Morton, W. H., 97
Moses, 1, 7, 15, *22*, 46, *47*, 93, 118, 127, 170
Moses, books of. *See* Pentateuch.
Mosul, *149*
Mot, 173, 175
mummy, 128
murals, *20*
murder, 16, *24*
musical instrument, *157*
Mycenaeans, 95
myrrh, *136*
myth, *114*, 173–180

N

Nabonidus, 69, 183–184
Nabopolassar, *29*, 64, 153, 182
Naboth, 30
Nabu, 157
Nadab, *25*, 42
Nahor, 51, *52*
Nahum, *149*
Nana, 144
Nanna, 104
Nanna-Sin, 104, 108
Napata, 136
Naples, 14
Napoleon Bonaparte, 71, 124, 127
Near East, *2*, 5, 7, 32, 67, 71, 82, 90, 96, 108, 120, 148, *159*, 176, 183

Nebo, Mount, *22*
Nebuchadnezzar I, *25*, *29*, 64, 69, 139, 150, 186
Nebuchadnezzar II, 8, 153, 159
Necho, *133*, 138, 153, 194
Nefertiti, 118, 168
Negev Desert, 74, 78, 83, 91
Negroid race, 123
Nehemiah, 31, 66, 98, 181, 198
Nekau. *See* Necho.
Neo-Hittites, 7
Neolithic Period, 3, *4*, 10, 81
Neptune, 104
neutron activation, 78
Nig-gina, 108
Nig-sisa, 108
Nikkal, 177
Nile River, *22*, 71, 84, 125–127, *131*, *133*, 194, 200
Delta, 71, 93, 125–128, 134, 142
Nimrod, 149. *See* Sargon of Agade.
Nimrud, 155
Nineveh, *12*, *29*, 34, 71, *149*, 152, 183
Nin-gal, 144
Ninsun, 114
Nippur, *12*, 108, 145
Niqmad II, 167–168
Niqmad III, 167–168
Niqmepa, 167–168
Nisan, 33, 35
Noah, 3, 18, *52*, 56, 116, 149
ark, 4, 17
non-accession dating. *See* dating, non-accession.
Nubia, 124, *136*, 195
See also Ethiopia.
Nubians, 124
Nun, 110
Nut (god), 110, *111*
Nuzi, 91–92

O

obelisk, *34*, *136*
Ochus, 200

Odyssey, the, 8
Old Stone Age. *See* Paleolithic Period.
Old Testament, *141*
    history, 15–32
    manuscripts, *11*
Ombos, 128
Omri, *25, 29,* 40–41, 98
oneiromancy, 117
Ophel, 97
Oppenheim, Leo, 118
Osiris, 107, 121–122, 133–134
ossuary, 83
ostracâ, 98
Othniel, 26, *48*

P
Padriya, 174
Paebel, 178
pagan religion, 5, *17, 22,* 104–122
paleography, 77
Paleo-Hebrew script. *See* Hebrews, script.
Paleolithic Period, 81
Palestine, 2–5, 12, 19, *29,* 70, 81, 123, 130, 140, 153, 172, 181, 189, 193, 196, 201
    archaeological periods, *73*
    See also Canaan.
Palestine Exploration Fund, 74
Panehsi, 135
pantheon, 104
papyrus manuscripts, 13, *111, 124*
parchment scrolls, *11*
Parthia, 183
Pasargadae, 201
Passover, 23, 35
patriarchs, 3, 14, 48, 91
Paul the apostle, 9, 14
Pekah, *25, 58,* 61–62
Pekahiah, *25, 58,* 61
Peleg, 51–52
Pentateuch, 7, *22*
    See also Samaritans.
Persepolis, *191,* 195
Persia, 8, 71, *106, 133, 159,* 181–203

Persian Empire, 8, 32, 65, 84, *185, 188*
Persian Gulf, 143, 191
Persian Period. *See* Iron Age.
Persians, 8–9, 138, 155, 182–203
    kings, 8, *159*
    language, 84
    religion, 109, 202
Peter the apostle, 14, 102
Petrie, W. M. Flinders, 72, *73*
Pharaoh, *20, 22, 29, 49,* 128–142
Philip II of Macedonia, 9
Philistines, 48–49, 95, 135, 170
Philo Judaeus, 142
philosophy, 108
    See also Greeks.
Phoenicia, 70, 86, 90, 98, 161, 183, 189
Phoenicians, 169
Phraortes, 182
Pigat, 179
Pindar, 13
Pithom, 45
plagues, the ten, *22,* 23
Plato, 13
Platonism, 142
polytheism, 5, 104, 109, *118*
    See also monotheism; pagan religion.
Pompeii, 14
Pompey, 140
Poseidon, 104
postal system, *185*
potsherd, 12, 75
pottery, *71, 73, 76*
pre-history, 1
Processional Street, 159
Promised Land, *17, 22,* 46
prophet, 26, 31
    false, 30
proton magnetometer, 78
Proverbs, Book of, 141, 180
Psalms, Book of, 141, 180
Psamtik I, 138

Pseudo-Smerdis, 192
Ptah, 108, 140
Ptolemy I Soter, 142
Ptolemy V Epiphanes, 124
Ptolemy dynasty, 128, *133,* 190
Punt, *133, 136*
pyramid, 5, *131*

Q
Qarqar, Battle of, *29,* 35, 37, 59
Qumran, *11,* 13, 54, 98, 101
    See also Dead Sea Scrolls.

R
Rachel, 20
Rahab, 175
rainbow, 18
Rameses I, 95, 133–134
Rameses II, 45, 95, 135, 168
Rameses III, *49, 96,* 135
Rameses XI, 135
Rameside dynasty, 95, 134
Rawlinson, Sir Henry Creswicke, *71*
Re, 109, 130, 135
Redeemer, 16–17
    See also Jesus Christ.
Red Sea, *22,* 123, *133*
redemption, 16
Re-Harakhti, 134
Rehoboam, 8, *25,* 40, 42
Rehoboth-Ir, *149*
Reisner, G. A., 72
religions. *See* Christianity; Jews; pagan religion.
Resen, *149*
Reu, 51–52
Rich, Claude J., 71
Robinson, Edward, 74
Robinson's Arch, 100
Roman Catholic church, 10
Roman Empire, 10, 70, 99, 142
Roman Period, 9, *73*

Romans, 190
  army, 32, 140
  emperors, *133*
  religion,109
Rome, 9–10, 140, 181
Rosetta, 125
Rosetta Stone, 71, 124
Russia, 181, 195
Ruth, 26

S

Sabbath, 199
sackcloth, *185*
sacrifice, 107
  pagan, 106–107
Sahara Desert, 125
Saint Anne's Church, 100
Sais, 138
Salah, 52
salvation, 16
Samaria, *29*, 42, 72, 98, 152, 196
Samaritans, 102, 198
  Samaritan Pentateuch, 54
  temple, 102
Samarra, 144
Samson, 26
Samuel, 26, 48
Sanballat, 98, 198
Sardis, *159*
Sargon of Agade, 6, *12*, 145, 148, 153
Sargon II, 62, *149*
Satan, 16
Saul, king of Israel, 8, 26, *42*, 151
Savior, 16
  See also Jesus Christ.
Schliemann, Heinrich, 76
scriptorium, 101
scroll, Isaiah, *11*
Scythians, *149*, 154, 182, 195
Sedeq, 109
seer, 26
Sekhmet, 106, 113
Seleucids, 32, 140, 190
Semites, 6, 14, *49*, 84, 106, 144
Semitic languages, 11, 86, *159*, 164
Senmut, *136*
Sennacherib, *29*, *57*, 63, *149*, 153

Sennacherib Prism, *57*
Senwosret pharaohs, 130
Sepharvaim, 145
Septuagint, 53–54, 57, 142
Serbonian Bog, 127
serpent, 26
Serug, 51
Sesostris I, *133*
Seth (god), 121, 128
Seth (person), 17, 54, *56*
Sethi I, 134
Sethnakht, 135
Shallum, 58, 61
Shalmaneser I, 148, 168
Shalmaneser II, 151
Shalmaneser III, *29*, *34*, 35
Shalmaneser IV, 152
Shalmaneser V, 62
Shamash, 104, 108, 144, 157
Shamshi-Ramman IV, 151
shappatu, 120
Shechem, *76*, 91, 96
Shem, 18, *52*, 53
Shemesh, 105, 109
Sheshbazzar, 31, 187–188
Sheshonk I, 137, *139*
  See also Shishak.
Shiloh, 97
Shinar, 143
  See also Sumer.
ships, *136*
Shishak, *29*, 137, *139*
  See also Sheshonk I.
Shu, 105, 110, *111*
Shuppiluliuma, 168
Shushan, *185*, *188*
Sidon, *29*, 170
Sidonians, 170
Siloam, Pool of, 97
silver, *76*, *124*
Simanu, 35
sin, 16
Sin (god), 144, 157, 184
Sinai, 12
Sinai Desert, *22*
Sinai Peninsula, 123, 138
Sivan, 33

skull, *74*
slavery, *20*, *22*, *49*, *141*
Sodom, 89, 144, 170
soldier. *See* warfare.
Solomon, 8, 27–28, 35, *40*, *42*, 43, 96, 119, *121*, 136, 151, 172
  stables, 97
Somaliland, *133*, *136*
Son of God. *See* Jesus Christ.
Son of Man. *See* Jesus Christ.
Son of Re, 132
Spain, 10
Sparta, 200
spectography, 78
Sphinx, *132*
star, *35*
states, multi-national, 7–8
stele, *134*
Stoicism, 142
Stone Age. *See* Mesolithic Period.
Strabo, *133*
stratigraphy, 72, *73*, 75
stratum, 72
Suez Canal, *133*
Suez, Gulf of, 123, 194
Sumer, 4, 11, 19, *55*, 144
  See also Shinar.
Sumerians, 1, 6, 11, 156
  clothing, *2*
  genealogy, 54–57
  king list, *55*, 57
  language, 11, 14, 84
  religion, 104, 107
Sumero-Babylonian history, 11
Sumero-Babylonian texts, 10
Sun of Righteousness, 108
sun worship, 108, *118*
Susa, 146, *188*, 192, 198
  See also Shushan.
Sybaris, 78
Syria, 6, 70, *87*, 89, 93, 130, *162*, 183, 189
Syrians, 41
Syria-Palestine, 7–8

T

Table of Nations, 145
Talliya, 174
Tanis, 92
Taru, 105
Tatnai, 194
Tefnut, 110
Tehran, 158
Teima, 184
Tel Aviv, 83
Telipinu, 105
tell, *75, 87,* 89
Tell Asmar, *2*
Tell Beit Mirsim, 72
Tell el-Amarna. *See*
   Amarna.
Tell el-Farah, *71*
Tell Judeideh, *87*
Tell Mardikh. *See* Ebla.
temple, Jewish, 65,
   186, 201
   destruction, 66
   Solomon's, 43, 101,
      137
temple, pagan, 4, 107
   Babylonian, *150*
   Egyptian, *49, 136*
Ten Commandments,
   22
Terah, 51, 144
Thebes, Egypt, 108,
   110, 129, *131*
thermoluminescence,
   77
Thoth, 108
Thrace, 195
Thutmose I, 46, *47,*
   136
Thutmose II, *47,* 132,
   136
Thutmose III, *20,* 47,
   93, *131,* 132, *136*
Tiamat, 110–113, 120
Tibni, *40,* 42
Tiglath-Ninib, 149
Tiglath-Pileser I, 151
Tiglath-Pileser II, 151
Tiglath-Pileser III, 152
Tigris River, 143, *149,*
   190
Tigris-Euphrates Val-
   ley, 10, 84
Timsah, Lake, *133*
Tirzah, 42, *71,* 88
Tishri, 33, 35, *38*
Titus, 101
Tobiah, 98, 198
Tolah, *48*

tomb, *20, 49, 174*
   robbery, *131*
tomb of the kings, Je-
   rusalem, 12
tool, *136, 164*
Torah, 201
Trajan III, *133*
Transjordan, 74, 78,
   89
tree of knowledge of
   good and evil, 16
tribute, *29, 34*
Troy, 76
Tukulti-Ninurta I, 168
Turkey, 8
Tutankhamen, 7, *131,*
   133
typology, 75
Tyre, *29*
Tyropean Valley, 100

U

Ubaid, 144
Udum, 178
Ugarit, 161–180
Ugaritic language, 164
   literature, 166,
      173–180
Umman-Manda, 154
underworld, *114, 124*
Ur (place), 17, 19, 69,
   144, *157,* 170
Urban Period, 85
Uru. *See* Ur.
Uruk, 114, 144
Utnapishtim, 115, 120
Utu Shamash, 104
Uzziah, 54, 60–61
   See also Azariah.

V

vase, *106*
Vesuvius, Mount, 14
Via Dolorosa, 102
Virolleaud, Charles,
   164

W

Wailing Wall, 100
warfare, *46, 57, 133,*
   136, 164
water, *22, 73,* 174
weapon, *164*
   See also warfare.
weights and measures,
   141
Wenamon, 161

wife, *178*
Winged Bull, *154*
wisdom, *141*
Wisdom Literature,
   141
wise men. *See* magi.
women and woman-
   hood, *136*
Wood, Leon, 23
World War II, 1
worship, 103, *162*
Wright, G. E., 72
writing, 5
Wurusemu, 105

X

Xenophon, *149*
Xerxes, 66, 190, *191,*
   195, 201
   See also Ahasuerus.
Xerxes II, 200

Y

Yahweh (YHWH), 22
   See also God;
   Jehovah.
Yam, 105
Yanoam, 135
Yareah, 105
Yarih, 177
Yassib, 178
Yatpan, 179
YHWH. *See* Yahweh.
Young, Thomas, 124

Z

Zababa, 147
Zagazig, *133*
Zagros Mountains,
   143, 148
Zanoah, 197
Zarephath, 29
Zeboim, 170
Zechariah the king, *25,*
   58, 61, 65
Zechariah the prophet,
   31, 193
Zedekiah, *25, 60,* 64
Zerah, 138
Zerubbabel, 31, 188
Zeus, 104, *106,* 107,
   140
ziggurat, *17,* 155
Zimri, *25, 40,* 42
Zipporah, *22*
Ziv, 43
Zoroastrianism, 203